The
AMERICAN
ESSAY
in the
AMERICAN
CENTURY

The
AMERICAN
ESSAY
in the
AMERICAN
CENTURY

Ned Stuckey-French

UNIVERSITY OF MISSOURI PRESS
COLUMBIA AND LONDON

Cataloging-in-Publication data is available from the Library of Congress
ISBN 978-0-8262-1925-1 (hard cover: alk. paper)
ISBN 978-0-8262-2015-8 (pbk: alk. paper)

♾™ This paper meets the requirements of the
American National Standard for Permanence of Paper
for Printed Library Materials, Z39.48, 1984.

Designer: Stephanie Foley
Typesetter: FoleyDesign
Printer and Binder: Integrated Book Technology, Inc.
Typefaces: Adobe Garamond and Palatino

To my gals: Elizabeth, Flannery, and Phoebe

Contents

PREFACE

T his book grew out of a love of the personal essay and a desire to figure out why middle-class Americans like to read magazines that contain essays. I grew up middle class myself (or more specifically, white, Protestant, and middle class) in a small town in Indiana in a 1950s ranch house—twenty-one hundred square feet with four bedrooms, three baths, a knotty-pine rec room, and a screened porch. My parents built the house using a floor plan my mother adapted from one she found in the *Ladies' Home Journal*. In that house I watched *Omnibus* and the Young People's Concerts on Sunday afternoons and read my mother's Book-of-the-Month Club selections when she was done with them—Marchette Chute's *Shakespeare of London*, Jim Bishop's *Day Lincoln Was Shot*, Theodore White's *Making of a President, 1960*. It was there I first read James Baldwin's *Fire Next Time* and some borrowed copies of the *New Yorker*. My parents were Stevensonian Democrats and thoroughly middlebrow.

During the spring of 1968, when Martin Luther King Jr. and Bobby Kennedy were shot, the Students for a Democratic Society (SDS) occupied buildings at Columbia, students and workers struck in Paris, and I registered for the draft and graduated from high school, my allegiance to my class began to erode.

I went away to college at Harvard that fall, disillusioned by the assassinations and the hypocritical mess that was the Chicago Democratic Convention. Nixon's election in November sealed the deal. I started to go to SDS meetings. The following spring, we occupied University Hall, the administration called in the police, people got clubbed and arrested, and the whole campus went out on strike. I came home for the summer feeling angry, cynical, revolutionary, and full of myself, and I turned on my parents and their home. In one nasty argument I meanly dismissed their Utrillo prints and Paul McCobb

furniture as "no different than what's in every Holiday Inn in America," a dig
that left my mother in tears and my father fuming.

A few years later, I dropped out of graduate school, joined the new communist movement, lied about my Ivy League education, and got a job as a
janitor in a Boston hospital in order to organize the unorganized. For the next
decade, I mopped floors, cleaned bathrooms, talked union during the day,
and went to meetings at night.

I remember two moments in particular from those meetings. The first
occurred when some national leadership came to town to check on us.
During a moment of downtime after a formal meeting I was talking with
an important African American comrade from Philadelphia. His credentials
were impressive. He'd been a Student Nonviolent Coordinating Committee
organizer in Georgia, had served more than two years in prison for draft
resistance during the Vietnam War, and his brother, a Vietnam vet who'd
been exposed to Agent Orange, was recently dead from cancer. I was eager
to impress him and somehow postured, making a point of my choice to leave
my privileges behind and work at the hospital. He let me know in a good-
natured way that while he respected my decision, I didn't need to talk it up.
Then he added with a laugh, "It seems sometimes like you Ivy League guys
join the working class so you can get less out of life, but I think most working-
class people want more."

At another meeting, this one of a Marxist study group that included cell
members and potential recruits from the working class, we were discussing
the dictatorship of the proletariat and the transition to socialism. The group
leader, a red-diaper baby whose father had been forced underground during
the McCarthy era, was talking about his recent trip to Cuba. He mentioned
how the Cuban government used wage controls as incentives to promote,
indeed enforce, equality. The government had decreed that no one could
earn four times more than anyone else. What did we think of this? My mind
began to churn: correct or incorrect? Ultra-left adventurism? Right-wing
economism? Before I could say anything a Puerto Rican woman we were
trying to win over, a single mother of two who worked as a legal secretary,
fairly shouted, "Four to one! Sounds good to me. What's our ratio? A thousand to one? A million to one? Hell, people I know won't even talk about
what they make."

A friend of mine who died not long ago, the essayist Carol Bly, once told
me, "Nobody knows anything until they've left their class for a while—up
or down, it doesn't matter." I think she was right, and I think I learned three
things from those two incidents when I tried to leave my class: first, some
people (my young self, for instance, and many academic Marxists) are too

quick to dismiss the middle class as merely smug, always conventional, and something to avoid; second, working-class people don't necessarily see the middle class that way and would like to have some of the security and leisure that come from being a part of it; and third, it is the ruling class, not the middle class, that is the real source of inequality.

When I started this project, it was to be primarily a study of a genre I love—the personal essay—and in many ways, that is what it has remained. The book offers close readings of personal essays, studies of individual essayists, and a survey of what American critics have had to say about essays and their role in our culture. But my life history has led this to also be a book about the American middle class and its culture—middlebrow culture.

My time as an organizer was bookended by two trips to graduate school, and it was a desire to study the essay—the genre of Montaigne and Thoreau, Baldwin and Didion—that led me back to school. I was intrigued by the story of a mind remembering and thinking. I began to write essays as well as study their history. Essays offered a way to think independently. In his defense of the essay, Theodor Adorno claimed, "The essay shies away from the violence of dogma."[1] Perhaps, but by saying "shies away," Adorno wisely suggests that it would be dogmatic to hold that any form is inherently, always, and definitely *not* dogmatic. Still, the essay's birth in skepticism, in an individualism distrustful of individualism, seemed to me then and seems to me now a good way to proceed.

If I wrote this book to understand the American essay in the twentieth century and its middle-class readers, I found that I was also writing about myself (and perhaps, dear reader, about you as well), for I am a product of twentieth-century American middlebrow culture. My family's journey is the journey of America's new middle class. It began with my grandparents who were, on both sides, midwestern farm couples and moved through my mother, the Book-of-the-Month Club member, and my father, a G.I. Bill intellectual and college professor, arriving finally at me, my wife, and our daughters, who live in a 1950s ranch house—twenty-one hundred square feet with four bedrooms, three baths, a knotty-pine rec room, and a screened porch.

⚬━┿━⚬

This book has been long in the works, and there are many people to thank. In my two trips to graduate school I was lucky enough to study with two scholars who are themselves friends and collaborators—Bob Scholes and Carl Klaus. Their rigor, encouragement, and love of the essay have been indispensable. Bob said good-bye to me when I quit the academy to become an organizer and (along with Ed Ahearn and Brent Harold) left the door open; Carl was there to welcome me back. A mutual friend said to me, "I love the essay, but Carl would kill for it." I have been inspired by Carl's level of commitment, his friendship, and the many conversations about the essay we have had over the years.

If Carl kept me focused on form, Tom Lutz has been the one who has always reminded me that close reading does not mean that we need to abandon context and history—that, in fact, the opposite is true. Carl and Tom along with Bob Sayre, Garrett Stewart, and the late Janet Altman helped me more than they will ever know by being the first readers of a manuscript that would become this book. Others at Iowa who generously read early versions of some of this book include Martha Patterson, Carol Spaulding, and Susanna Ashton. Much of my understanding of the form of the essay was hammered out in a stimulating and long-standing essayists-on-the-essay study group at the University of Iowa that included Maura Brady, Cassie Kircher, Michele Payne, John Price, and Dan Roche. The University of Iowa supported me with a Seashore Dissertation-Year Fellowship.

Since leaving Iowa I have been fortunate to teach at two other universities that are strongly committed to the study of the essay. At St. Lawrence University, I was lucky enough to work with two great memoirists and essayists—Natalia Rachel Singer and Bob Cowser—and to meet a student of theirs who has since become a terrific essayist, scholar, and friend, Bill Bradley. At Florida State University (FSU), I have been welcomed by the creative writing program as a practicing essayist and by the literature program as a scholar of the essay. I owe special thanks to my nonfiction compatriots Bob Shacochis, Diane Roberts, David Vann, and the late Wendy Bishop. Many other colleagues have read portions of my work or discussed it with me in faculty symposia. Special thanks to Robert Olen Butler for his friendship, generosity, and the gift of his art; to Janet Burroway and Peter Ruppert for their love, conversation, and opportunities to collaborate; to Barry Faulk for friendship, helpful readings, and good talk about music and middlebrow; to Bruce Bickley for close readings of my first chapters and help with nineteenth-century America; to Andrew Epstein, Paul Outka, Meegan Kennedy, Cristobal Silva, and Doug Fowler for sage advice and helpful reads; to Leigh Edwards for walking the line; and to Robin Goodman and Dan Vitkus for keeping things organized. Thanks also to our FSU American literature reading group, especially its intrepid organizers—Catherine Altmaier, Lucy Rhyne Littler, and Jennifer Moffitt. Two wonderful research assistants—Eileen Reynolds and Alison Voorhees—read the entire manuscript with much care; another—Peggy Wright-Cleveland—helped immensely by tracking done primary sources.

Wayne Toberman and the International Press Club of Chicago helped track down information about the Whitechapel Club. Martha White, granddaughter of E. B. and Katharine White, was wonderfully helpful and supportive.

Several kind and generous administrators have become friends and mentors. I could not have done this work without the support of Hunt Hawkins, Don Foss, Joe Travis, Kathi Yancey, and Ralph Berry. Florida State supported my work with a Personal Development Grant and a First-Year Assistant Professor Grant.

I was welcomed to Tallahassee by a local writing group: Michael Trammel, Terry Schneider, Joe Clark, Virgil Suarez, Russ Franklin, Mike Rychlik, and Dean Newman. Thanks, Wingsters, for admitting a newcomer and giving of your good humor and fine insights.

Good friends from the past and accomplished scholars of twentieth-century American culture Alan Nadel and Judy Smith have supported my work for years.

Clair Willcox helped this book find a wonderful home, the University of Missouri Press, where Sara Davis and Annette Wenda expertly moved it through the production process. Bob Atwan and an anonymous reader provided insightful, indeed indispensable, readings of the manuscript.

As an editor at *Fourth Genre: Explorations in Nonfiction,* I have had the privilege of working with some of the nation's foremost scholars and writers of nonfiction. I want to thank especially editor in chief Marcia Aldrich; the magazine's founders, Mike Steinberg and David Cooper; my predecessor as book review editor Jocelyn Bartkevicius; and interview editor Bob Root. Bob, who, like Jocelyn and I, studied with Carl Klaus at Iowa, is the author of our best critical study of E. B. White. He has shared his work with me and been an inspiration.

Librarians at Florida State's Strozier Library, Harvard's Houghton Library, and Yale's Beinecke Library all gave generously of their time and knowledge. Friends and relatives including Kent French and Robert Guthrie, Kimberly French and Michael Rozyne, Peter Sims and Amy Peters, and Tom and DeeDee Hamilton opened their homes to me while I was on research trips. Charles Witmer and Miriam Gurniak, Mitch Ross and Eddie Lueken, and Mary Wilson Lovelady all gave me beautiful secluded places where I could write undisturbed. Much of this book was written while I was a fellow at the Lillian E. Smith Center for the Creative Arts on Screamer Mountain near Clayton, Georgia. Lillian Smith was a major figure in American letters and politics; a friend of Eleanor Roosevelt, Carson McCullers, and Martin Luther King Jr.; and civil rights activist, teacher, editor, camp director, and author of such important books as *Killers of the Dream* and *Strange Fruit.* When the latter was banned in Boston, she was concerned that it would be misrepresented and so wrote to her editor, "The book is cheap in the eyes of the middle classes—the very people whom we wanted to read the book and take it seriously for these are the people who can do something about both race and the church in the South—and indeed in the whole country. We can't dismiss them as the rabble, the fools. They are 'our people' whether we like it or not; and they are the people who determine the quality of our national life. I think it is very important that we change their idea of the book."[2] Lillian Smith's novel went on to sell three million copies and change the way Americans think about race. I feel honored to have been able to write where she wrote, and I want to thank Robert Fichter and Nancy Smith Fichter for that opportunity.

Earlier versions of parts of this book appeared in *American Literature, culturefront,* the *CEA Critic,* and *The Encyclopedia of the Essay,* or were presented at the Modern Language Association and Bedell NonfictioNOW conferences. I would like to thank my editors, conveners, and fellow panelists, especially Michael Moon, Jay Kaplan, William A. Tanner, Tracy Chevalier, Lynn Z. Bloom, Doug Hesse, and Rebecca Faery.

Finally, I am blessed to have a wife and two daughters who make all this worth doing. They are patient when I disappear into my head, the 1920s, or the mountains of North Georgia. They keep me honest with their honesty; they keep me laughing with their silliness. Elizabeth's experience as a writer and her fine eye as an editor have made this a better book, but her love has made it possible.

The
AMERICAN
ESSAY
in the
AMERICAN
CENTURY

Introduction:

Defending the Essay

> The perfect essayist could write a good essay on Hitler or on hogs, and I should be enchanted to read it—but he has not done it yet, and I am not yet enchanted.
>
> —Katharine Fullerton Gerould, "Information, Please! A Call for a Plebiscite of Magazine Readers"

> Once in everyone's life there is apt to be a period when he is fully awake, instead of half asleep. I think of those five years in Maine as the time when this happened to me. . . . It was one of those rare interludes that can never be repeated, a time of enchantment. I am fortunate indeed to have had the chance to get some of it down on paper.
>
> —E. B. White, in 1982, about the years (1938–1943) when he wrote *One Man's Meat*

The dates and titles tell the tale—"The Passing of the Essay" (1894), "The Survival of the Essay" (1897), "The Prosperity of the Essay" (1905), "Once and for All" (1929), "A Disappearing Art" (1932), "A Little Old Lady Passes Away" (1933), and "The Lost Art of the Essay" (1935). A debate over the "death" of the essay simmered on from the end of the nineteenth until well into the twentieth centuries. What was dying, however, was not the essay, but a particular kind of essay and the America of which it had been a part. Simultaneously, a new kind of personal essay was coming into being. This book describes that moment and in so doing engages in an act of recovery. By revealing this previously unrecognized aspect of American literary history it seeks to dispel the lingering myth that the essay is old-fashioned and less literary than other genres. In short, it offers a defense of the essay.

During the debate over the demise of the essay, some writers and critics argued that in an age of commercialism, mass culture, and shrill polemics the essay was the last bastion of tradition, standards, and independent meditative thought. Others countered that the essay was inherently genteel, hopelessly obsolete, and foolishly enamored of English upper-class conventions. But a third group chose to write essays that responded to the concerns of America's expanding, increasingly cosmopolitan, and largely middle-class readership. It was in this zone of contention where older forms of the essay and self, forms that we associate with the Genteel Tradition, were giving way to new ones that modern America was written.

A new kind of American personal essay appeared first in the syndicated columns (or "colyumns" as they were called then) of the New York papers during the 1920s. Written by men such as Franklin Pierce Adams, Heywood Broun, Don Marquis, and Christopher Morley, this new kind of essay was more ironic and streetwise than its genteel predecessor, and its influence would become wide reaching. It helped spark the "magazine revolution," launch radio book shows, and give voice to the new and ascendant middle class. Genteel essayists continued to chat by the fireside about Art and old books, but in book reviews, Sunday supplements, and popular magazines, a new group of essayists tried to make sense of modern life. Their readers included small-town girls recently arrived in the big city, Pullman porters carrying the news between North and South, recent immigrants assimilating to the New World, eager young men on their way up, and husbands and wives in suburban starter homes. They read over hurried cups of coffee in diners and at family breakfast tables; they read while hanging onto straps in the subway or on trolleys. These consumers of culture had some new money, but little cultural capital. The new essays appealed to them because they were brief and accessible, and their writers were neither old-school Brahmins nor snooty "custodians of culture," but friendly generalists and savvy insiders who knew the city, offered opinions, recommended books, and modeled a witty and useful brand of sophistication.[1]

The new essayists found their first alternatives to the genteel essayists in the wild transcendentalism of Ralph Waldo Emerson and Henry David Thoreau, the satire of Mark Twain and H. L. Mencken, and the Progressivism of John Jay Chapman, Randolph Bourne, and Jane Addams. They included, in addition to the colyumnists, modernists such as Edmund Wilson, Gertrude Stein, and F. Scott Fitzgerald; Harlem Renaissance writers such as Zora Neale Hurston, Langston Hughes, Richard Wright, and W. E. B. Du Bois; and Algonquin Wits such as Robert Benchley, Dorothy Parker, and Alexander Woollcott.

These new voices helped open the way for E. B. White, who is arguably the greatest American essayist of the first half of the twentieth century and who will be the focus of the last two chapters of this book. Certainly, White is well known, but his great work as an essayist has too often been buried under the tremendous success of his children's books and his handbook on style. An important handful of his essays are taught in college writing classes, but rarely do students study his entire oeuvre and learn about the distinctly American voice he brought to bear on basic human problems and critical global issues. White, like so many middle-class liberals, struggled to find his way through both the high times of the twenties and the fierce arguments of the thirties. By 1937 White had been writing for the *New Yorker* for more than a decade. He had grown tired of the magazine's weekly deadlines, short paragraphs, dry irony, and anonymous editorial "we," which he called "a cloak of dishonesty."[2] Fascism was on the rise in Europe, and he wanted to write about it, something he could not do at the *New Yorker*. Finally, in 1938, he left New York for Maine and the *New Yorker* for *Harper's*, which had offered him a signed monthly column of twenty-five hundred words. Those columns would be collected in *One Man's Meat*, a book in which White battled the isolationists and advanced the cause of the Popular Front against fascism. White's work in this book connected with a country that had moved from the Victorian parlor to the bungalow living room, where the hearth had been replaced by the radio and Americans listened to their president deliver fireside chats. *One Man's Meat* also signaled a breakthrough for the American personal essay. In it White developed a new voice that retained the warmth, self-deprecation, and irony he had honed in the *New Yorker*'s "Notes and Comment" and "Talk of the Town," but was now more serious and possessed of a greater sense of citizenship.

Later, at the end of his career White wrote that he was "not fooled about the place of the essay in twentieth-century American letters—it stands a short distance down the line. The essayist, unlike the novelist, the poet, and the playwright, must be content in his self-imposed role of second-class citizen" and should not dream of "the Nobel Prize or other earthly triumphs."[3] Nor should we be fooled by the self-pity White is ironically adopting here. By 1977, when he was seventy-eight years old and wrote this passage, he was successful and as comfortable as a man who had always battled depression could be, but what he wrote about the hierarchy of genres is true.

There are several reasons for the essay's lowly status during the twentieth century. First of all, essayists themselves must share some of the blame, for they were slow to modernize. On the eve of the First World War, when fiction had already turned toward realism and naturalism, and poetry toward imagism, many essayists were still emulating Charles Lamb. The old-fashioned, genteel essay of the Victorian and Edwardian ages had surprising holding power. As late as 1988, in the preface to his book-length study *The Observing Self: Rediscovering the Essay*, Graham Good admitted that he was launching his project with some trepidation because the word *essay* still "conjures up the image of a middle-aged man in a worn tweed jacket in an armchair smoking a pipe by a fire in his private library in a country house in England, in about 1910, maundering on about the delights of idleness, country walks, tobacco, old wine, and old books."[4]

A second reason for the essay's second-class citizenship flows from the first, for if the essay was not modernist, neither could it be considered truly difficult and "literary." Modernism was not much interested in the personal essay. On the whole, the high modernists chose to hide confession behind metaphysical conceits and difficult allusions. As a movement, modernism sought detachment and obliqueness—goals that have generally lain outside the province of the essay. The personal essay is a genre that employs a familiar style and addresses the common reader, but New Criticism, modernism's handmaiden, focused its attention on "purer," more closed forms such as the lyric poem. The essay, like the lyric, speaks personally and out of a moment, but it is a lower genre—mixed, messy, digressive, and written in prose. Essays appear first in magazines and on op-ed pages. Even when they are later collected in anthologies or collections of the author's own work, they continue to be associated in the minds of many readers with fish-wrap journalism. They are seen as a product of memory and reporting rather than imagination and intellect. All of this is compounded by the form's reverence for clarity and familiar language. The trope of the essay as a conversation began with Michel de Montaigne's decision to write in French rather than Latin, continued through the coffeehouse table talk of the London periodical essayists, and was codified by William Hazlitt in his 1821 essay, "On Familiar Style." White's own preference for windowpane prose and simple diction animates every page of his revision of *The Elements of Style*, which began as the classroom handbook of his college composition teacher, Will Strunk.

This clarity and ability to communicate has led to a third black mark against the essay. In an age of specialists, it is seen as the work of generalists. Essays often give the inside dope on this or that subculture, specialty, or scientific breakthrough, yet they are written for general readers and appear in general magazines. If a real man of letters indulges in the form, he is excused for he is a novelist or poet first, momentarily off-duty and writing with his left hand, and for money. Guiltily, we grant him this chance to earn a dime, but a full-time essayist writing regularly for a check is considered a hack, and because he spouts off about anything and everything, he's considered a dilettante.

Finally, their intended audience has also stigmatized essays. Suzanne Ferguson has argued, "Like societies of people, the society of literary genres has its class system, in which, over time, classes reorganize themselves, accept new members, and cast old members into the dustbin. It has its aristocracy, its middle classes, and its proletarians."[5] In the society of genres, the essay—especially the modern American essay—is decidedly middle class and middlebrow.

Pierre Bourdieu offers an explanation as to why. There is a "duality," Bourdieu argues, to the literary field in which genres reside, for that field is at once economic and symbolic. From the economic point of view the hierarchy of genres is "simple and relatively stable"—drama is at the top, and poetry is at the bottom. People pay more money to see plays (and films) than they do to attend poetry readings. On the other hand, a genre tends to move up the symbolic hierarchy to the extent that it expresses a "disavowal" or "refusal" of the economic. If a genre is seen as difficult, it is more likely to be associated with "art for art's sake," and as such it accrues more symbolic capital. From this point of view—the point of view of the symbolic—the hierarchy is inverted: poetry moves to the top precisely because its audience is small and select, and plays and movies slide to the bottom because they are popular.[6]

The essay, according to Bourdieu, is (like the novel) a mixed or middle genre. It is less pure or "artistic" than most poems but not as massively popular as Hollywood films, network television, or Broadway plays. Middle genres, in Bourdieu's scheme, are especially malleable or adaptable. They are able to reach out to different audiences depending on how they deploy their own "hierarchy of specialties," or subgenres.[7] Just as the novel ranges from literary fiction to genre fiction, so does the essay range from the formal essays that appear in literary quarterlies to the popular columns that appear in newspapers.

Bourdieu also argues that new class formations require new genres and subgenres, and middle genres are especially adept at satisfying these needs. During the twentieth century, the American class structure underwent a radical change. The old middle class of artisans, small-town entrepreneurs, independent professionals, and farmers gave way to a new middle class of salaried professionals and wage-earning clerks, nurses, public school teachers and technicians—what John Ehrenreich and Barbara Ehrenreich have called the professional-managerial class.[8] In order to hail each other and consolidate as a class, the members of the PMC developed a new culture—middlebrow culture—and it required new genres. The "producers . . . of middle-brow culture," according to Bourdieu, constituted a new set of "cultural intermediaries" that included radio and public television producers, "the critics of 'quality' newspapers and magazines," and various "writer-journalists and journalist-writers," and these intermediaries invented "a whole series of genres, half-way between legitimate culture and mass production." Notable among these genres are "'essays.'"[9] Bourdieu's enclosure of the term in quotation marks makes clear that these contemporary versions of the essay may or may not conform to traditional, more literary definitions of the term.

So why focus on this belittled, second-class genre? In one sense, the answer is simple: the essay is not second-rate, and the belittling has been unfair. Not only is the tradition of Montaigne, Sir Francis Bacon, Ralph Waldo Emerson, James Baldwin, and Joan Didion long and rich, but it is also vibrant and vital, and the American essay in particular is undergoing a renaissance. Robert Atwan has edited the Best American Essays series annually since 1986. Several historical anthologies of essays have appeared since 1993.[10] Important new magazines focus on the genre.[11] A growing number of scholarly journals and conferences focus on the essay.[12] The Association of Writers and Writing Programs (AWP) lists 310 graduate programs in creative writing. Almost all of them offer courses, and almost half of them offer concentrations or graduate degrees in creative nonfiction. Over the past twenty years these nonfiction programs have been the fastest growing of all graduate writing programs.[13]

The traits of the essay that are often perceived as weaknesses have also been strengths and assets. Its clear and familiar language has left it relatively jargon free and open to the American idiom. Its broad appeal has attracted specialists who want to share their expertise with a wider readership. Its kinship to journalism has required it to be current, but it has not followed that it is inevitably ephemeral; currency has also meant that essays have been relevant and engaged. Indeed, it will be my argument that engagement can and has served the American essay well and helped it break out of the cozy complacency in which it sometimes wrapped itself.

Within the humanities and the human sciences, few issues are more current and controversial than that of subjectivity, yet the literary genre most explicitly focused on subjectivity, the one that claims on the one hand to create the subject and on the other to issue directly from it—the essay—has not received much scholarly attention. Michel Foucault and Raymond Williams have both remarked on the irony inherent in the term *the subject*, which refers at once to the subject of political and ideological domination (for example, a

British subject) and to "the active mind or thinking agent" of classical German philosophy.[14] This book, like the essay itself, embraces that irony and explores a moment in history when American essayists, led by E. B. White, appropriated and were appropriated by the Genteel Tradition. The attitude of even the most radical of these new essayists toward Victorian gentility was conflicted and ambiguous. Each of these writers was struggling to find a single confident voice, but in that struggle their essays were invariably caught between retreat and departure, between America's past and its future. That tension is the subject of this book.

∘━✦━∘

A few notes on methodology, beginning with periodization. *The American Century* was a contested term from the moment Henry Luce coined it in 1941. Luce and Franklin Roosevelt were both interventionists, but Luce disagreed with the way in which Roosevelt's Lend-Lease proposal would put Great Britain on more or less equal footing with the United States. Luce's famous "American Century" article in the February 17, 1941, issue of *Life* was an answer to Roosevelt's Four Freedoms speech of the previous month and Lend-Lease, which was being debated in Congress. Luce's article described what he hoped would be a century of U.S. hegemony rather than an alliance of equals. This disagreement between Roosevelt and Luce was the latest round in an argument about America's role in the world that had begun at Versailles with the debate over the League of Nations. I have appropriated Luce's term because it is both potent and contested. New Deal supporters tried almost immediately to counter it. Just weeks after Luce's article appeared, Max Lerner called for a "people's century." In May 1942 Henry Wallace declared the "century of the common man."[15] Neither formulation found traction.

Luce's term continues to prompt (and even frame) an argument about our national character and the role of the United States in the world, both of which have been indelibly linked to America's new middle class. Warren Susman argued that at the end of the Great Depression, America's "enormous" middle class "felt themselves suspended between two eras" and surprised that their "progress" had not yielded the results they once expected. "The story of American culture," wrote Susman, "remains largely the story of this middle class."[16] During the American Century the essay was one of the central organs through which the American middle class told its story.

But if there was an American Century, when did it begin, and has it yet come to an end? Luce meant his term to refer to the twentieth century, and some scholars have agreed with him, though others have not. Harold Evans saw the

American Century as being the country's second. He dated it from the centennial of Washington's inauguration to 1989. Biographers David Levering Lewis and Ronald Steel linked it to the lives of their subjects—W. E. B. Du Bois (1868–1963) and Walter Lippman (1889–1974), respectively. Joshua Freeman and his collaborators believe it ended with the fall of Saigon and the embarrassment of Watergate, David S. Mason with 9/11. William Kristol's neoconservative cohorts launched their Project for the New American Century in 1997, suggesting that they agreed with Luce but saw the millennium as a time to re-up.[17]

My own position is that the American Century (like the Genteel Tradition before it) was over almost as soon as it was named. America's involvement brought an end to World War II, a war that left the United States as the only world power with its industrial base unbombed and intact. America also had sole possession of the atomic bomb and had twice shown itself willing to use it. Yet the postwar era of American hegemony that Luce envisioned did not happen. Instead, the United Nations succeeded where the League of Nations had not, the cold war began, and colonial empires fell apart. If there was an American Century, it was a short one. It encompassed roughly the last two decades of the nineteenth century and the first four of the twentieth, and while my epilogue will bring this study up to the present, the book's focus is the period 1880 to 1940.[18] Many of the essayists discussed in this book served as major figures in important middlebrow institutions, including magazines such as the *New Yorker* and the *Saturday Review of Literature;* the Book-of-the-Month Club and Literary Guild; radio talk and quiz shows; book publishing ventures that produced outlines, digests, reprints of classics, and popular anthologies; and adult education programs. Some of them also wrote for Broadway, helped administer the arts projects of the Works Progress Administration and the Office of Wartime Information, edited the postwar quality paperback series, and appeared on the early educational programming of the television networks.

Alan Trachtenberg and Michael Denning have distinguished two approaches to the politics of culture: "cultural politics," on the one hand, which focuses on the politics of organization, institutions, alliances, and affiliations, and "aesthetic ideologies," on the other, which takes up the politics of genres, taste, aesthetics, and form.[19] Scholars have sometimes discussed literary genres, including courtship stories, Broadway musicals, and "women's novels," as distinctly middlebrow,[20] but the bulk of the work on middlebrow culture has focused on institutions and alliances. I will engage in both kinds of analysis, but my focus is on the essay. Many figures familiar to scholars of middlebrow culture will reappear here, but this time as essayists. I will examine Heywood Broun and Christopher Morley not primarily as Book-of-the-Month Club judges but rather as columnists and Henry Seidel Canby, Carl Van Doren, Amy Loveman, Katharine Fullerton Gerould, W. E. B. Du Bois, and Stuart Sherman not mainly as editors and critics but rather as essayists and theorists of the essay.

Though I talk primarily about America this is, to some extent, a transatlantic story. Montaigne, Bacon, La Bruyère, and the English periodical and romantic essayists (especially Lamb) have been models for America's essayists. Nineteenth-century American essayists traveled and published in Europe. Washington Irving and James Russell Lowell served as ambassadors to Spain and the Court of St. James, respectively, and many of the American genteel essayists launched their careers by writing up their grand tour as a book of travel essays. Conversely, English essays were widely reprinted in American magazines, especially prior to the International Copyright Act of 1891. Englishman Leslie Stephen was one of the first critics to bemoan the "death" of the essay. Stephen's youngest daughter, Virginia Woolf, was arguably the greatest essayist of the twentieth century, wrote insightfully about the essay, and will appear often in this book.

Finally, however, the essays on which I focus most closely are American. Many, as I have suggested, are objects of retrieval, including most of the essays from the ongoing debate over the death of the essay. These "essays upon essays," as Hilaire Belloc referred to them, constitute a buried archive.[21] They appeared in turn-of-the-century reviews such as *Outlook* and the *Bookman* and later in middlebrow magazines such as the *Saturday Review of Literature* and *Ladies' Home Journal*, and though controversial and much discussed at the time, few of them have been studied since they first appeared.

Essays by other writers are better known. They have stayed in print in collections of those authors' work and in popular and important anthologies as Gerald Early's two-volume *Speech and Power: The African American Essay and Its Cultural Content from Polemics to Pulpit* (1992), Phillip Lopate's *Art of the Personal Essay: An Anthology from the Classical Era to the Present* (1994), and Robert Atwan and Joyce Carol Oates's *Best American Essays of the Century* (2000). Canon formation is a vexed and contentious issue, and particularly so for the essay. As Lynn Z. Bloom has demonstrated, the essay canon as we presently know it is primarily a teaching—rather than a historical, critical, or national—canon, and so while most of the essays discussed here are familiar, some readers may not have revisited them since they read them in their freshman composition class.[22] I will discuss the implications of this quarantining of the essay in first-year writing anthologies more in my epilogue.

A term that recurs in this book is the *site of the essay*, by which I mean several things. Most literally, it refers to the setting of the individual essay (assuming it has one). Where is its narrator located? Does that location bear an important relation to the place where the essay was actually composed? And because the essay is often characterized as a conversation between author and reader, how does the imagined site of the essay relate to the place where the essay is being read? By examining a variety of such sites, including Victorian parlors and gentlemen's clubs, public school classrooms, the living rooms of suburban bungalows, the Algonquin Round Table, Jim Crow cars, and the Roosevelt White House, I hope to deepen our understanding of the essay's history and its role in American culture. The term *site* can also refer to the places where these essays first appeared in print (magazines, journals, newspapers, book reviews, Sunday supplements) and the places where they were later collected (anthologies and textbooks). By studying the essay in relation to America's evolving text technologies, I also hope to extend our understanding of the cultural work of the essay, especially the role it played in the construction of the new middle class during the first half of the twentieth century.

That class, as Janice Radway has noted, is "the class . . . that always insists it is not a class," or, as Anthony Giddens has written, the middle class is "aware" of itself as a class, but not "conscious" of itself as a class, a distinction that he says is important "because class awareness may take the form of *a denial of the existence or reality of classes.*"[23] Middle-class people valorize meritocracy and all the beliefs and metrics that follow from it: self-improvement, personal accomplishment, autonomy, academic degrees, professional titles, and distinctive taste. But this "ideology of social atomism," as Stuart Blumin calls it, can be a thin glue that must be supplemented by something else—a belief that everyone, or almost everyone, is middle class and so can get along, even when we are not all middle class and are not getting along.[24]

A term that helps illuminate the essay's relationship to the middle class is *friendship,* which is meant to get not only at the friendly relationship between essayist and reader but also at the complicated and contradictory ways in which friendship has functioned in twentieth-century America. Friendship is not merely ideology, but sometimes it is. Sometimes it becomes a way for middle-class people to make their employees or subordinates, their business associates or supervisors, into friends—something they are not. Sometimes, it becomes a word meant to displace other words such as *comrade, brother and sister,* or even *compañero y compañera*—words that because they are inflected by class, race, ethnicity, or gender tend to expose the myth that we are all "one big happy family."

Friendship can function in these ways because it signifies so much more than this ideology. Friendship also refers to a universal and essential human relationship, and the contradictory nature of the term, the way it can toss us between delusions and dreams, is at the heart of this book. Montaigne conceived of the *Essais* as a conversation between friends, and his great essay "Of Friendship" is a tribute to his friend Étienne de La Boétie. It was in that essay that Montaigne, writing more than fifteen years after La Boétie's death, famously struggled to define friendship: "If you press me to tell why I loved him, I feel that this cannot be expressed, except by answering: Because it was he, because it was I." American essayists have also focused often on the intimacy and openness that constitute true friendship. Certainly, the genteel essayist chatting at the fireside was constructing himself and his readers as friends. "A friend is a person with whom I may be sincere. Before him I may think aloud," wrote Emerson. Or as White had Wilbur put it at the end of *Charlotte's Web*: "It is not often that someone comes along who is a true friend and a good writer. Charlotte was both."[25]

But to imagine the essay as a conversation between friends also has its problems. Following the lead of Walter Pater, essayists have conceived of their form in terms of a Platonic dialogue, but the truth is, it is usually only the essayist who is talking.[26] In the genteel essay of nineteenth-century America, not only was the conversation a monologue, but the essay's false coziness presaged the next century's marketing of friendship. Warren Susman saw America's move from the nineteenth to the twentieth centuries as being marked by a shift from a culture of character to one of personality, and that shift affected America's view of friendship as well. Americans in the twentieth century became obsessed with personality, friendship, and the relationship between the two. By 1925 Fitzgerald, in describing Gatsby's appeal, defined personality as "an unbroken series of successful gestures."[27] The rise of mass consumer society and the advertising that came with it moved Americans away from self-control, duty, and restraint toward self-expression and the cultivation of a personality designed to make friends. The colyumnists of the 1920s, for instance, wrote essays meant to make New York seem a friendlier place.[28] Then, in 1937, a former soap salesman and actor turned public speaker named Dale Carnegie published *How to Win Friends and Influence People*; the book went through seventeen printings in its first year. A key to the success of would-be columnist Franklin Roosevelt's fireside chats was that he opened them not with the speechified greeting of "My fellow Americans," but rather with the quieter and more intimate phrase "My friends."[29]

When the era of character gave way to that of personality has been a point of much contention.[30] Beginnings and endings become "clear" only in retrospect. I argue that the new American essay began with the appearance of colyumnists like Broun and Morley during the 1920s but am aware that cultural history, like all history, evolves. Fixed moments of origin lead to creation myths, and so this book reaches past the colyumnists through the Progressive Era and genteel essayists to Washington Irving, Nathaniel Hawthorne, and Fanny Fern for antecedents. It effectively ends in 1944 when White, having just published a revised edition of *One Man's Meat,* stops writing his column for *Harper's* and returns to the *New Yorker,* where he negotiates an arrangement with the magazine's editor, Harold Ross, that allows him to write longer pieces than he had before. During the next two decades White would write some of his greatest essays, including "Death of a Pig" and "Ring of Time," but his first assignment took him to the Allied conference at Dumbarton Oaks and a subsequent meeting of fifty nations in San Francisco where plans were laid for the organization that would become the United Nations.

From the beginning of World War II the Allies had been thinking about what the goals of the war were and what the postwar world would look like. In his dispatches from Dumbarton Oaks and San Francisco, White argued for a world government in which the United States was one nation among all nations. He believed that a United Nations organized along democratic and federalist principles in which no nation possessed a veto power could be the first step toward what he called "supranationalism." It was a goal he had been thinking about for a while and one that was for him bigger than politics. Just three days after Pearl Harbor he wrote about it in decidedly Thoureauvian terms:

> Before you can become a supranationalist you have first to be a naturalist and feel the ground under you making a whole circle. It is easier for a man to be loyal to his club than to his planet; the by-laws are shorter, and he is personally acquainted with the other members. A club, moreover, or a nation, has a most attractive offer to make: it offers the right to be exclusive. There are not many of us who are physically constituted to resist this strange delight, this nourishing privilege. It is at the bottom of all fraternities, societies, orders. It is at the bottom of most trouble. The planet holds no such inducement. The planet is everybody's. All it offers is the grass, the sky, the water, the ineluctable dream of peace and fruition.[31]

White collected his essays from the period in a book called *The Wild Flag* that proved to be a harbinger of writing he would do during the 1950s when he argued against nuclear testing and his environmental writing inspired Rachel Carson. He revealed in *The Wild Flag* that the title came to him in a dream just before Christmas 1943. In his dream a third world war had left fewer than two hundred people on earth. Delegates from the world's eighty-three nations gathered after the war to make a lasting peace. All arrived carrying their nation's flag except the Chinese delegate, who had a shoe box containing what he called "a wild flag, *Iris tectorum*." He brought the wild iris, he said, because it is "very beautiful and grows everywhere in the moist places of the earth for all to observe and wonder at. I propose all countries adopt it, so that it will be impossible for us to insult each other's flag."[32]

In spite of these editorials, his pamphlet for Roosevelt, his service in the army as World War I came to an end, and his work as a civilian defense spotter on the Maine coast during World War II, White always claimed he was not a joiner, though he admitted to joining one group. It was an act that suggested how expansively a true essayist might conceive of friendship. He was a charter member of America's first environmental organization—the Friends of the Land.[33]

┌─────────┐
│   1   │
└─────────┘

THE GENTEEL ESSAY AND
THE GENTLEMAN AT THE FIRESIDE

The Genteel Tradition had been waiting for someone to name it, but by the time George Santayana did, it was already in decline. It had to be, for when a culture is hegemonic and fully naturalized, it is everywhere and, therefore, hard to see. But when Santayana delivered his lecture "The Genteel Tradition in American Philosophy" in 1911, the culture of the Gilded Age had receded sufficiently so that when he pointed toward it, it stood out, wholly revealed.

Yet gentility persisted, though it was no longer dominant and still in the process of being displaced by modernism. In fact, as Joan Shelley Rubin has argued, "genteel values" did not die in America at the turn of the century but "survived and prospered, albeit in chastened and redirected form" well into the 1940s. As late as 1935, for example, Nathaniel Peffer, editor of *Collier's* magazine, was still railing against "the cult of the genteel essay."[1]

The author and narrator of the genteel essay was a particular type—a gentleman, often a professor or bachelor, chatting amiably at the fireside about his books, his garden, or whatever topic his mind wandered to. Philip Rieff and Warren Susman have argued that as cultures change, so do the "modal types of persons who are their bearers," and the gentleman at the fireside was a modal type in Victorian America.[2] He emerged first in the sketches of Washington Irving, was an uneasy presence in the essays of Hawthorne and Melville, and is most commonly associated with later figures such as Oliver Wendell Holmes and James Russell Lowell.

Adherents of the Genteel Tradition, such as Holmes and Lowell, argued for an art that reflected upper-middle-class values, Christian morality, the classical unity of truth and beauty, and a belief in the progress of (Anglo-American) civilization. Organizationally, they formed an interlocking network of literary

critics, magazine editors, and Ivy League English professors. These "custodians of culture" (as Henry May famously referred to them) were motivated by
a desire to protect art from the vulgar commercialism of the Gilded Age.[3] The
New York wing of this priesthood, which included George William Curtis,
Richard Henry Stoddard, and E. L. Godkin, self-identified as "The Band" and
expressed themselves through magazines such as *Century, Scribner's, Harper's,*
and the *Nation.* The Boston, or Brahmin, wing—sometimes more liberal politically and usually more rigorous intellectually—included Charles Eliot Norton
as well as Lowell and Holmes, and was associated with the *Atlantic* and the
North American Review.

The two groups were distinct but marked by crossover and shifting alle-
giances.[4] Individually, they saw themselves as men of letters—poets, scholars, teachers, critics, editors, and publishers. They were also essayists and did
much of their cultural work in that genre. That work consisted of advancing
an aesthetic and an ideology that were conventional, sentimental, and didac-
tic. Beauty, for them, was not only objectively definable in classical terms but
also integrally related to decorum. They held tight to Christian (especially
Protestant) traditions and Anglo literary conventions, distrusted the incom-
ing waves of immigrants as well as the new rich, and were uncertain about
America's growing role as a leader in international affairs. They revered
Matthew Arnold and enlisted as the "apostles of culture" he called for in
his 1869 book *Culture and Anarchy,* pledging to defend what he deemed the
"touchstones" of Western culture, "the best that has been thought and said in
the world." His happy conjunction of "sweetness and light" confirmed their
own belief in the unity of beauty and truth, and they were much moved by
his 1883 and 1884 lecture tour of the United States during which he warned
against confusing popularity with greatness.[5]

The essay was under particular pressure from popularity. As early as 1881,
another English idol of the American apostles, the eminent Victorian Leslie
Stephen, had bemoaned the passing of the "old-fashioned essay," which he
believed was being drowned out by a new kind of essay that seemed akin
to "the address of a mob-orator."[6] By the end of the century, as fiction was
turning toward realism and naturalism, and journalism toward muckraking,
genteel essayists were holding especially tight to the literariness of their form.

They also tried to be the real Victorians, acting more "English" than the
English. It was a phenomenon still apparent in 1916, when Owen Wister, writing in a preface to a collection by Henry Dwight Sedgwick titled *An Apology
for Old Maids, and Other Essays,* claimed that America's essayists were more
accomplished than its novelists and that they were the ones who "save our
face." "We can point to them without blushing," wrote Wister. "[I]t is their

books mainly that we send to friends in the civilized world, because they show that all of us do not live in the best-seller belt, that some of us are writers and readers with civilized intelligence. . . . They are our vindicators."[7]

Stephen's youngest daughter, Virginia Woolf, disagreed. In a review of Sedgwick's book, she argued that the genteel essayists were especially responsible for the hardening of American gentility. Sedgwick's own essays, she remarked, felt like some eighteenth-century contributions by a "country clergyman to the *Gentleman's Magazine*." The "studious refinement" of America's essayists seemed to grow from a "determination to show the stranger that they are people of civilized intelligence," and such insecurity led them to raise gentility to a dictum: "The men of genius and learning are to constitute a priesthood, held in special reverence; and the intellectual traditions of generations of educated men should be taught by them as a special cult. Was there ever a plan better calculated to freeze literature at the root than this one?"[8]

Here, then, are some of the traits of the genteel essay, traits its inheritors will grapple with well into the next century—a reverence for English and European high culture, an almost religious faith in the possibility of progress and reform, a belief in the sanctity of Art, and a deep familiarity with the warmth, intimacy, and geniality of the hearth.

THE GENTEEL ESSAY AND THE HEARTH

From its beginnings the essay has been an examination of the self. Montaigne's goal was to write "a book consubstantial with its author, concerned with my own self," though he understood that self was multifarious and changing. As he put it, "I do not portray being: I portray passing." It was in conversation he hoped to find this mutable self. To one reader he wrote that should his book of essays eventually come into her hands, "You will recognize in them the same bearing and the same air that you have seen in his [the author's] conversation." If he could have adopted some style other than that of his conversation, Montaigne claimed to her that he would not have done so, "for I want to derive nothing from these writings except that they represent me to your memory as I naturally am."[9]

In Victorian America the hearth was where the most unencumbered and intimate conversations took place. It was where people could be themselves, but by midcentury both the hearth and those selves were changing. As early as 1843 in an essay titled "Fire Worship," Nathaniel Hawthorne found himself waxing nostalgic for the loss of the fireside. Having recently installed woodstoves (invented in 1742 by fellow essayist Benjamin Franklin) in his home,

Hawthorne admits, "I, to my shame, have put up stoves in kitchen and parlor and chamber" and so participated in the "almost universal exchange of the open fireplace for the cheerless and ungenial stove." He apostrophizes the "brilliant guest" whom he has "thrust" into "an iron prison," apologizes to it, and foresees an almost apocalyptic set of losses: "The easy gossip; the merry yet unambitious jest; the life-like, practical discussion of real matters in a casual way; the soul of truth which is so often incarnated in a simple fireside word,—will disappear from earth. Conversation will contract the air of debate, and all mortal intercourse will be chilled with fatal frost."[10]

Soon after, intent on resisting progress and simplifying his life, Thoreau made the same mistake at Walden. In his "House-Warming" chapter, he reveals that while first building his cabin, he "lingered most about the fireplace, as the most vital part of the house," telling us that he even studied masonry so as to get the chimney right, but admits that later he switched to "a small cooking-stove." He soon found it "did not keep fire so well as the open fire-place," and even cooking became, "for the most part, no longer a poetic, but merely a chemic process." Then, in language reminiscent of Hawthorne's, he reveals the larger loss: "The stove not only took up room and scented the house, but it concealed the fire, and I felt as if I had lost a companion. You can always see a face in the fire."[11]

A few years later in his hilariously suggestive story "I and My Chimney" (1856), Herman Melville created a narrator whose massive chimney is being challenged by his youthful and aggressive wife. Unable to leave well enough alone, she wants to modernize their house by remodeling his patriarchal, authoritative, and phallic chimney. The husband opens by telling the reader he likes to sit at his hearth, "pipe in mouth, indolently weaving my vapors" and admiring his fireplace, the chimney of which is so impressive, he says, that when greeting his guests, "I stand not so much before, as, strictly speaking, behind my chimney, which is, indeed, the true host." Yet he and his chimney are aging. They are both "old settlers," and, he admits, even his "huge, corpulent old Harry VIII of a chimney," which "rises full in front of me and all my possessions," now "settles more and more every day."

But the narrator embraces this oldness and all that he associates with it: "For that cause mainly loving old Montaigne, and old cheese, and old wine, and eschewing young people . . . new books, and early potatoes, and very fond of my old claw-footed chair, and . . . my betwisted old grape-vine . . . and . . . high above all, am fond of my high-mantled old chimney." In punning language that fulsomely suggests homoeroticism, onanism, and backwardness, the narrator makes it clear that he would like to be left alone with his chimney. His chimney is his "superior," which he "ministers" to by "bowing over."

His young wife, on the other hand, "takes the Ladies' Magazine for the fashions," "likes a young company; and offers to ride young colts." In time she also enlists the help of a young architect to help her take down her husband's chimney. This man—named "Hiram Scribe"—suggests that a rumored "secret closet" is hidden in the chimney, built by the narrator's bachelor ancestor. When he finds that his wife has actually explored this secret space, the shocked husband wonders what would prompt her to "crawl into" this cavity that he sees as merely a "secret ash-hole" connected to the "queer hole" where they dispose of their ashes. Under assault by his wife, her hired scribe, and a "Ladies' Magazine" view of progress, the narrator engages at the story's end in a kind of sit-down strike, refusing for seven years to leave his house in order to stand "guard over my mossy old chimney."[12]

Melville turned his irony on his characters, but he may also have been turning it on himself. Feeling a failure as a novelist and deeply ambivalent about his success with short magazine pieces (his editor at *Putnam's Magazine*, George W. Curtis, had just declared "I and My Chimney" a "capital, genial, humorous sketch" and "thoroughly magazinish"), Melville had just suffered a breakdown and his family had called in Dr. Oliver Wendell Holmes to check on him, ostensibly for sciatica. His narrator turns to the past (as represented by the essays of Montaigne), and his wife turns to the magazines of the time; Melville seems to have felt caught between the two.[13]

In language less charged than Melville's, Lowell also discussed what was at stake in preserving a certain kind of hearth and its intimacy. Lowell, who entitled a collection of his essays *Fireside Travels*, wrote in 1867 that the first difficulty in finding a good essay was finding a "perfectly sincere and unconscious man." Such a man, he claimed, "is even more uncommon than a genius of the first order. Most men dress themselves for their autobiographies, as Machiavelli used to do for reading the classics, in their best clothes; they receive us, as it were, in a parlor chilling and awkward from its unfamiliarity with man, and keep us carefully away from the kitchen-chimney-corner, where they would feel at home, and would not look on a lapse into nature as the unpardonable sin."[14]

Ironically, the task of finding one's true self among the roles one must perform in the parlor was made more difficult by the rules of cultural decorum enforced by Lowell and his fellow custodians of culture. The parlor table, they decreed, was to hold only those books and magazines that a father could read aloud to a daughter and that would be proper for a guest to see. "It is the 'young girl' and the family center table," complained Frank Norris, "that determine the standard of the American short story."[15]

Genteel essays were geared to take readers into the intimacy of the hearth, whether it be that of the chilly parlor or that of the warmer kitchen-chimney-corner. Lowell himself may have felt more comfortable at yet a third fireplace, for his essays, according to Walter Blair, were written "as if he were putting down on paper the sort of talk an informed professor, blessed with a good sense of humor, might deliver to an intelligent college student who had dropped in for an evening chat by the library fire in Elmwood [Lowell's home in Cambridge]."[16] And though Lowell does not say it, any of these three inglenooks probably felt warmer and friendlier to him than the large and troubled outside world of immigrants, robber barons, busyness, and greed.

Titles of collections from the period confirm the preoccupation essayists had with the hearth. Authors and titles, in addition to Lowell and his *Fireside Travels* (1881), included Harriet Beecher Stowe (as "Christopher Crowfield"), *The Chimney Corner* (1868); Harriet Prescott Spofford, *Home and Hearth* (1891); Charles Dudley Warner, *Back-log Studies* (1894); Hamilton Wright Mabie, *My Study Fire* (1899); Agnes Repplier, *The Fireside Sphinx* (1901); and Samuel McChord Crothers, *By the Christmas Fire* (1908).

EMERSON AND THE PROBLEM OF CONVERSATION

Others looked on fireside talk less ironically than Melville had, more philosophically than Lowell had. Lawrence Buell has claimed that for the Concord transcendentalists, "conversation was not just a pastime but also a fine art and fit subject for philosophy." Certainly, it was for Emerson, who considered it the highest art: "But there is an art which is better than poetry, painting, or music, or architecture, better than botany, geology, or any science, namely conversation: wise, cultivated, genial conversation. Conversation is the last flower of civility, and the best result which life has to offer us; a cup for gods, which has no repentance. It is our account of ourselves. All we have, all we can do, all we know, is brought into play, and is the reproduction in finer form of all our havings."[17]

In 1832, twenty months after his first wife's death, Emerson resigned as minister of the Second Church and began to remake himself as a lecturer. Over the next five years he struggled with his faith, remarried, and along with his fellow transcendentalists explored the possibilities of conversation. In the mid-1830s he met Bronson Alcott, whom he considered the greatest of talkers. Alcott's conversation, Emerson rhapsodized, was "so lucid, so playful, so new and disdainful of all boundaries of tradition and experience, that the hearers seem no longer to have bodies or material gravity, but almost they can mount in the air at pleasure, or leap at one bound out of this poor solar system."[18] Emerson introduced Alcott to Margaret Fuller, who was working on the first

English translation of Johann Peter Eckermann's *Conversations with Goethe*. On Saturdays she conducted a series of what she called "conversations" at her friend Elizabeth Peabody's bookshop. The mix of readings, lectures, and discussion provided Boston's female intellectuals, transcendentalists, and social activists with a new educational opportunity. Fuller supported herself for five years with the conversations, which Emerson's wife Lydia attended regularly.

Emerson aspired to the same elevated state of conversation that he saw Alcott and Fuller practicing. "I lie torpid as a clod" until a friend arrived with whom he could really talk, he confided to his journal in March 1839, but once lost in conversation, he felt "the presence of a new and yet old, a genial, a native element." He was revived: "The effect of the conversation resembles the effect of a beautiful voice in a church choir . . . which insinuates itself as water into all chinks and cracks and presently floats the whole discordant choir and hold it in solution in its melody."[19]

He tried to capture such exalted conversation in his lectures and was full of hope that it could be done. In the summer of 1839 he declared: "A lecture is a new literature. . . . It is an organ of sublime power, a panharmonicon for variety of note." His talks at the lyceum, he believed, might offer "[a]ll the breadth & versatility of the most liberal conversation." But soon they began to feel repetitive, merely a way to make money. By October he was resigned: "So I submit to sell tickets again." He wondered if he had, in his lectures, set himself an impossible goal, but his "objection" to the lectures, he concluded, was "not to the thing but the form" and the commercialization of that form. His still wanted to capture the sound and roll of conversation in writing, but by the end of the winter, he had all but given up on the lecture as a way of attaining that goal: "These lectures give me little pleasure. . . . I have not once transcended the coldest self-possession. . . . I dared to hope for ecstasy & eloquence." In February he wrote to his brother William, "Ten decorous speeches and not one ecstasy, not one rapture, not one thunderbolt. Eloquence, therefore, there was none."[20]

Robert Atwan has illuminated what eloquence and ecstasy meant to Emerson. According to Atwan, ecstasy for Emerson is "more than an exalted state of feeling." It is the escape from self that happens in the spontaneous exchange of conversation and as such is connected to eloquence. For Emerson, says Atwan, eloquence "was not a matter of smooth and decorous speech" that adhered to traditional notions of rhetoric but something new—a mix of high and low, "a wide variety of articulation." A learned man like Alcott could be eloquent, but eloquence was not just fancy speech with elaborate subordination and elevated diction; in fact, it was more likely to be found in the easy flow of vernacular, the new talk of America's cities and frontier. "For blacksmiths and teamsters do not trip in their speech; it is a shower of bullets. It is the Cambridge men who correct themselves and begin again at every half sentence, and, moreover, will pun, and refine too much, and swerve from the matter to the expression." In the summer of 1840, Emerson shifted his focus from lectures to essays and tried to infuse those essays with American colloquialisms. "The language of the street is always strong," he wrote in his journal that June in an entry that focused on Montaigne. "*Guts* is a stronger word than intestines."[21]

He thought there were very few models for such writing, but Montaigne was one of them: "I know not anywhere the book that seems less written [than Montaigne's *Essays*]. It is the language of conversation transferred to a book. Cut these words, and they would bleed; they are vascular and alive." Another model for this kind of writing was Carlyle: "I know nobody among my contemporaries except Carlyle who writes with any sinew & vivacity comparable to Plutarch & Montaigne." Carlyle, he believed, "has seen as no other in our time how inexhaustible a mine is the language of Conversation. He . . . draws strength & motherwit out a poetic use of the *spoken* vocabulary, so that his paragraphs are all a sort of conversation."[22] But the road from speech to writing was a hard one to travel. It ran through journals and lectures and revisions and essays, and Emerson could not always reach his destination. A transcription or a draft was one thing, but revision could either draw out the essence of the draft or kill it. It was a difficulty Thoreau had warned him about. Fuller's writing, Thoreau wrote to Emerson in an 1843 letter, is "rich extempore writing, talking with pen in hand," but he cautioned that they should not fooled into thinking it was easy to achieve such effects: "In writing, conversation should be folded many times thick. It is the height of art that, on the first perusal, plain common sense should appear; on the second, severe truth; and on the third, beauty; and having these warrants for its depth and reality, we may then enjoy the beauty for evermore."[23]

Emerson knew he was not achieving the conversational effects that he had hoped for in his own essays. They offered a mind thinking and were rich and dense, but unlike Montaigne's book, they felt written. They were full of beauty, learning, knottiness, and thought—a lot of thought—but like the lectures before them, they were not what he was after. In the fall of 1840, he confided to his journal:

> I have been writing with some pains Essays on various matters as a sort
> of apology to my country for my apparent idleness. But the poor work
> has looked poorer daily as I strove to end it. My genius seemed to quit
> me in such a mechanical work, a seeming wise—a cold exhibition of dead

thoughts. When I write a letter to any one whom I love, I have no lack of words or thoughts: I am wiser than myself & read my paper with the plea-sure of one who receives a letter, but what I write to fill up the gaps of a chapter is hard & cold, is grammar & logic; there is no magic in it; I do not wish to see it again.[24]

It was not as bad as all that. Indeed, in a sense, it was not that at all, for Emerson is the great American essayist. But he is a particular kind of essayist. He is a Baconian, not a Montaignean. His essays are formal, careful, aphoristic, removed, impersonal, and even, sometimes at least, impenetrable. Discussing his principles of selection in the introduction to his sweeping anthology, *The Art of the Personal Essay: An Anthology from the Classical Era to the Present*, Phillip Lopate was quite direct about the difference: "Though it nearly killed me to leave out Bacon and Emerson, I decided in the end that they were not really personal essayists but great formal essayists whose minds moved inexora-bly toward the expression of impersonal wisdom and authority, regardless of flickering references to an 'I.'"[25]

This high formality compromised Emerson's persona and his style. His essays do not flow in the way that conversation flows or connect in the way conversation connects. Of his *Essays*, Carlyle famously told Emerson, "It is a *sermon* to me, as all your other deliberate utterances are. . . . I have to object still . . . that we find you a Speaker indeed, but as it were a *Soliloquizer* on the eternal mountain-tops only, in vast solitudes where men and their affairs lie all hushed in a very dim remoteness." As a consequence, wrote Carlyle, the "sentences . . . did not . . . always entirely cohere for me." They were "strong and simple" and possessed "of a clearness, of a beauty—But they did not, sometimes, rightly stick to their foregoers and their followers; the paragraph not as a beaten ingot, but as a beautiful square *bag of duck-shot* held together by canvas!"[26] These interrelated problems made it difficult for Emerson to find followers. His work is difficult, even inaccessible. He was admired and respected, but he was not loved. He was not read widely in the way that lesser nineteenth-century essayists such as Nathaniel Parker Willis and Donald Grant Mitchell were read.

Again, the problem is both one of personality and writing. Even as cold a fish as Henry James felt he could call Emerson a cold fish. Of the Emerson that emerged in James Eliot Cabot's memoir, James wrote, "We get the impression of a conscience gasping the void, panting for sensations, with something of the movement of the gills of a landed fish." Alcott, who was Emerson's close friend, concurred. Alcott tried to be circumspect and offer but a single hesita-tion, but in the end he called both Emerson's conversation and his writing into question: "I know of but one subtraction from the pleasure of reading of his books—shall I say his conversation?—gives me,—his pains to be impersonal or discrete, as if he feared any the least intrusion of himself were an offence offered to self-respect, the courtesy due to intercourse and authorship; thus depriving his page, his company, of attractions the great masters of both knew how to insinuate into their text and talk without overstepping the bounds of social or literary decorum."[27]

Emerson's difficulty and his impersonality have led to what Joel Porte famously referred to in a 1973 article as "the problem of Emerson." Porte opens with a quote from Emerson scholar Stephen Whicher that sounds almost like one of Emerson's own aphorisms: "The more we know him, the less we know him." Porte finds this statement both enigmatic and true and sees it as a clue to why "Emerson has become the least appreciated, least enjoyed, least understood—indeed, least read—of America's unarguably major writers." Porte's answer is that Emerson is not really an essayist, not in the sense that Lowell and Holmes were essayists—amicable and accessible—but is instead "fundamentally a poet whose meaning lies in his manipulations of language and figure."[28]

Atwan comes to a similar conclusion. "Emerson's essays," he decides, "did not lead to a flowering of the essay form in American; in fact, they may have been a dead end. If the essay is the one genre that did not make a notable transition into twentieth century modernism, the reason may be that Emerson's radical departures from conventional literary orderings had already taken it to that stage. After Emerson, the American essay (with the exception of Santayana's work) grew increasingly personal and moved far closer to rhetoric than to poetry." Emerson's essays led not to more essays, says Atwan, but to "the ecstatic rhythms of American eloquence in our long poems."[29]

If Emerson led to Whitman, Crane, and Williams, then he led also to the kind of careful reading that those modernist poets required. With Emerson, says Porte, we are almost forced to "focus our attention on his writing *as writing*." We are forced onto the page. We must puzzle out the tropes and assemble the duck-shot sentences ourselves as they unfold illuminations of the Oversoul or Nature or some other transcendental abstraction. There is pleasure in this, but it is pleasure of a different sort. In essays, at least in Montaignean essays, we have the illusion that we are sitting down with the author to talk; in Emerson, the pleasure comes from another source. With Emerson, says Porte, if we are to go "in search of the living Emerson," we must realize that it is on the page, not at his fireside, that we will find him. As Porte puts it, "Emerson *is* a great writer. He has only to be read."[30]

TWO GENTLEMEN: WASHINGTON IRVING AND
GEOFFREY CRAYON

The essay tradition of the late nineteenth century did not, then, grow out of Emerson. It grew out of Washington Irving instead and found its exemplars in Lowell, Holmes, and a coterie of lesser genteel essayists. The Victorian essay as fireside chat evolved from (and was occasionally still called) the sketch. Popular during the late eighteenth and early nineteenth centuries, the sketch was brief and light. Irving's *Sketch Book of Geoffrey Crayon, Gent.* included thirty-five entries, averaging just ten pages apiece. A sketch usually appeared first in a periodical and was meant to render a single scene, character, or incident. It was to the writer what a preliminary study in chalk, charcoal, or wax was to a painter. Irving used the name of Geoffrey Crayon for his persona to indicate the broad, quick strokes he would employ. Often, sketches were travel pieces that offered moments from a sojourn—a view of a country church here, a character type there. Such scenes were picturesque rather than sublime, focusing in rather than panning out. Sketches captured the familiar rather than the historic or the grandiose. They noticed a babbling brook or a conversation at a country inn.

Just as the sketch's subjects were small, so too (at least ostensibly) were its goals. In rendering a single setting or evoking a particular mood, the sketch made no attempt to capture the whole. They were, in the tradition of the earliest English essays, "imperfect offers" meant to be provisional and even disposable—individual takes rather than parts of a grand system, the occasional jottings of an idler, as personal as a diary entry. If they evolved into a book, so much the better. Charles Brockden Brown, in "The Man at Home" (1798), sounded a note of ambivalence (or perhaps disingenuousness) on this subject: "It is not my intention to compose a book; unless the papers that day after day may be scribbled over shall gradually enlarge into something that may merit the name. . . . I write to myself. The pen is not, in this instance, an instrument of communication."[31]

Colonial America had few essayists. Franklin was one of the first, and his career reflected the halting development of the form in the colonies—oscillating as it did between politics and lightness, argument and humor. His early essays were amusing bits of advice that he signed first as "Silence Dogood" and then more famously as "Poor Richard." After 1736, however, he was a public servant, and he published essays (and pamphlets) with such ponderous titles as "A Dissertation on Liberty and Necessity, Pleasure and Pain" and "Rules for Reducing a Great Empire to a Small One." At the end of his career, while ambassador to France (1776–1785), he published *Bagatelles*, light and witty pieces done up for various Parisian salons.

Some American writers imitated Joseph Addison, Richard Steele, and the other great English periodical essayists of the early eighteenth century. In the manner of the Spectator and the Tatler, they even adopted pseudonymous personae. Most notable among these were the Connecticut Wits, especially John Trumbull, who wrote first as "The Meddler" (1769–1770) and then as "The Correspondent" (1770, 1773–1774).

After the Revolution, American writers were preoccupied with politics, focusing in particular on the first party debates. Among essayists, the Federalists dominated. They included most prominently Trumbull and the Connecticut Wits, but also Joseph Dennie, Brockden Brown, and later, Irving. Soon political invective, though still popular, began to give way to the lighter, less biting, and more whimsical tone of the sketch. Brockden Brown's work as "The Rhapsodist" led the way, but Irving perfected the form.

Early in his career Irving wrote biting political satire. With the publication in 1820 of *The Sketch Book of Geoffrey Crayon, Gent.*, however, he adopted a more genial and sentimental tone. The book, which appeared serially in New York but was collected (with Sir Walter Scott's help) in England and published by the powerful London house of John Murray, was a breakthrough success. Irving soon made more money from his writing than had any American author before him (or, for that matter, any English author other than Scott) and eventually was able to retire to a comfortable estate named Sunnyside.

As an essayist, Irving's accomplishments were twofold. First, the magnitude of his success began a renegotiation of America's cultural relationship with England. *The Sketch Book* was widely read, earned a lot of money, and made Irving famous. He was very much an American—a biographer of Columbus and Washington and ambassador to Spain—but he also loved England. *The Sketch Book* is best remembered for two great American characters—Rip Van Winkle and Ichabod Crane—but most of its thirty-five pieces were written in England, and all but four have English subjects.[32]

America in 1820 was a young nation with an emerging economy and nascent publishing industry. Of his own and any American author's predicament at the time, Irving wrote, "Unqualified for business in a nation where everyone is busy; devoted to literature where literary leisure is confounded with idleness, the man of letters is almost an insulated being, with few to understand, less to value, and scarcely any to encourage his pursuits." Irving's solution was to live in Europe and immerse himself in its past. In "The Author's Account of Himself," Irving (as Crayon) admits, "Europe held forth the charms of storied and poetical association. . . . My native country was full of youthful promise; Europe was rich in the accumulated treasures of age. . . . I longed to escape . . . the commonplace realities of the present and lose myself among the shadowy grandeurs of the past." With a deference that foretells that of genteel essayists toward Matthew Arnold, he advised, "We are a young people, necessarily an imitative one, and must take our examples and models, in a great degree, from the existing nations of Europe. There is no country more worthy of our study than England."[33]

The unprecedented and international success of *The Sketch Book*, however, made it influential on both sides of the Atlantic. During the summer and fall of 1853, for instance, when he was reeling from the commercial failures of *Moby Dick* and *Pierre*, and trying to decide whether to take up magazine writing, Melville received a two-volume edition of Irving's collected works, which he seems to have reread continually over the next three years while writing "Bartleby the Scrivener," "I and My Chimney," "Jimmy Rose," and "The Paradise of Bachelors." As Bruce Bickley has pointed out, all of these essayistic stories have very Crayon-like narrators—sentimental outsiders (often bachelors or henpecked husbands) who "reveal more about themselves than about the external reality they pretend to describe."[34]

Irving's sketches were also used as models in English schoolbooks and influenced English writers, most notably Charles Dickens. Dickens studied *The Sketch Book* and corresponded with Irving about it. Dickens's first major work, *Sketches by Boz, Illustrative of Every-Day Life and Every-Day People* (1836–1837), owed a great deal to Irving. Boz, Dickens's persona, strolls the streets of London as Crayon did before him, taking in the shops and their tenants. The two narrators share what Irving (as Crayon) calls his "sauntering gaze."[35] Their apparent idleness belies the fact, however, that each of them is (in Walter Benjamin's formulation) a kind of "strolling commodity," a professional pretending to be an amateur, a "man of letters" who "goes to the marketplace as a *flâneur*, supposedly to take a look at it, but in reality to find a buyer."[36] These lurking tensions between literary leisure and commercial demands would continue to surface as the century proceeded, the nation incorporated, and more American writers began to earn their livings—as Irving had, as Melville wanted to—by their pens.

Irving's second great accomplishment in *The Sketch Book* was his creation of Geoffrey Crayon. Irving's Anglophilia was a major help in doing this, for English essayists had been experimenting with cleverly named personae for a century or more, though it was the French essayist Jean de La Bruyère who had gotten them started. Inspired by a new translation of Theophrastus and then the vogue of La Bruyère, English essayists of the early seventeenth century began to write "characters" in which a vice or virtue was personified—the busybody, the vain fop, the happy milkmaid. A century later, the periodical essayists adapted this device to their own ends, using it to write gossipy "papers" about London's coffeehouse scene that became tremendously popular among the city's newly arrived middle class. Though Addison and Steele individualized their characters more completely than their predecessors had—often basing them at least in part on real people—Will Honeycomb remained primarily a fop, Sir Roger de Coverley an eccentric country gentleman, and Squire Bluster and Mrs. Busy the people their names implied.

More important, the English periodical essayists adopted personae for themselves, sometimes in a serial manner, sloughing one off in order to take up another. Steele used five different ones over the course of one decade. The papers of Steele, Addison, Oliver Goldsmith, and Samuel Johnson were hybrids that mixed real and imaginary characters and folded what Addison called "serious essays" in among the gossip, conversation, and anecdotes they garnered from London's coffeehouses and streets. The essayists' personae provided a brand name, a narrator who knitted the whole mélange together, and the protection and distance of a mask, which granted them the freedom to be more honest and precise in their observations. Goldsmith, for instance, put on the mantle of a "Chinese philosopher residing in London" in order to defamiliarize his hometown in *Letters from a Citizen of the World* (1760–1761).

By 1820, when *The Sketch Book* appeared, American essayists and their readers were quite familiar with personae and the ironic distance they allowed. In 1808, for instance, Dennie stepped for a moment out of his persona of "The Lay Preacher." Invoking the available tradition, winking at his savvy readers, and punning wonderfully on the various definitions of the word *muffle* (warmth and coziness, veil and mask, silencer), he spoke directly about the possibilities of the persona as a literary device: "I hope that this style of speaking occasionally in the first person will be forgiven, even by the most fastidious of readers, when he adverts to the custom of my predecessors. A periodical writer can hardly avoid this sort of egotism, and it is surely very harmless when its employer muffles himself in the mantle of concealment and in the guise, whether of shrewd Spectator or a simple Lay Preacher, walks unobtrusively abroad."[37]

Irving was, then, hardly the first essayist to employ a persona, but in Crayon he created an especially full, timely, and appealing one. It was a creation, however, that did not happen overnight. By the time he published *The Sketch Book*, Irving had already spent most of two decades working with the persona as a device. He had published his first essays in 1802 in the *New York Chronicle* as "Jonathan Oldstyle, Gent." (itself a takeoff on another of Dennie's creations—"Oliver Oldschool"). He then moved from that nostalgic old gentleman to a younger, more ironic gay blade in 1809 with the publication of *Diedrich Knickerbocker's a History of New York* (1809), in which he skewered Jefferson and Jeffersonians.

Next came Crayon, and now Irving was able to pile persona on persona. Crayon, for example, supposedly finds the tale of Rip Van Winkle among the "papers of the late Diedrich Knickerbocker," the "author" of Irving's previous book. Irving relied on Crayon's presence to hold together a book that included everything from short stories such as "The Legend of Sleepy Hollow" to sketches such as "A Sunday in London" to critical pieces such as "English Writers on America."

THE GENTEEL ESSAYIST AS REFORMER

Geoffrey Crayon's personality became more influential than the inside jokes or narrative complications he made possible. He was an amiable, sentimental, ironic, sometimes snobbish, middle-class bachelor who loved all things English.

Ann Douglas has identified the influence Irving's career and his narrator's personality had on the work of three of the most important genteel essayists of the rest of the century—Nathaniel Parker Willis, George William Curtis, and Donald Grant Mitchell. Like Irving, all three of these men broke through as travel writers, presenting themselves as casual amateurs, young men who jotted down impressions while on their grand tours. They may have made "apparently aimless wandering a vocation," as Douglas put it, but they also made it a lucrative profession.[38]

Thoreau, on the other hand, may have traveled far in Concord, but his own first book—an American volume of travel writing titled *A Week on the Concord and Merrimack Rivers* (1849)—was a commercial failure. A first printing of a thousand copies did not sell well. Thoreau had to take on extra work as a surveyor to pay the printer, and when in 1853 he could finally retrieve the unsold copies he joked in his journal, "I have now a library of nine hundred volumes, over seven hundred of which I wrote myself."[39]

Irving's followers, on the other hand, were motivated by reverence for all things English—Willis declared in 1839 that London was the center of "a new literary empire, and America is a suburb"—but even while longing for the storied past of Europe, they recognized that exoticism might sell better than nostalgia. A sexy description of a belly dancer in the young George William Curtis's *Nile Notes of a Howadji* (1851) shocked his father, but Curtis countered in a letter that the book is "precisely what I wish it. I would not have toned down, for I toned it up intentionally."[40]

Launched by their travel books, they all went on to successful careers as writers, educators, lecturers, and editors. Willis's *Pencillings by the Way* (1844) was excerpted in more than five hundred newspapers nationally, and he became one of the highest-paid authors of his time. He worked on several journals, including the popular *Home Monthly*, and he was editor of the *New York Mirror* from 1823 to 1857, which was the nation's leading weekly for most of that time. Curtis played an important role (along with Godkin, Norton, and Lowell) in what David Hall has called "the Victorian connection," a group of transatlantic intellectuals who, when their Christian faith was shaken, turned toward culture and liberal politics instead. In time, according to Hall, they helped shape "a new cultural system in which the university replaced the church and the serious writer found a means of reaching a wide audience." They advocated for civil service reform, public parks, museums, libraries, and magazines of higher journalism. Their commitment to public service, says Hall, "flowed from a sense of their own firm social placement in the middle class."[41]

Curtis, as we have seen, was also an associate editor at *Putnam's Magazine*, where, in 1856, he recommended publishing Melville's "I and My Chimney" because it was "thoroughly magazinish." In 1865 he became a founding editor of the *Nation*. A few years later, he moved to *Harper's*, where he succeeded Mitchell as conductor of its "Easy Chair" column and served as political editor. Success enabled all three men to retire to picturesque Sunnyside-like estates in the English manner: Willis first to Glenmary and then Idelwild outside New York City, Mitchell to Edgewood in Connecticut, and Curtis to a retreat in the Berkshires.

Yet there were contradictions. They embraced democracy, community, and progressive reforms, but they also saw themselves as part of a cultural elite who sided with Truth and Progress against dogma and superstition. The very personae they adopted in their essays were the sources of success and influence, but also brought them into conflict with other more hard-nosed spokesmen of "the people." Curtis was successful, prominent, and well connected—he would serve eventually as chancellor of the State University of New York and was offered the ambassadorship to the Court of St. James—but he ran into trouble when he took up the cause of civil service reform and challenged Tammany. As a *Harper's* editor during the 1860s, he encouraged cartoonist Thomas Nast to skewer Boss Tweed. Then, in the early 1870s, he became involved in the Liberal Republican reform movement. But after the Compromise of 1876 when the Republican leadership traded Reconstruction for Tyler's presidency, the forces of reform within the party were weakened, and he found himself under attack. Part of the problem was that his personae as an essayist preceded him. These included the wealthy young traveler of *Nile Notes of a Howadji* (1851), the idler of *Lotus Eating: A Summer Book* (1852), and the self-indulgent young husband fantasizing about other women in *Prue and I* (1856).

Richard Hofstadter tells the story of how Curtis and his magazine were emasculated at the 1877 New York State Republican Convention by Roscoe Conkling, a flamboyant member of the faction that defended the patronage system. At a pitch point in the battle between the reformers and the bosses, Conkling rose and asked imperiously, "Who are these men who, in newspapers and elsewhere, are cracking their whips over Republicans and playing school-master to the Republican Party and its conscience and convictions?" Immediately, he answered his own question: "Some of them are the man-milliners, the dilettanti and carpet knights of politics," who trumpet their own "superior purity" and "rancid, canting self-righteousness," while forgetting that "parties are not built by deportment, or by ladies' magazines, or by gush."[42] With the "man-milliner" crack, explains Hofstadter, Conkling was referring to the fashion articles Curtis had recently begun to publish in *Harper's* and reducing that organ of reform to a mere "ladies' magazine."

Douglas rightly emphasizes the deeply ambivalent attitude toward women maintained by the genteel essayists, who regularly portrayed themselves as bachelors or henpecked husbands, but in Hofstadter's anecdote we can see how these issues of gender intersected with those of party politics and class. Curtis, Willis, and Mitchell (again, like Irving before them) were all, as Douglas points out, sickly, precocious children; belittled by stern, pious fathers; and indulged by sunny, overprotective mothers. As a result, she says, they "chronically postponed adulthood," and when they finally pursued their careers as writers, they carried into their essays the persona of "a perpetual child" who "pleaded implicitly for a special status."[43]

It is little wonder, then, that tough adversaries like Conkling, or George Washington Plunkitt of Tammany Hall who called on "plain American citizens" to "whip the dudes who part their name in the middle," or the fiery Republican senator John J. Ingalls of Kansas—who dismissed apparent party traitors as a "third sex . . . effeminate without being either masculine or feminine; unable either to beget or bear; possessing neither fecundity nor virility; endowed with the contempt of men and the derision of women, and doomed to sterility, isolation, and extinction"—would wield the weapon of sexual innuendo in their attacks on the genteel essayists and their allies in the reform movement.[44]

DEFENDING "FANNY FERN"

Perhaps the most popular essayist of the middle of the nineteenth century was Nathaniel Parker Willis's sister Sara, who became famous as "Fanny

Fern." She wrote widely on crime, poverty, corruption, prisons, and especially the rights of women and children, and although she was not an active member of the reform movement, she was, like Curtis, an enemy of Tammany Hall. Writing in the *New Yorker* in 1936, her granddaughter Ethel Parton described her as "a columnist before columnists were heard of." Parton recalled growing up in her grandmother's house in Stuyvesant Square, where one of her playmates was Julia Nast, whose father, Thomas, was married to her cousin. She recalled walking down Fifth Avenue with her grandmother and playing a game in which they tried to imagine who lived in each of the fabulous houses and what their lives were like. As they approached one enormous mansion, the little girl wondered who lived in it. "A thief," her grandmother snapped. Having always thought of thieves as "homeless wretches," she pressed her grandmother for an explanation and found out it was the home of Peter Sweeny, one of Boss Tweed's Tammany Hall gang.[45]

As a little girl herself Sara Willis had been bright and independent. She attended Catharine Beecher's boarding school, published some of her school compositions in the local paper, and helped edit (without pay) her father's Christian newspapers before marrying a bank cashier named Charles Eldridge and beginning a family. For seven years the couple lived in the Boston area and raised three young daughters. Then in 1845 their oldest daughter, Mary, died suddenly of meningitis, and a few months later Charles succumbed to typhoid fever. Sara's tragic situation was compounded by the fact that a lawsuit against her husband had recently wiped out his estate. Sara's family and in-laws quarreled over the cause of her dire straits—Charles's risky real estate speculation or her extravagant spending habits. They talked with each other, she later wrote, only "to decide which family need do the least."[46] The agreed-upon contributions forced Sara and her children into a cramped boarding-house. Her moralistic and tightfisted father told her she could improve her lot only by remarrying, and soon a widower named Samuel Farrington asked for her hand. At first she refused, admitting to him she did not love him, but he persisted and she gave in. It was a mistake. He was insanely jealous of everyone (including the deceased Charles) and enlisted his daughters to spy on their stepmother. After two years of this treatment, she sought legal counsel, left her husband, and moved out. She had taken a most modern and unusual step. Farrington was furious and tried to tarnish her name but found no support, as even his brother took her side. In a huff he fled Boston in order to avoid supporting her and her children.

Sara was forced to leave her older daughter with her in-laws while she and her youngest moved into cramped quarters and she tried to figure out what to do next. She took to writing and soon published some articles under pseudonyms in the *Olive Branch,* a Boston weekly. One of these, a satirical piece entitled "The Model Husband," was popular enough to be pirated immediately and reprinted by another Boston paper. Feeling some new confidence, she sent a few writing samples to her brother, now a famous poet and essayist who was editing the *Home Journal* in New York, to see if he might help. It was a risk, for he had disapproved of her decision to leave her second husband and not come to her defense when Farrington had tried to slander her. Nathaniel not only refused to publish any of her work, but he also took a haughty tone in his rejection letter: "You overstrain the pathetic, and your humor runs into dreadful vulgarity sometimes. I am sorry that any editor knows that a sister of mine wrote some of these which you sent me."[47]

A fog of sanctimoniousness and paternalism may have blinded Willis to his little sister's talent, but she was quite clear about the nature of his rebuke and never forgave him. She kept writing, and almost immediately editors in New York and Boston began to publish her sketches. Middle-class readers loved her honest and irreverent mix of instruction, sentiment, satire, and advice, and within a year she was writing a regular column as "Fanny Fern" for the New York–based *Musical World and Times.* A collection of her early pieces, *Fern Leaves from Fanny's Portfolio,* appeared in 1853, was widely advertised by its publisher, and became one of the nation's first best-sellers, with seventy thousand copies sold the first year.

Traveling in the Caribbean for his health, Nathaniel Willis had left the *Home Journal* in the care of his young assistant, James Parton. Parton gave *Fern Leaves* a favorable review in the magazine, celebrating its originality. "Fanny Fern," he wrote, "is a voice, not an echo."[48] Like most everyone, he knew her only by her pseudonym and had no idea she was his boss's sister, the former Sara Willis. He contacted her through her publisher and began to publish some of her work in the *Home Journal.* Next, he invited her to New York, introduced her to the city, and urged her to relocate from Boston. When her brother returned, he discovered who Fanny Fern was and forbade Parton from publishing any more of her work. Parton resigned in protest.

By now Sara and Farrington were divorced, and she and Parton were falling in love. She had moved to New York, where her royalties enabled her to buy a house. Still known publicly as Fanny Fern, she published a novel entitled *Ruth Hall* based on her recent experiences with Farrington, her in-laws, and various editors, including her brother. One editor, upset because she had left his paper and portrayed him unfavorably in the novel, revealed her identity in his paper and published a pirated edition of her sketches, interspersing them with unflattering commentary and a "true" biography of the author. Threatened by the success of this scribbling woman and her attempt to take control of her life by that scribbling, male critics chastised her as unfeminine, egotistical, and spiteful, but the resulting publicity only boosted sales of the novel. Readers loved to decode the roman à clef, sympathized with its heroine, and enjoyed Fern's portrait of her brother as an arrogant dandy named Hyacinth Ellet, who "recognizes only the drawing-room side of human nature. Sorrow in satin he can sympathize with, but sorrow in rags is too plebeian for his exquisite organization."[49]

The controversy established Fanny Fern as an author, and Sara adopted the name as her own, even protecting it and any future earnings from it in a prenuptial agreement with Parton before their marriage in January 1856. The earnings would be considerable. She had recently agreed to write a weekly column at one hundred dollars a week for the *New York Ledger*, which made her the highest-paid columnist in the United States. In time her publisher would transport her about the country in a railroad car with her name emblazoned on its side. The *Ledger* copyrighted the columns and worked to prevent unauthorized reprint editions of her work, but in July 1856 a Philadelphia publisher, William Fleming, published a slipshod knockoff and called it *Fanny Fern's Cookbook*. Backed by the *Ledger*, Fern brought suit to stop the book and, invoking the rhetoric of both women's rights and abolitionism, used her column to win support for her cause. She won the case and the exclusive right to her pseudonym, but as Melissa Homestead reminds us, it was James Parton who actually "brought the suit because she, as a wife, had no separate legal existence. Even though Fern and her husband entered into a prenuptial agreement that allowed her to maintain ownership of and control over her copyrights, she still could not bring suit against Fleming without her husband's consent and full cooperation."[50]

IK MARVEL'S FIRESIDE REVERIES

Sara Willis Parton was at home with the name Fanny Fern. She adopted it as her own and defended it in the courts. Donald Grant Mitchell was more ambivalent about Ik Marvel. Mitchell's *Reveries of a Bachelor; or, A Book of the Heart by Ik Marvel* sheds light on the way in which genteel essayists of the late nineteenth century appropriated the Crayon-like persona of the pensive bachelor at the fireside, and were appropriated by it.

Reveries of a Bachelor seems an odd and antiquated book to us now, but it was tremendously popular in its time. First published in 1850, it went through more than a hundred printings (fifty of them pirated) and sold more than a million copies for Scribner's, whose list it led for fifty years.[51] The book is narrated by a twenty-six-year-old bachelor with the improbable name of Ik Marvel, a persona Mitchell employed elsewhere in pieces for *Harper's* and the *Atlantic* and in books such as *Wet Days at Edgewood.*

In the book Mitchell offers four "reveries." These are not exactly "essays," as he has Marvel confess in his preface, but "whimseys" or "reflections" that were "written to humor the world."[52] A glance at the table of contents reveals immediately how thoroughly this book-length essay is a fireside chat. The first reverie, titled "Over a Wood-Fire," is divided into three parts: "Smoke—Signifying Doubt," "Blaze—Signifying Cheer," and "Ashes—Signifying Desolation." This is the story of a fireside as trope. The fire provides both form and content. Hearth is both *fabula* and *sjuzet.* The flaring and dwindling of the fire correspond to the narrator's mood and tell the story of his meditation.

The subject of the meditation is marriage. Nearly alone at the fire (only his dog, Carlo, keeps him company), the bachelor resolves to take a wife but quickly begins to question himself (quite literally, for he poses twenty-one questions in three pages). He considers the problems raised by in-laws, money, the inevitable decline in his wife's beauty, whether she'll be a good cook, and whether a deceitful affair on her part would be worse than cloying loyalty. Discouraged, he decides Carlo is more steadfast and less demanding—truly man's best friend.

But then he pokes the fire, settles back into his chair, and as he looks "straight into the leaping and dancing flame" decides "love is a flame," and he thinks about "how a flame brightens up a man's habitation." Carlo is not enough after all; if Marvel is to become giving, benevolent, and truly loving, he must take a wife. But as the ensuing rumination on romantic love turns to the comforting thought that if he were to sicken, his wife could nurse him, he stops to consider the horrifying possibility that she could precede him in death. What if they had children and he had to suffer their loss as well? What if he lost his fortune and dragged his family down with him? And so, back to Carlo—how much easier to confine your responsibilities and potential losses to your replaceable dog alone, Marvel decides, and, having decided, he feels grateful to have escaped such a close call: "I dashed a tear or two from my eyes; how they came there I know not. I half ejaculated a prayer of thanks that such desolation had not yet come nigh me, and a prayer of hope that it might never come. In a half an hour more I was sleeping soundly. My Reverie was ended."[53]

This back-and-forth, this resolve and retreat, this oscillation between power and powerlessness, and the sexually confused and ambivalent feelings it evokes, the "half ejaculated" and masturbatory prayer that bring sleep and relief (or perhaps just postponement), are indicative of what Vincent Bertolini has called "bachelor sentimentalism." The voice of the essayist as sentimental bachelor, alone by the fire at night, letting his thoughts and emotions wander where they will—to despair and hope, to control and release, to anger and regret, or, as the bachelor himself puts it later, to a fire that is "half smoke, half flame—love and hate, canker and joy"—undoubtedly appealed to different readers for different reasons.[54] Some probably found satire in Ik's musings (it is hard to avoid doing so today), but others felt pathos and pain.

Certainly, the readers were many and seem mainly to have been young. Mitchell admitted, in an 1898 preface written forty-eight years after *Reveries* first appeared, the book no longer appealed to him and suggested he had written better ones since (even if "the world of book-buyers will not agree"). But he granted that there must have been something in it that was "new" and that "it made easy reading for young folks; it laid strong hold upon those of romantic appetites."[55] One suspects young girls saw the narrator as a project, a wayward soul to save, and maybe gave the book to young boys as a cautionary tale; the boys for their part may have cheered the bachelor as he struggled to remain independent.

Later in the book, Marvel engages in an idle affair with a young girl in Europe while simultaneously writing letters home to string along his devoted American cousin Isabella who is taking care of her sick and dying mother. The fling in Europe over, he returns home to find Isabella has died.

Douglas proposes that essays like Mitchell's created a male persona that was "overtly emasculated and covertly vengeful." But if much of their emotional appeal lay in the turbulent swirl of sentiment, so also must such essays have fostered a longing for a certain kind of comfortable middle-class life. On the first page of *Reveries*, Marvel reveals that he is visiting his country home "to look over the farm accounts." He downplays his parlor as merely "cozy" but then itemizes its contents—"heavy oak floor," "arm chairs," and "brown table with carved lions' feet." Marvel is a twenty-six-year-old bachelor who owns a country house where he rents rooms to tenants, he travels widely on the Continent, and his range of allusions suggests considerable leisure time. His second reverie takes place in his city apartment, where the "wide country chimney" of the first reverie is replaced by "a snug grate, where the maid makes for me a fire in the morning, and rekindles it in the afternoon."[56] The "romantic appetites" that Mitchell identified in his readers may have included desire for a comfortable middle-class lifestyle. It is as if the window-shopping Boz and Crayon, having made their fortunes, have now made their purchases as well. Benjamin's "strolling commodities" have returned to the comfort of their middle-class homes.

PERSONALITY AND CHARLES LAMB AS
THE IDEAL BACHELOR

Leisure and reading were not, of course, reserved completely for gentlemen of wealth like Ik Marvel, but they were much harder to come by for the busy clerks, journalists, admen, engineers, and accountants who were beginning to populate the offices of corporate America in the late nineteenth century. Many essayists and readers among these several Bartlebys celebrated Charles Lamb, himself an unpretentious clerk. Crayon, Marvel, and the other bachelor idlers were popular, but Lamb's Elia was canonized, at least in part because of Lamb's own life story—itself an exemplary case of "bachelor sentimentalism."

Lamb was born in 1775, the son of a barrister's clerk in London. Of his parents' seven children only he, one brother, and their sister, Mary, survived. Poverty forced Lamb to give up a scholarship, quit school, and begin work at the age of fourteen. A few years later, the family was struck by worse tragedy. Mary had a breakdown and in a fit of madness stabbed their mother to death and wounded their father. Charles wrestled the knife from her, dissolved into tears, and soon lapsed into despondency. After a time he rallied, and the courts, having judged Mary insane, placed her in his custody. They lived together for the rest of their lives, collaborating on a famous children's book, *Tales from Shakespeare*. Charles remained a bachelor, struggling to write and to help Mary during her several relapses into madness, while also working as a clerk at the East India House.

This sad, Dickensian story touched the sentimental side of Victorian America and its genteel essayists, who felt, from his essays, that they knew Lamb personally. Witness the effusive testimony in this May 1888 piece from the *Critic* in which an anonymous writer (identified only as "M. E. W.") is leafing through some old copies of *London Magazine* from the 1820s and comes across some essays by Lamb:

> Charles Lamb. What a rush of memories comes with the mere utterance of the name! How thoroughly we seem to be at home with the man whose intense individuality was so strongly marked, even in those times of remarkable men. . . . There is no time when he is hidden from our sight. We can follow him as a lad of one-and-twenty, "starving at the India House seven o'clock without any dinner," getting "overworn and quite faint," and then returning to the desolate household where the bent figure of his old father was not a more actual presence to him than the remembrance of his murdered mother and his poor banished sister. We can be with him through the long home evenings when his whole spirit rebelled against his

thralldom and cried fiercely for the necessary leisure in which to frame his
glowing thoughts into words. We can be close to him in the long years that
followed, when he chose to burden himself with the charge of his sister,
rather than cherish the love-hopes that were springing into life.[57]

The degree of transference here is extreme, the quashed "love-hopes"
familiar. A similar identification with Lamb (and conflation of Lamb and Elia)
became commonplace at the end of the century but probably reached its apo-
gee in a thirty-one-page illustrated two-part piece by Benjamin Ellis Martin
for *Scribner's* in the spring of 1890, titled "In the Footprints of Charles Lamb."
In it Martin follows Lamb from his birthplace to the burial plot he shares with
Mary. Like M. E. W., the writer in the *Critic*, Martin seems drawn to Lamb's
personality as much as to his writing: "And Lamb, central and dominating
personality of all these strong characters [of the romantic era] towers above
them all, not only and not so much by the greatness of his gifts as of his character. Alone among them he was known by his first name; even as at school he
had been called, 'Charles,' as he best liked."[58]

But of all essayists over whom Lamb towers there is one name that comes
up more than any other at the turn into the twentieth century: William Hazlitt.
The two men were friends, but the late Victorians chose the cherubic, genial
Lamb over the more engaged and acerbic Hazlitt. M. E. W., for instance,
while looking through those old copies of *London Magazine*, also comes across
a piece by Hazlitt about English politics but decides to "do not more than
glance at the account and pass on." Hazlitt may be a "brilliant colorist," but
"we do not sufficiently care for Hazlitt to appreciate or to sympathize with
him." The slide into first-person plural magnifies the way the comment dis-
misses Hazlitt. Such dismissals were common. Two years later a reviewer of
a book on Hazlitt in the *Critic* admits, "Hazlitt has not the reputation which
he deserves," but then damns him with faint praise, claiming "he has wit,
humanity and a raciness all his own, that bring him nearer to Lamb than
almost any other writer."[59]

This choice of Lamb over Hazlitt reveals much about the genteel essay and
its practitioners. Lamb was consciously and avowedly old-fashioned, looking
back to the ornate prose of the Elizabethans for models; Hazlitt believed in
a cleaner, more modern idiom, and he argued his case in an essay titled "On
Familiar Style." Lamb was a bachelor, apparently celibate, and sexually ambivalent, acknowledging of Elia (and perhaps, with a wink, himself), "He is too
much of the boy-man. The *toga virilis* never sate gracefully on his shoulders.
The impressions of infancy had burnt into him, and he resented the imper-
tinence of manhood." Hazlitt was married twice, indulged in a scandalous

infatuation with a barmaid, wrote about prizefights, and elevated "gusto" to a critical principle. Lamb, bruised by the events of his life that forced him into a long domestic responsibility, was a clerk and stay-at-home who retreated into the past and his books; Hazlitt was a man of his day, politically active and full of opinions. He fell out with old friends like Wordsworth (though never Lamb), wrote an essay titled "The Pleasures of Hating," and criticized Irving as early as 1825 for being unaware of the changes the Industrial Revolution was bringing to England and for indulging in "literary anachronisms."[60]

These many differences led the genteel essayists to side with Lamb, but it is this last, this contrariness of Hazlitt's, they cite most often. Hazlitt himself admitted in "On Depth and Superficiality," "I am not in the ordinary acceptation of the term a good-natured man."[61] His candor is to be admired, but the late Victorians wanted geniality more than candor.

Hamilton Mabie, in an important two-part survey of contemporary essayists that appeared in the *Bookman* in 1899, was the first of several writers who would cite the following anecdote: "'How could I hate him?' said Lamb of an acquaintance, 'Don't I know him? I never could hate any one I knew.'"[62]

Lamb certainly earned the right to hold on to optimism as a way to stave off hate, but whether such sunniness should be a defining trait of the essay is another question. Many genteel essayists seem to have found it indispensable. "The poet's work is treasured," wrote Tudor Jenks in 1893, "the novelists are greatly remembered, the historian and the scholar are admired, but the essayist becomes our friend." Then, in case we missed the implications, he added, "The surest way to put an end to all hopes of mutual understanding is to argue; and the next, to instruct and preach." An anonymous reviewer writing in the *Outlook* was not quite so prescriptive and allowed for some dissent, but not much, positing that the "true essay" consists of "opinions pleasantly offered on subjects to which every cultivated reader might bring a predisposition and a taste." In the *Atlantic Monthly*, a reviewer personified the entire genre and claimed that the "best test of essays" is that they "prove themselves to be good comrades."[63]

Titles of essay collections from the period show how extensively it was believed that essays and essayists should be friendly and cheerful: *On Making the Best of Things, and Other Essays* (1891) by E. Condon Gray; *The Happy Life* (1896) by Charles W. Eliot; *The Sunny Side of Shadow* (1897) by Fannie Nichols Benjamin; *The Optimist* (1897) by Charles Frederic Goss; *Cheerful Yesterdays* (1898) by Thomas Wentworth Higginson; *The Great Optimist, and Other Essays* (1903) by Leigh Mitchell Gray; *Cheer Up and Seven Other Things* (1904) and *Cheer Up and Eight Other Things* (1905) by Charles Austin Bate; *Cheeriness* (1906) by W. R. Rutherford; *Adventures in Contentment* (1907) by David Grayson; and

A Happy Half Century by Agnes Repplier (1908). In her *Atlantic Monthly* review of *Adventures in Contentment*, Florence Converse praised its author not for his thought but for his sunny personality: "He does not meditate, he sentimental-izes. . . . He has no depths except of enthusiasm. He is not urbane, he is genial. . . . His opinions are entirely without distinction, but he hugs each rural experience to his breast with a gush of gratitude and a twinkle of humor. Frankly, it is the twinkle that fetches us."[64]

According to Carl Klaus, the "role of the essayist in the essay" has two components—personality and thought—and essayists during this period displayed a "preoccupation with an author's implied personality" rather than "the flow of an author's thoughts." Indeed, the personality of the essayist comes up time and again at the turn into the twentieth century. The "form" of the essay, wrote Mabie in 1899, is "an expression of personality. The historian and philosophical writer obliterate themselves; the essayist emphasizes himself." Three years later Jennette Barbour Perry wrote, "Personality is the keynote of the Romantic essay," adding that by "Romantic essay" she meant "the modern essay" with its "Hegelian emphasis of the personal over the impersonal or classic." The "familiar essay," claimed Louise Collier Willcox in the *North American Review* in 1906, is the literary form toward which we "should turn, in these days for that proper study of mankind, the presentation of personality."[65]

Personality may be integral to the essay, but when it is too much separated from and elevated above thought, the essay is reduced to mere emotion. Richard Burton took the position to its extreme. In a 1902 piece titled "The Essay as Mood and Form," he defined the genre as follows: "Slight, casual, rambling, confidential in tone, the manner much, the theme unimportant in itself, a mood to be vented rather than a thought to add to the sum of human knowledge; the frank revelation of a personality—such have been and are the head marks of the essay down to the present day." When the essay becomes the mere venting of a mood and is emptied of thought, the essayist is reduced to happy idiot. That Burton has brought things to such a point becomes that much clearer when we look at the way he elevates (and reduces) Lamb, who, he says, is "the most brilliant exemplar of the essay, prince of this special literary mood; not primarily a thinker, a knowledge-bringer, a critic, but just a unique personality expressing his ego in his own fascinating way, making the past pay rich toll, yet always himself; and finding the essay accommodative of his whimsical vagaries, his delicious inconsistencies, his deep-toned, lovable nature." For Burton, Hazlitt is, after Lamb, an "anticlimax," who did "good work in extending the gamut" of the essay but was finally nothing more than a "helper."[66]

Again, personality itself is not to blame here. The problem is that personality is elevated above thought, and only one kind of personality is deemed appropriate. The insistence that the essay be light—an expression of a friendly personality, but not an exploration of thought—cut it off from other kinds of discourse, including political argument or the more detached and mannered discussion we carry on with those outside our own circle of friends. Friendship itself became a tyranny when it required the essayist (or, for that matter, the reader) to be always happy, always friendly. Malcolm Cowley was right (if somewhat reductive) when he later criticized gentility as having been "an attempt to abolish the evils and vulgarities and sometimes the simple changes in American society by never talking about them."[67]

This dogmatic coupling of the essay with emotion and decorum led it to become associated with women, femininity, and domesticity. This was the problem Curtis ran into when he entered the nasty, bruising world of politics and debate. By the end of the century, however, criticisms of the genteel essays as sissified were coming from literary critics and other essayists, not just from Tammany Hall hacks. In 1904 F. M. Colby complained of a recent crop of essays, "They have the air which we have learned to expect in the prolonged spinsterhood of American letters, wherein bloodlessness is taken for refinement and reduced vitality for a judicial mind." Critics argued for a new, more masculine essay. In an 1897 review of *American Ideals,* an essay collection by his friend Theodore Roosevelt, Brander Matthews asserted, "Mr. Roosevelt is a robust writer, not afraid of clear thinking and of plain speaking, and all these essays are stamped with his vehement sincerity." The whole book, according to Matthews, was stamped with a "manly and self-respecting Americanism."[68]

The essay was in the throes of a change that might bring with it special dangers—associating manliness with thought, for instance, or blood with Americanism—but opportunities as well. But for those who had for the past century associated the essay with Charles Lamb's genial stoicism, Geoffrey Crayon's sentimentality, and Ik Marvel's reveries, the move toward "manliness" and "plain speaking" meant the essay, as they knew it, was dying.

2

The "Death" of the Essay

For most of the nineteenth century the genteel essay featuring a learned gentleman digressing amiably at a fireside was read by a relatively small, well-educated group of people, usually after dinner by lamplight at a parlor fireside. Reading was often a communal activity. Depending on the length, difficulty, and appropriateness of the essay, it might well be read aloud by the father to the rest of his family. These essays appeared mainly in the print-heavy, advertising-free pages of literary journals.

After the 1870s, genteel essayists began to give way to a new kind of professional writer who published regular columns and articles about practical features of modern life. These pieces appeared in profusely illustrated magazines full of advertisements. Busy middle-class people read these new magazines at the breakfast table or while holding onto a strap in a train or trolley during their daily commute. Electric lights and central heating meant that these magazines could be read in one's own bedroom. Editors started to aim essays, articles, and whole magazines at specific family members.

The new essayists began to think of themselves as middle class as well. They saw themselves less and less as gentleman amateurs writing for elite northeastern readers and rather as trained professionals writing for a nationwide reading public. Essayists and their readers were part of that new class the Ehrenreich and Ehrenreich called the professional-managerial class, or PMC. During the closing decades of the Gilded Age, salaried writers, managers, engineers, marketing specialists, salesmen, clerks, teachers, librarians, nurses, and other professionals joined the PMC and quickly began to outstrip the old "middling sorts"—the farmers, urban artisans, and small-town entrepreneurs who had come before. As Ehrenreich and Ehrenreich succinctly put it, "The PMC emerged with dramatic suddenness in the years between 1890 and 1920."[1]

THE "DEATH" OF THE ESSAY, 1849–1897

As early as 1849 W. Alfred Jones had fretted about the "decline" and "gradual extinction" of the essay, but concern began in earnest in 1881 when Leslie Stephen announced that essay writing "is as much one of the lost arts as good letter-writing or good talk." In 1893 Tudor Jenks wrote that he preferred essays to all other genres, but admitted, "Essays are unsalable. The public does not want them. Anybody can write essays." Competition seemed to come from all sides. Richard Burton, in an 1894 article in the *Dial*, claimed, "At present the novel is the all-engulfing form. . . . Fiction . . . draws the natural essayist away from his *métier* . . . [and] this modern maelstrom, with its secret undertow, has drawn the essayists into its potent circle, to the impoverishment of the essay." Societal changes, most often associated with a new, faster pace of life, were seen as the biggest threat. As Stephen put it, "We are too distracted, too hurried."[2]

Many essayists tried to put a good face on the situation, but they were not always convincing. In an 1894 review essay titled "The Passing of the Essay," Agnes Repplier (already the grand dame of the form in America) argued that even though the essay had been "warned that it is not in accord with the spirit of the age, and that its day is on the wane," it would survive. "The essay may die," she admitted, "but just now it possesses a lively and encouraging vitality." To prove her point, she cited the popularity of seven essayists. Unfortunately, they were all British, three were dead, and two more would die within the year.

On the eve of the Fordist revolution and its mass production of automobiles, which would make longer travel more widely available, Repplier declared with characteristic certainty, "There was never a day when by-roads to culture were more diligently sought for than now by people disinclined for long travel or much toil." The modern essayist "feels as a carpenter might feel were he told that chairs and doors and tables are going out of fashion, and that he had better turn his attention to mining engineering, or a new food for infants." But essays will survive, she asserted, because "there are still readers keenly alive to the pleasure which literary art can give," and part of that pleasure is reading an essay in which "one saunters lazily along with a charming unconsciousness of effort."[3]

Repplier's discourse in this passage links her (and the essay) to the Arts and Crafts movement, which T. J. Jackson Lears has characterized as an "antimodern" reaction to the corrupting influences of mass production and consumer culture.[4] Paradoxically, while Repplier may have called for a return to fine carpentry and lazy saunters, she herself wrote fast and short. During her fifty-year career she published more than a thousand essays.[5] This contradiction was not lost on her contemporaries. In 1897 Clara Laughlin wrote, "Ours is an age of fragments of time. All too few of us have long quiet winter evenings beside the blazing fire when we may sit us down to three or four hours with Walter Pater or Sainte-Beuve." Instead, snipped Laughlin, "the average man of affairs . . . is more frequently now to pick up a magazine with his after-dinner cigar and find a little essay by Agnes Repplier." Despite the dig, Laughlin did support Repplier's view that the situation was not as dire as some believed: "The hue and cry about the passing of the essay has been out of all proportion to the gravity of the case."[6]

Benjamin Wells agreed. Speed kills and Repplier was falling prey to its dangers, but the essay was still alive. In an 1897 review essay in *Forum*, Wells proposed that both essayist and reader need "the pause of reflection" and "the backward gaze," but, he averred, such leisure is hard to come by in an age in which "the intellectual life" has become "more intense" and art oscillates so quickly between creation and "critical assimilation." Repplier's career, he believed, had succumbed to these pressures. "One is constantly, and not always willingly, diverted from her own thought to that of others," and she seems to have "read more than she has assimilated." But the country, he argued, was now turning back to the essay after the Civil War and the long rush west, and "the novelist has yielded somewhat his dominant place to . . . the essayist."[7]

Defenders of the essay appeared throughout 1897. First, there was Laughlin's assessment in May, then Wells's in June. In July, H. A. Clarke published a piece titled "The Survival of the Essay" in *Poet-lore*. "There has been much talk lately in certain quarters about the revival of the essay as a form of literature," he wrote before arguing (somewhat metaphysically), "Rebirth is a better term than revival, because it implies the reincarnation of the essence in new variations of the form to suit the knowledge and temper of the times." That November Brander Matthews closed out the year with a piece in *Harper's Weekly*, in which he proclaimed the "vitality of the form" even if "the essay as we know it now, at the end of the nineteenth century, is necessarily not just what it was at the beginning of the eighteenth."[8]

FORDISM AND THE ESSAY

The changes felt by Matthews and the other critics were a consequence of Fordism and the modern consumer society it brought with it. At the turn of the century railroads were still America's largest industry, buying more iron, steel, and coal and employing more workers (1.7 million as late as 1910) than any other industry.[9] Soon, however, they were replaced by the automobile, which offered Americans not just speed but also autonomy and flexibility.

Henry Ford famously maintained that he was producing "a motor car for the great multitude" so that it could "enjoy . . . the blessing of hours of pleasure in God's open spaces."[10] Leisure in the open spaces, however, was not the same as leisure with a book at the hearth, and many Americans thought automobiles, with their noise and fumes, threatened family life and the sanctity of the parlor. Angry farmers scattered broken glass on roads in order to sabotage the horseless carriages. As George Amberson Minafer put it in Booth Tarkington's *Magnificent Ambersons* (1918), "Automobiles are a useless nuisance. . . . They had no business to be invented."[11] But Minafer was the voice of the past; Henry Ford spoke for the future.

Three months after Ford opened his Highland Park assembly plant in January 1914, his workers were able to make a car in a tenth of the time it had taken previously.[12] His new plant turned out 1,000 cars a day—a total of 263,210 in 1914, more than were made by the next ten automakers combined. By developing standardized parts and constantly tinkering with the assembly line, Ford was able to double his production every year for the next decade and drop the price of the Model T by two-thirds.[13] By 1920 one American household in three had its own car, and by the end of the decade, the figure was four out of five. Detroit and its attendant industries and enterprises— sales, advertising, financing, steel, glass, rubber, and oil—dominated the American economy. By the mid-1920s one in eight Americans was involved directly or indirectly in the automobile industry.

The pace of these changes was disconcerting. Even Ford grew nostalgic for the rapidly receding past. He created a theme park, called Greenfield Village, near his Michigan plant, for which he bought and relocated almost one hundred landmarks of small-town American ingenuity, including the Wright brothers' bicycle shop, Thomas Edison's Menlo Park laboratory, and William Holmes McGuffey's birthplace (as well as his own).

America's essayists also felt anxious about the speed at which change was coming. They too struggled with the rationalization of their work, the dislocations of mass culture, the relentlessness of mass production, and the arrival of a mode of production that would be summed up as Fordism, a phenomenon Antonio Gramsci would say was synonymous with Americanism, the new century's dominant ideology.[14] As automobiles came to symbolize the acceleration and standardization of modern life, the language used by defenders of the contemplative essay became infused with references to roads, speed, noise, and automobiles.

In 1907 an anonymous reviewer in the *Outlook* wrote, "One may rush through a story as an American in an automobile often goes through Europe, with no other purpose save to get to the end as soon as possible . . . [b]ut no one reads an essay at breakneck speed." That the essay persists, said the writer, is testimony to a lingering "desire for interpretation of experience" and "for a margin of ease and leisure around the story of life." Another reviewer, writing in the May 17, 1913, issue of *Harper's Weekly*, worried that the entire project of publishing might soon be pushed out of commission by the automobile: "In place of the old-time quiet hours when the leisurely classes spent their time reading before the open fire, or in the hammock on the green-shuttered verandah, the world is now whizzing over the earth sampling scenery and taking the air. . . . The great truth for the contemplative essayist to learn, wherever he exists, is that the world is in far too great a hurry to think about what he is doing."[15]

⊶—✦—⊷

The industrial model we associate with Ford also transformed the publishing industry. Increases in literacy laid the groundwork for this growth in publishing. More people were reading, and they were reading more. Shortly after the Civil War, states began to pass compulsory education laws, and by the 1880s truancy laws were on the books and being enforced nationwide. Elementary school enrollment rose from 57 percent to 75 percent between 1870 and 1918. The number of public high schools tripled during the 1890s alone.[16] By 1880 the goal of national literacy seems largely to have been won, at least for white Americans. That year approximately 90 percent of all native-born white Americans and 88 percent of all foreign-born white Americans claimed to be literate, though the percentage for African Americans was less than 40.[17] Illiteracy continued to fall during the Progressive Era, declining from 20 percent to 6 percent between 1876 and 1915.[18]

Increased literacy laid the groundwork for the growth in publishing, but that growth was kicked into gear by new technologies and modes of production (the cylinder press and Linotype machine), and by the 1890s steam-driven "lightning" presses, time-production scheduling, and conveyor systems had revolutionized publishing, especially the newspaper industry.[19] A revolution in distribution enabled the printed word to be moved faster and cheaper than ever before. The completion of the transcontinental railroad in 1869 did away with the Pony Express, relegated Wells Fargo to special regional delivery, and helped establish publishing as a national business. After the Postal Act of 1879, magazines could be mailed coast-to-coast at the same low rate long enjoyed by newspapers.

Work within the industry was also organized along modern, Fordist lines. Newspapers moved to multiple editions and rapid deadlines and developed a thirst for scoops. American publishing became a big business. Between 1880 and 1900 the number of titles produced by American book publishers increased threefold; between 1890 and 1905 magazine circulation increased more than three and a half times.[20] To facilitate and accommodate this growth the industry began to rely on incorporation, Taylorization, specialization, and the "scientific management" of the labor process. Reporters were assigned to particular departments and beats such as sports, city hall, or theater. Specialization required coordination and planning. Editors anticipated and assigned stories; reporters phoned them in; rewrite men worked them over. Newsmakers responded with the creation of public relations firms and press agents. Increasingly, magazines felt themselves in competition with newspapers, and they became less literary and more journalistic. Their editors also chased scoops, developed staff systems, farmed stories out to freelancers, and assigned more investigative pieces. The age of muckraking had arrived.

The influence of newspapers and the design elements made available by new technologies also changed the way magazines looked. Editors increased their use of headlines, halftones, pulled quotes, and sidebars. They began to edit more heavily and emphasize a consistent, accessible, and recognizable house style. Deadlines, design, and subject matter took priority over literary, or authorial, style. Don Seitz, city editor of the *Brooklyn Eagle* and business manager of *New York World,* declared there is "no place in journalism for the leisurely, reflective writer, carefully cultivating style. Speed governs."[21] Editors wanted a simpler, more "readable" style.

No one argued this position more aggressively than Edward Bok, editor of *Ladies' Home Journal.* Bok maintained, "The message itself is of greater import than the manner in which it is said. . . . A readable, lucid style is far preferable to what is called a 'literary style.'"[22] As a boy, however, he collected letters and autographs from famous people (including essayists such as Emerson, Carlyle, Twain, Howells, Eugene Field, and Holmes, who offered to write an introduction to a collection of Bok's "personality letters") and became transfixed by the power of personality. As a result, he recognized that a transparent style could also be flat and impersonal. His solution, however, was not to publish writers noted for their style but to create for the magazine its own corporate style. Even in the "Editor's Personal Page" that opened every issue and in which he replied to readers' letters, Bok used the indefinite "we."[23] When it came time to write his autobiography, he was unable to find the first person and opted to write in the third person instead. This was not the subtle and ironic use of persona that we saw with Dennie, Irving, or even Mitchell, but the awkwardness of a man who had become a projection of his corporation. Here, in *The Americanization of Edward Bok: The Autobiography of a Dutch Boy Fifty Years After* (1920), "Edward Bok" discusses how he and the *Ladies' Home Journal* became one and the same: "Edward Bok's biographical reading taught him that the American public loved a personality. . . . He felt the time had come—the reference here and elsewhere is always to the realm of popular magazine literature appealing to a very wide audience—for the editor of some magazine to project his personality through the printed page and to convince the public that he was not an oracle removed from the people, but a real human being who could talk and not merely write on paper."[24]

FROM THE GENTLE READER
TO THE READING PUBLIC

If corporate or house style was staging an assault on the more personal or literary style of the individual writer, so also were the individual readers becoming more faceless. Things were changing on both sides of the traditional essay-conversation. Increasingly, publishers were treating writers, including essayists, as middle-class professionals, putting them on staff, paying them salaries, and expecting them to write on assignment and employ house style. Similarly, writers and publishers began to think of their readers less as individuals and more as a collection of consumers—a demographic or market.

One can witness this change in the terms employed by Holmes in a series of prefaces he wrote to *The Autocrat of the Breakfast Table*. These prefaces accumulated in several editions over a thirty-five-year period during the last half of the century. The preface to the first edition appeared in 1858, and in it he looked back at the early pieces that had been serialized in the *New England Magazine* in 1831–1832. He was not pleased. After a twenty-five-year interlude he had relaunched the series in the *Atlantic Monthly*, and it was there that he really developed the autocrat's witty and dominating persona. Because he was embarrassed by the early attempts, Holmes promised not to reprint them in their entirety, but asked the forbearance of "the gentle reader, if that kind being still breathes," while he reproduces just "a sentence or two."[25]

Twenty-five years later in the preface to the 1882 edition, Holmes noted that the generation for whom he had originally written his essays was one "which knew nothing or next to nothing of war, and hardly dreamed of it," and that his current readers included their children. Though much time has passed and much had changed, Holmes hoped to continue to experience the "friendship of my readers." He chose not to revise the text, believing "the sensible reader [will] take it for granted that the author would agree with him in changing whatever he would alter." He did add a few notes that he hoped would "not interrupt the current of the conversational narrative."[26]

A decade further on, in his preface to the 1891 Riverside Edition, Holmes noted that the book, which he feared would now be seen as "old-fashioned" and "outworn" in an age of "new miracles" such as the telephone, electric lights, and electric trolleys, had found yet another generation of readers for whom he was most appreciative: "I can only repeat my grateful acknowledgments to the reading public at home and abroad for the hospitable manner in which my thoughts have been received."[27] The move in these prefaces from antebellum to turn-of-the-century America is also a journey from a friendly, innocent, and possibly antique "gentle reader" through a war-weary, mature, and scrutinizing "sensible reader" to a global "reading public."

In 1903 Holmes's biographer, essayist and Unitarian minister Samuel McChord Crothers, wrote a book titled *The Gentle Reader* in which he too worried about the future of reading. Crothers feared that the Gentle Reader had "passed away with the stagecoach" only to be replaced by "the stony glare of the Intelligent Reading Public," adding that even "reading, in the old-fashioned sense, may become a lost art." He connected the passing of the Gentle Reader to the passing of the essay, that intimate form that linked writer and reader by means of conversation. Gone, he feared, were the "good temper, insight into human nature, a certain reserve, and withal a gentle irony" that were characteristic of essayists such as "Montaigne, . . . Addison, Goldsmith, Charles Lamb, . . . Irving and Dr. Holmes and James Russell Lowell." Gone, he feared, was the great writer in whose "speech we recognize a real person, and not the confused murmur of a multitude."[28]The multitude might read, but increasingly they seemed to be reading newspapers and magazines instead of books. In 1890 a writer in the *North American Review* described the changes:

> What does the average American read, morning and evening, on the train or ferry, by the fireside, at the breakfast- or dinner-table, in the office and counting-room, at the street corners and in public houses? What but daily papers, from Christmas to Easter, and from Easter to Christmas again? Every spare moment is filled with the perusal of papers of some kind. The breakfast-table becomes a silent hour for the family, so that the father may read the news of a great world, and an evening paper claims the later hours of the day. Opportunities for social intercourse, for the cultivation of home friendships, for the exercise of helpful, neighborly influences are all sacrificed at the feet of this huge, inexorable Juggernaut of Newspaper-Reading.[29]

Workers carried dime novels in their pockets, commuters folded the big-city tabloids, and housewives discussed the latest "best-sellers" at coffee, but, according to Christopher Wilson, "the medium most often singled out as responsible for reshaping reading was the 'cheap' magazine, which rose to cultural prominence after 1885."[30]

THE MAGAZINE REVOLUTION

Frank Luther Mott called the arrival of this new medium "the magazine revolution" and linked it to the "remarkably aggressive drive for self-improvement which characterized middle-class society" during the 1890s.[31] Richard Ohmann has argued that these new magazines signaled the arrival of mass culture, which he dates quite specifically to October 1893 when Frank Munsey, in desperation, dropped the price of his struggling magazine from a quarter to a dime, miraculously tapped into a new middle-class readership, and increased his circulation from forty thousand to a half million in just six months. The new price did not cover his production costs, but he more than made up the difference in increased advertising revenues. With this move, he changed the paradigm. He was no longer selling magazines to readers; he was now selling consumers to advertisers.[32]

Others quickly followed suit. By 1900 the ten-cent magazines Munsey had introduced accounted for more than 80 percent of all magazines sold, though circulation of all kinds of magazines exploded.[33] At the end of the Civil War the total circulation of all monthly magazines had been perhaps four million; by 1890 it had increased to eighteen million and by 1905 was up to sixty-four million.[34] In 1880 no magazine had a circulation equal to 1 percent of the nation's population; by 1920 eight did.[35]

Not only were there more of them, but the new magazines looked different as well, largely because they needed to draw the reader's eye to their advertising. There were more images than ever before, and they were juxtaposed with words in new ways. The gentleman essayist had mainly appeared in literary journals such as *Harper's New Monthly Magazine, Scribner's* (later *Century*), *Putnam's,* and the *Atlantic Monthly.* These four big "family house" journals were owned respectively by Harper and Brothers, Charles Scribner's Sons, G. P. Putnam's Sons, and Ticknor and Fields, publishers who used them to promote their own catalogs in a single advertising section confined to the back of the book. Now, ads appeared throughout the magazine, jostling with illustrations and essays for space. Editors of the dime magazines rethought design so as to "scientifically manage" the reading process and attract advertisers.

They developed techniques to hurry the reader's eye across a busier page and through a magazine full of new departments. In 1896 Bok introduced "ad-stripping," or "tailing," in the *Ladies' Home Journal,* a process in which articles were cut and continued on the back pages, where the layout switched from a three- to a four-column format so the continued articles could be more easily surrounded by advertisements.[36] Relevance and speed defined the new magazines. The literary essay came increasingly into competition with illustrations, advertisements, and timely articles, and often it seemed to be losing the battle. Walter Hines Page, editor of the *Atlantic, Forum,* and *World's Work,* argued that a magazine should "have a higher aim than to fill an idle hour, and a more original aim than to thresh over the old straw and call the chaff 'Literature.'"[37]

In the past, especially on farms and in small towns, families had made their own clothes, canned their own food, and generally provided for themselves. Now, people turned to the commodities provided by mass retailers to satisfy their needs. Department stores and mail-order companies filled the magazines with advertisements that used celebrities or made-up company spokespersons to sell these products. Henry Ward Beecher (America's most famous preacher) praised Pears' soap; Uncle Ben sold rice. Richard Ohmann describes this advertising strategy as one that uses a "personalized text."[38] Often, these advertisements employed rhetorical devices common to the essay, including a form of direct address in which the second person, as Judith Williamson has pointed out, is a "you" that while "transmitted plural" is received "as singular."[39] The rhetorical questions, familiar voice, and strong first person that had been associated with a friendly and learned personal essayist now took on an accusatory, anxiety-inducing edge ("Oh! Why don't you use Pears' Soap?").

The magazines continued to publish essays, but the essays looked different in their new context. They were illustrated, interspersed among articles, and interrupted by advertisements. As Tom Reynolds has pointed out, in these new magazines, "prose appears as one element in a larger communicative field," making reading into a "richer semiotic activity in which a number of different bits of information were part of the whole text."[40]

WILLIAM DEAN HOWELLS ON THE PROFESSIONAL ESSAYIST

No one was better situated to understand what the magazine revolution meant for the essayist and his reader than William Dean Howells. Like many editors of the new mass-market magazines, he was an outsider with training in public relations as well as publishing. As an ambitious young man from Ohio, he wrote a campaign biography of Lincoln that earned him enough money to travel to Boston in 1860 for the first time, where he introduced himself to Lowell, then editor of the *Atlantic Monthly*. He impressed Lowell, and after four years as U.S. consul to Venice (a reward for his work on the Lincoln campaign), he returned to serve as assistant editor (1866–1871) and then as editor (1871–1881) of the *Atlantic*. In 1886 he left Boston for New York, where he became editor at *Harper's New Monthly Magazine*, writing that magazine's "Editor's Study" column from 1886 to 1892 and its "Editor's Easy Chair" (a position held earlier by both Willis and Curtis) from 1899 to 1909.

Howells collected much of his thinking about American authorship in an 1893 piece for *Scribner's* titled "The Man of Literature as a Man of Business." Literature, like the essay, consists of "the mind speaking to the mind," and no "man ought to live by an art." But, added Howells, the "man of letters" was now becoming "a man of business." The International Copyright Law brought protection against piracy, so writers were no longer forced to seek patrons or live in poverty. They had entered the new middle class:

> Many authors live now, and live prettily enough. . . . They do not live so nicely as successful tradespeople, of course, or as men in the other professions when they begin to make themselves names. . . . Still, they do very fairly well, as things go; and several have incomes that would seem riches to the great mass of worthy Americans who work with their hands for a living—when they can get the work. Their incomes are mainly from serial publication in the different magazines; and the prosperity of the magazines has given a whole class existence, which as a class, was wholly unknown among us before the war.

Many Americans, said Howells, were reluctant to accept these changes. Essayists now found themselves caught between genteel readers of the old school and a new kind of reader, who was more interested in the pictorials, gossip, and sensationalism of the mass-market magazines. Magazine articles on "timely topics," he believed, were crowding out "belles-lettres," including "humorous sketches of travel, or light essays."

Serialization, newspapers, and the new magazines, continued Howells, had changed the way Americans thought of their culture and its relationship to Europe: "We do not think the Old World either so romantic or so ridiculous as we used; and perhaps from an instinctive perception of this altered mood writers no longer appeal to our sentiment or our humor with sketches of outlandish people and places. . . . When one thinks of the long line of American writers who have greatly pleased in this sort, and who even got their first fame in it, one must grieve to see it obsolescent." The writers who had gotten their starts looking to the Old World and appealing to the sentimental side of their readers, wrote Howells, were often essayists, including Irving, Curtis, "Ik Marvel," and Lowell. The trend away from that kind of travel writing had led in turn to the more recent decline of what Howells called the "light essay," and he associated that form with the fireside chat:

> We have essays enough and to spare, of certain soberer and severer sorts, such as grapple with problems and deal with conditions; but the kind that I mean, the slightly humorous, gentle, refined, and humane kind, seems no longer to abound as it once did. I do not know whether the editor discourages them, knowing his readers' frame, or whether they do not offer themselves, but I seldom find them in magazines. I certainly do not believe that if anyone were now to write such essays as Mr. Warner's "Backlog Studies," an editor would refuse them; and perhaps nobody really writes them. . . . Without a great name behind it, I am afraid that a volume of essays would find few buyers, even after the essays had made a public in the magazines.[41]

Nearly a decade later, in 1902, Howells turned again to the effects magazines and newspapers were continuing to have on the essay, this time looking more fully at the question of form. In his "Editor's Easy Chair" column for the October 1902 issue of *Harper's,* he argued that the "old-fashioned essay" had been defined by its "lyrical sense" and its "wilding nature." Such essays had "no central motive," and although they might be prompted by a specific subject, they soon "gadded about at their pleasure, and stopped as far from [that originating subject] as they chose." But things had changed. The essay, said Howells, had "begun to have a conscience about having a beginning, a middle and an ending, like a drama, or a firstly, secondly, and thirdly, like a homily." And more recently, "the moment came when the essay began to confuse itself with the article, and to assume an obligation of constancy to premise and conclusions, with the effect of so debasing the general taste that the article is now desired more and more, and the essay less and less."[42] The situation, according to Howells, was dire—taste had been debased, literature confused with journalism, and the essay outstripped by the article.

3

THE ESSAY IN THE PROGRESSIVE ERA

The world of the late Victorians produced the mix of whimsy, quiet reflection, and good manners associated with the genteel essay, but that world was never as ordered and sedate as it sometimes seemed to be. Certainly, by the turn of the century, industrialization, incorporation, a flood of new immigrants, increasing labor unrest, the first wave of feminism, and the revelations of the muckrakers had challenged its complacency. These changes, coupled with the magazine revolution and the rise of consumer culture, forced essayists out of their libraries and gardens and into the streets and newsrooms. Meanwhile, the lives of their readers—the rapidly expanding cohort of young professionals—were changing in two important ways. Their parents had lived in small towns or the walking neighborhoods of big cities, and their fathers had owned a shop or read for the law on their own, but this new generation was going to college and moving to the suburbs. These two changes meant that the essay would now be read by a new cadre of readers for new reasons in a new setting. Middle-class readers began to read essays in living rooms instead of parlors, and they read them in order to better understand the demands of modern urban and exurban life.

HOME OWNERSHIP AND AMERICA'S NEW MIDDLE CLASS

In 1890 Howells had written a novel about a middle-class editor like himself who leaves Boston for New York and a job in modern publishing. In *A Hazard of New Fortunes*, Basil March takes on the editorship of *Every Other Week*, a magazine Phillip Lopate describes as a kind of "precursor to *The New*

Yorker" that tried "to be light and informative, and to catch the Gotham spirit, mainly for readers outside the city limits."[1] From the start March's life in New York is rife with contradictions, and the demands of the market force him into a number of editorial compromises. He claims to be "not ashamed" of his literary choices for the first issue, which include a "sketch of travel," "a literary essay and a social essay," and "dashing criticism of the new pictures, the new plays, the new books, [and] the new fashions," but he quickly realizes that "the number would be sold and praised chiefly for its pictures." His backer is "extremely proud" of the issue, but decides "it was too good" and they had given the public "too much" for "their money."

March and his wife, Isabel, spend six chapters at the beginning of the novel house hunting. Their long journey from property to property is a downward spiral of useless real estate agents, misleading advertisements, and lowered expectations that leads finally to a small, grim, furnished apartment and the realization, in Isabel's words, that "life isn't what it seems when you look forward to it," for Americans are driven by the "superstition that having and shining is the chief good" and so end up "moiling and toiling on to the palace or the poorhouse."[2]

A Hazard of New Fortunes was Howells's first full experiment in the unflinching realism he had been advocating for some time in the pages of the Atlantic. The novel was colored by the disenchantment Howells felt after the hangings of the Haymarket anarchists in 1887, whom he felt had been executed for their beliefs. His pessimism about America's persistent inequalities may have led him to the stark carrot-and-stick of the palace or poorhouse, but at the time the new middle class saw the rising rate of home ownership as proof of their country's unique role in the world. Home ownership was increasing (though until 1950 it stayed below 50 percent), class composition changed, and a new, simpler house became the rage. Historians, economists, and sociologists use various criteria to identify the new middle class, including occupation, income, standard of living, and aspiration, but one could argue that at the turn of the century, no criterion was more telling than home ownership. Buying a house became an expected life stage, a gateway to the middle class. As Clifford Clark has noted, "Owning one's own home was evidence both of a certain level of income and of a particular outlook on life."[3]

Home ownership was the way the middle class saved money and protected itself. Farm life had required a family to raise its own food, dig its own well, and make its own clothes. Such work was hard, but leaving it behind was hard too, for the land had provided self-sufficiency. Owning a home eased the transition into an age of urbanization and manufactured goods, for it provided some measure of security when the economy cycled downward.

In an era without pensions or Social Security, it was the only way most people could accumulate enough wealth to remain secure and independent, especially in old age. Hispanic and Asian and African Americans encountered housing discrimination unknown to others, and home ownership remained low for younger couples and recent immigrants, but the aspiration to own one's home was strong across all segments of the population.

Despite slumps and dislocations, the Gilded Age was, for many, a time of opportunity. Technological developments and assembly lines raised productivity and reduced prices. Workers' real wages rose more than 50 percent between 1860 and 1900.[4] The per capita gross national product nearly doubled in the last thirty years of the century.[5] This rise in real income coupled with lower down payments, the advent of building-and-loan associations, friendlier mortgage plans, and an increase in the number of employees who earned salaries (as opposed to wages) created a housing boom. In the three decades after the Civil War, America built more houses than it had during the previous 250 years of European settlement.[6] Home ownership, estimated at 20 percent in 1870, increased to nearly 48 percent by 1890.[7]

Increasingly, it became possible for skilled laborers as well as for professionals and managers to own homes. In fact, it became almost un-American not to make the attempt. In a Centennial Day speech, Henry Ward Beecher, the brother of Catherine and Harriet, and Congregationalist reformer, declared, "The laborer ought to be ashamed of himself who in 20 years does not own the ground on which his house stands . . . who has not in that house provided carpets for the rooms, who has not his China plates, who has not his chromos, who has not some books nestling on the shelf."[8]

The housing boom brought with it not only a new conception of middle-class life but also a new kind of house. Electrification, indoor plumbing, and central heating became commonplace and changed the way families lived. Though their homes were quieter and more private, individual family members found themselves scattered about the house and less governed by the natural rhythm of night and day. Gone were the regular rituals: candle making, the trimming of lamp wicks, and each evening's stoking of the fire. "Central heating and electrical lighting tended to disperse such family circles," says Thomas Schlereth. "Centrifugal privacy replaced centripetal intimacy."[9] These changes were closely connected to the magazine revolution. There were magazines for each member of the family—*St. Nicholas* for the kids, *Ladies' Home Journal* for Mother, and *Field and Stream* for Father.

These new kinds of houses were also constructed differently. On the frontier and in rural America people had built their own houses with local materials and the help of neighbors or a few craftsmen. Now, in a precursor to the

Fordist revolution, planning and execution were separated. Catalogs, such as *Bicknell's Plan Book*, offered blueprints for everything from two-room laborers' cottages to large Queen Anne–style homes with turrets, porte cocheres, and wraparound porches. At first wholesalers dealt only in mass-produced lumber and nails, but soon they sold all sorts of prefabricated and standardized parts, including everything from joists and rafters to door frames and window sashes. In time, the construction business integrated vertically. Developers such as Samuel E. Gross made "dream houses" available to all, offering new home owners everything from designs to prefabricated materials, furnishings, and lots in newly subdivided suburbs. During the 1880s and 1890s (before the recession of 1907 wiped him out), Gross developed sixteen towns and 150 subdivisions in the Chicago area, selling more than forty thousand lots and seven thousand houses, ranging from eight hundred–dollar workers' cottages to five thousand–dollar middle-class manses.[10]

FROM PARLOR TO LIVING ROOM

Most of the new homes, whether tiny or spacious, contained a parlor. According to Schlereth, parlors "transcended social class, economic status, or geographic location."[11] They were less elegant, private, and English than drawing rooms. Both terms were used on either side of the Atlantic, but *parlor* was more American. A Pullman "parlor car" in the United States was called a "drawing-room car" in England. During the Gilded Age wealthy Americans built houses with drawing rooms, but such homes existed mainly in exclusive suburbs and weekend resorts like Newport, Tuxedo Park, and Bar Harbor, or on a city's most posh streets—Summit Avenue in St. Paul, for instance, or Euclid Avenue in Cleveland.

The two terms—*drawing room* and *parlor*—were sometimes conflated, but historically the term *drawing room* was short for *withdrawing room*. In England it was the room to which the ladies withdrew after dinner, while the gentlemen took their port and cigars in the billiard room or library. Later, all parties reconvened in the drawing room for polite conversation. Such subtle and decorous transitions required a house with several single-purpose rooms, but of course not everyone lived in such a house. The new middle class, even some of the working class, might have a parlor, but not a drawing room, billiard room, conservatory, and library.

In the homes of the rich, the drawing room lay toward the back of the house near the dining room, where it was serviced by the kitchen, multiple hallways, and perhaps a butler's pantry. A parlor, on the other hand, was situated toward the more public front of the house, though there was an attempt to retain for it some of the drawing room's sense of removal and elegance. It was separated, for instance, by doors from the entrance hall on one side and the dining room on the other. The drawing room's fireside had been the traditional site of conversation. It was also where essays were read and where, as we saw in the case of Ik Marvel, they were set. A parlor could not accommodate a fireplace as large as the one in a drawing room, but it did try to replicate it. "A middleclass cult of the fireplace," says Schlereth, "emerged concurrently with and, in part, because of the practicality of central heating. . . . Home owners did not seem to mind if hearths came with artificial logs, were often gas fired, or hid a furnace register," for it did provide a "ritual center" that helped draw the family back together each evening, thus countering the centrifugal forces that pulled them toward their own rooms.[12]

Outside the house there were forces that felt even more threatening to the family's cohesion. The "cultured home," says Alan Trachtenberg, served "as middle ground, a domestic island of virtue and stability," and refuge from "the cultural degradation and alienation produced by industrial life and immigration." The parlor was where the family kept itself "cultured." It was there that they read, prayed, talked, sang, and insulated themselves from the larger "world of strangers."[13]

It was also there that they entertained, albeit selectively. Guests entered the parlor from the entrance hall, which provided a kind of screening area for assessing would-be visitors and deciding whether to admit them. This foyer was the site of the elaborate calling-card rituals satirized by Mark Twain and Charles Dudley Warner in *The Gilded Age*. When the guests did enter the parlor, Trachtenberg's "domestic island" became what Katherine C. Grier has called a "theater of culture." Parlors were the site of rituals as mundane as afternoon tea and as transformative as courtships, weddings, and funerals. Here the family displayed itself and its accomplishments. According to Ohmann, there was an eagerness, especially at first, among America's new middle-class families to show "how far they and their like had progressed from the rudeness of colonial and early republican home life, with its visual reminders of rural necessity and home production, toward cosmopolitan leisure and controlled beauty."[14]

In the 1890s, at the same time the genteel essay was beginning to be called into question, a new generation began to react to the clutter, ostentation, and showy style of their parents' houses. The move to the suburbs was now in high swing, and these suburbs segregated housing by class and ethnicity. In the Chicago area, for instance, Anglo-Saxon Protestants moved to Winnetka, European Catholics to Cicero, and Jews to Lawndale.[15] Sometimes written covenants and local ordinances enforced these divisions; more often rules were unspoken. Housing segregation meant there was less need for the overt social regulation that had been provided by the front hallway and the calling card.

Many of the new generation were born into the middle class rather than having risen to it. More accustomed to living in insulated suburbs, they felt less need to enforce formal codes or consume conspicuously. As early as the 1870s journalist Clarence Cook called for the abolition of the parlor in a series of articles in *Scribner's*.[16] According to Karen Halttunen, "Suburban social life helped usher in what Emily Post would soon call 'the era of informality.' From the 1880s on, the central ceremonial ritual of the Victorian parlor—the formal call—was coming under increasing attack; by 1895, according to *Ladies' Home Journal*, it survived only in the visit of congratulation or condolence." By 1916 Lillian Hart Tryon could write, "Life is too full to have patience with formalities. The cry of the time is for few friends and good ones," which meant to her that "we are fast becoming a parlorless nation."[17]

The end of the parlor came in stages. At first, parlor doors gave way to sliding separators, arches, or curtains. For a time, "cozy nooks" were the rage. A corner of the parlor was cordoned off with curtains, allotted its own divan, and given a Turkish or Baghdad look. Finally, in new houses the front hall was eliminated entirely, and in existing homes, the parlor was remodeled to accomplish the same end. Without its front hall and doors, the parlor became a living room. Almost forty years later, Henry Seidel Canby would remember, "It was a sign of change in the times when in thousands of homes parlors were made over into 'living rooms.' The date, which was the late nineties, is more significant than many better remembered."[18] It was significant, for it marked the move to a modern informality that transformed not just the parlor and the house but also the people who lived in the house, the way they spoke to each other, and what they read.

During this same period the marketing of house plans and manufactured parts by individual entrepreneurs gave way to the sale of homes that were completely fabricated by large corporations. This change was accompanied by a shift in domestic architecture from the elaborate "eclectic manse" to the clean and simple bungalow. The term *bungalow* derived from a Bengali word, *b angl a*. It entered English during the seventeenth century via Hindi, where it referred pejoratively to a low house with a thatched roof and porches all around in the Bengali style.[19] Big firms such as the Radford Company in Chicago; Gordon-Van Tine in Davenport, Iowa, and St. Louis; and Aladdin Homes in Bay City, Michigan, as well as mail-order giants Montgomery Ward and Sears, Roebuck, sold hundreds of thousands of these new, prefabricated homes.[20] According to Gwendolyn Wright, "By 1910 it was rare to have single-purpose rooms such as libraries, pantries, sewing rooms, and spare bedrooms, which had comprised the Victorians' sense of uniqueness and complex domestic life. In a moderate priced two-story house there were usually only three downstairs rooms: living room, dining room, and kitchen."[21]

VIRGINIA WOOLF'S DRAWING ROOM AND THE MODERN ESSAY

The year 1910 held a different significance for Virginia Woolf. For her it was when modernism arrived. She would remark later with famous and hyperbolic specificity, "On or about December 1910, human character changed. . . . All human relations have shifted—those between masters and servants, husbands and wives, parents and children. And when human relations change there is at the same time a change in religion, conduct, politics, and literature." In the 1924 Hogarth lecture in which she made this claim she focused on the arrival of the modernist novel, but added that "even in newspaper articles and essays" one could hear "the sound of breaking and falling, crashing and destruction" that announced new possibilities.[22]

Woolf had intervened as early as 1905 in the debate on the death of the essay in a short piece titled "The Decay of Essay-Writing." Like many of her counterparts in the United States, she saw the essay as suffering from lightness and a surfeit of geniality. Too many modern essayists, she said, wrote solely "because the gift of writing has been bestowed on them." As a consequence, the essay was beginning to amount to little more than "the amiable garrulity of the tea-table." Yet, she noted, the form still enjoyed wide popularity. No essayist could currently claim any "brilliant success," but that, she hoped, was because success comes hard in a form that requires so much honesty: "Confronted with the terrible spectre of themselves, the bravest are inclined to run away or shade their eyes."[23]

Over the next several years she would publish numerous reviews of essay collections, but her major statement on the form, a long review essay titled "The Modern Essay," appeared in 1925. This piece considered a five-volume set of essays written between 1870 and 1920, giving her an opportunity to talk once again about the arrival of modernism and changes in human character as well as the essay and the site of the essay. This last she described quite precisely: "The drawing-room is the place where a great deal of reading is done nowadays, and the essays of Mr. Beerbohm lie, with an exquisite appreciation of all that the position exacts, upon the drawing-room table. There is no gin about; no strong tobacco; no puns, drunkenness, or insanity. Ladies and gentlemen talk together, and some things, of course, are not said."

For Woolf, the essays of Beerbohm were conversation itself. Each one contained his voice and personality. With Beerbohm, she wrote, we are able to "look back upon essay after essay . . . knowing that, come September or May, we shall sit down with them and talk." He gives us "himself," she said; he gives us "Max." It is a remark that harks back to the genteel essayists' celebration of the tortured but genial "Charles." But such rooms, familiarity, conversation, and essays seemed to be over: "If it would be foolish to attempt to confine Mr. Beerbohm to one room, it would be still more foolish, unhappily, to make him, the artist, the man who gives us only his best, the representative of our age. . . . His age seems already a little distant, and the drawing-room table begins to look rather like an alter where, once upon a time, people deposited offerings—fruit from their own orchards, gifts carved with their own hands. Now once more the conditions have changed." In sentiments that echoed those of the American critics who considered what speed, Fordism, magazines, and the rise of the reading public might do to the essay, Woolf bemoaned the fact that a "small audience of cultivated people" was giving way to "a larger audience of people . . . not quite so cultivated," forcing the essayist "to write weekly, to write daily, to write shortly, to write for busy people catching trains in the morning or for tired people coming home in the evening, . . . a heart-breaking task for men who know good writing from bad."[24] For Woolf, the transition from the Victorian to the modern era was also personal. Her parents' house at 22 Hyde Park Gate in 1900 was, according to her, "a complete model of Victorian society" and a place of quiet, cultivated conversation. She and her sister, Vanessa, felt stifled by the Victorian code of manners enforced by their father and sexually abusive half brothers. She wrote that as early as 1900 she and Vanessa already "were living . . . in 1910," while her father and half brothers "were living in 1860."[25]

After Leslie Stephen's death in 1904, Virginia and Vanessa moved to 46 Gordon Square, their first Bloomsbury address. It was in the drawing room at Gordon Square where 1910 actually arrived. Critics usually associate Woolf's declaration about modernism and December 1910 with such public events as the death of Edward VII and accession of George V or Roger Fry's postimpressionist exhibition at the Grafton Galleries, but she was referring to private dislocations as well. At about this time her beloved brother Thoby began to bring home his Cambridge friends, many of whom were, as she put it, "buggers." Henry James, in a fit of what Eve Kosofsky Sedgwick has called "homosexual panic," said Thoby's friends were "deplorable" and wondered how Vanessa and Virginia could "have taken up with young men like that."[26] But the Stephen sisters found these visitors witty, stimulating, and safe. "The society of buggers," said Woolf, "has many advantages—if you are a woman." The conversation of Thoby and his friends was neither (heterosexually) flirtatious nor conventional; it was, she wrote, "abstract" and "philosophical."[27]

It was also irreverent. One afternoon in 1910, Lytton Strachey arrived to have tea with Vanessa and Virginia. As he came through the door into the drawing room, he noticed a stain on Vanessa's white dress. He pointed a finger at her and inquired wickedly, "Semen?" There was an uncertain pause before everyone burst into happy laughter. "With that one word," wrote Woolf, "all barriers of reticence and reserve went down."[28]

FLOOR PLANS AND ESSAYS IN THE *LADIES' HOME JOURNAL*

Edward Bok had no use for parlors, let alone drawing rooms, and he applauded the arrival of the new middle class, for they were the readers of his fabulously successful magazine—*Ladies' Home Journal*—a magazine in which he meant to sell houses and teach the middle class how to read essays.

Bok's *Journal* became known as "the monthly Bible of the American Home."[29] Along with the *Saturday Evening Post* (the other American magazine at the time with a circulation of more than one million and also published by Cyrus Curtis), it spoke directly to America's new middle class and those who aspired to it. As George Horace Lorimer, the editor of the *Saturday Evening Post*, pointed out, the *Post* would appeal "to two classes of men: Men with income, and men who are going to have incomes, and the second is quite as important as the first to the advertiser."[30]

Bok explained to his friend Howells that his magazine appealed "to the intelligent American woman rather than to the intellectual type." This "truest, best, and sweetest type of the American girl" represented "the great middle class," and it was that class, he added, "which teaches the manners of the drawing room, but the practical life of the kitchen as well." That same middle class, he believed, provided a buffer between "the unrest of the lower classes and rottenness among the upper classes."[31]

If the middle class provided an ideological buffer between capital and labor, then their new place of residence—the suburbs—provided a geographical buffer. Bok teamed with the big developers and mail-order firms to promote the suburbs and especially the bungalow. In 1896 he began publishing house plans in the *Journal*, a practice he continued until his retirement in

1919.[32] In his autobiography he wrote that he saw the *Journal* "as his medium for making the small-house architecture of America better." He placed two stipulations on the architects (including Frank Lloyd Wright) who submitted plans to his magazine: the houses must have cross-ventilation and no parlor, a room he considered "useless." By 1916 Bok claimed that nationwide at least thirty thousand houses had been built from plans published in the *Journal* and that every American probably knew someone who lived in one. "Entire colonies" and "complete suburban developments" of "'*Ladies' Home Journal* houses' have sprung up," he wrote.[33]

In 1903, the year the *Journal's* circulation surpassed the one-million mark, he estimated that 20 percent of all Americans and 60 percent of all American women read it.[34] Even if his figures are inflated, the magazine's role in Progressive Era reforms and the development of middlebrow culture is hard to overestimate. Many of the era's most important essayists and advocates of middlebrow culture were associated with it. Christopher Morley edited the magazine in 1917 and 1918. Bernadine Kielty Scherman, wife of Harry Scherman, who founded the Book-of-the-Month Club, wrote "Under Cover," the magazine's book-review column, for many years. Hamilton Wright Mabie, who as an editor of the *Outlook* had helped organize the debate over the death of the essay at the turn of the century, became a contributing editor of the *Journal* and between 1902 and 1912 wrote an influential literary advice column.

Bok's formula for the magazine included a mix of old pieties, modern advice, and celebrity authors, and contradictions were inevitable. In a schizophrenic mix of third- and first-person pronouns, he distinguished in his autobiography between his editorial front and his real self: "'Give the people what they want,' was his slogan. 'Give the people what they ought to have and don't know they want,' was mine."[35] The magazine advocated for women as domestic creatures at a time when many of them were entering the workplace. It argued against women's suffrage but for their liberation from the tedium of household tasks. It spoke for the future and the promises of consumer culture while holding on to the traditions, decorum, and discipline of the past.

Bok seems to have seen the genteel essay as a way to link the present to the past. In 1895 the *Journal* published *Five Thousand Books: An Easy Guide to the Best Books in Every Department of Reading,* which included six pages of titles by American essayists, including Curtis, Holmes, Irving, Lowell, Mabie, Mitchell, and Repplier. Henry Ward Beecher, pious apostle of the self-made man, had been a mentor to both Bok and Mabie. Bok had edited Beecher's sermons; Mabie had edited two of Beecher's publications, the *Outlook* and the *Independent*. Mabie was also a practicing essayist with strong connections to the Genteel Tradition, and his 1890 collection was titled *My Study Fire*. His career was devoted to middlebrow uplift. Mabie, wrote contemporary critic George S. Hellman, "represents perhaps more convincingly than any other of our essayists both the possibilities and limitations inherent in writers seeking to bring 'sweetness and light' to a generation of readers whose early education comes from the public schools, and who, for later enlightenment, turn to innumerable magazines."[36]

While Bok was peddling house plans in the *Journal*, Mabie was suggesting what kind of reading might take place in those houses. In a 1908 piece titled "Why the Essay Is Valuable as Reading," Mabie argued that the essay could serve as a guidebook to success. The first period of capitalism, he explained, "the age of the accumulation of capital," needed the "weighty essay, such as Bacon wrote," but America was now in "the age of seeking one's fortune," which called for the "lightly touched essay." This kind of essay "involves a self-restraint, a sense of relative values." Now, he argued, Americans must avoid "the mistake of youth, [which] through its very earnestness and sincerity, [tends] to bear on too hard, to push the moral too obviously and too fiercely, to be in too great a hurry either to persuade or to convince." Speak softly, he seemed to be saying; truth is a big stick.

America had finally arrived, mature and reasonable, on the world stage. The essayist, according to Mabie, also arrives late. He is, with his use of quotation and allusion, an educated man and a representative of a mature culture, and as such a model for the nation's new middle managers. "The essayist," wrote Mabie, "is the last to appear because he needs for his work experience and knowledge of life to observe, study, compare, set in order and make significant." Yet, lest his essayist sound so reasoned, evenhanded, and soft-spoken as to be buttoned-down and boring, Mabie made it clear that something more was needed: "The personality of the essayist is the prime element of his work; it gives color, variety, emotion, eloquence, humor, charm to his writing." To clarify what was at stake, he added a modern parable: "At a dinner one man tells a story with such monotony of voice and lack of selection of details that everybody is bored; the man next him describes a trivial incident in a trolley-car with such dramatic feeling and shading of emphasis that his hearers all hang on his words."[37]

In the next issue of the *Journal*, Mabie showed how the essay could also help young girls develop their personalities. In a piece titled "The Girl and Her Graduation Essay," he spoke against the tendency in schools to make composition a ponderous affair. Writing should be "as normal as talking," he said. Students should not use "long words" and try to "seem impressive." He

explained to his young readers, "If you do these things you will be as uncomfortable as a boy who is suddenly put into his 'company clothes' and told to
put on his 'company manners,' and you will be as dull to other people." The
same approach should be applied to one's school theme: "When your subject
has come to you treat it as an old friend; don't put on your Sunday clothes
and sit in the 'best parlor' with it." A relaxed, familiar style made sense, he
said, because it allowed authenticity: "In writing as in anything else, don't
try to be somebody else; be content to be yourself. Imitative people are never
interesting, nor are people who do things in a way which is not natural to
them." Simplicity is all and less is more, for a "bore is a man who never lets
anything go."[38] Be at home with your prose style, said Mabie, and you will be
at home with yourself, too.

As it turned out, changes in housing came faster than changes in the essay.
During the first decades of the century the bungalow swept west to east,
starting in California as a quick fix for the housing shortage brought on there
by rapid growth. It adapted to regional building materials as it came east
(redwood in the West, brick in the Midwest, clapboard in the East) and took
on different styles as well (Moorish, Mission, Swiss, and Japanese), but it
remained simple throughout and always suggested a fresh start. Bungalows
were ubiquitous and defining. People subscribed to *Bungalow Magazine* and
described their new neighborhoods as "bungalow cities" or "bungalow belt-
ways."[39] In time the people themselves would come to be described as the
"bungalow-owning middle class."[40]

These people, who were new to the middle class, joined book clubs, read
magazines, went to the movies, and sent their kids to college. Their homes
were more informal and open. Karen Halttunen has posited that this turn-
of-the-century shift from eclectic manse to bungalow, and parlor to living
room, indicated a transition from a culture of *character* to one of *personality*. Building on Warren Susman's well-known distinction between these two
understandings of self, she has argued that the ways in which domestic space
was designed, decorated, and used led to changes in how people hailed and
identified themselves. The more formal ways in which family and guests
encountered each other in the parlor—what Halttunen calls "the genteel performance"—were by this time giving way to less formal and more extempo-
raneous modes of self-expression.[41]

These changes in domestic architecture and the undoing of the "genteel
performance" that accompanied them would soon be reflected in the essay.
An 1893 piece by Tudor Jenks offered a first glimpse of what the changes in
middle-class family life might mean for the form. Jenks's essay on the essay
was one of many that Mabie published in the *Outlook*, Henry Ward Beecher's

magazine, around the turn of the century. In fact, it seems Mabie may have borrowed his metaphors of well-fitting, comfortable clothes from Jenks:

> Here now are some neighbors come in to talk with us. They wear their every-day clothes, and one does not even rise to receive them. They do not know what they are going to say; certainly they do not come to offer formalities either of congratulation or of condolence.
>
> Even should they be interrupted by the children's playing, there is no need of the imperative 'Hush!' What they will talk about depends upon the weather, the creak of a chair, the flapping of an awning, the twitter of a bird, the cackle of a triumphant hen. But there will be no wearisome frivolity, not dull posing, for these are our good neighbors the Essayists.[42]

Not everyone was happy with this new familiarity. For some, easy and impromptu conversation, especially if interrupted by noisy children, was neither conversation nor a model for the essay. They felt each step (from drawing room to parlor to living room) meant a degree of privacy and seriousness was lost. This was, for instance, the position of Henry James and Edith Wharton. Like Woolf, they mourned the loss of the drawing room and what it represented. Ambivalent at best in their attitude toward America's expanding middle class and the country's increasing separation from European culture, they saw the coming of the living room as a threat to polite conversation. In a widely consulted 1897 guidebook written with Ogden Codman Jr. and titled *The Decoration of Houses*, Wharton argued that privacy is "one of the first requisites of civilized life," and it is lost "if the drawing-room be a part of the hall and the library a part of the drawing-room."[43]

Returning to America in 1904 for the first time in twenty-one years, James saw these changes as a "provocation to despair." He feared that the arrival of the living room would bring an end "not only to occupation and concentration, but to conversation itself, the play of the social relation at any other pitch than the pitch of a shriek or a shout."[44]

Walls, doors, and dividers were coming down; drawing rooms and parlors were giving way to living rooms; quiet conversation by the fireside was drowned out by the hustle and bustle of modern life; gentle readers had vanished into that airy and abstract entity known as the reading public; publishing had become an industry; dime novels replaced books, and ten-cent magazines replaced quarterlies and journals; essayists were now brand names protected by copyright laws and painted on the sides of railroad cars; and essays were being lost in a clutter of ads, confused with articles, and asked to serve as guides for how to present one's self at a dinner party.

THE REFORM OF PUBLIC EDUCATION AND
THE TEACHING OF ESSAYS

The new middle class changed the schoolhouse as well as the house. The Progressive Era ushered in dramatic educational reform, including the expansion of public education, the rise of the research university, and the professionalization of the expert. These changes led to increased literacy and a larger reading public, but they also led to more specialization, valorization of the sciences at the expense of the humanities, and new kinds of middle-class status anxiety.

The first generation of the professional-managerial class did not go to college, but the next generation did. As the number of young middle-class managers and workers who acquired their expertise in colleges and universities increased, so too did the number of those institutions—from 563 in 1870 to 977 in 1900 and 1,409 in 1930.[45] This increase was made possible by the surplus generated during the economic growth of the Gilded Age. Wealthy families established private universities, which often bore their names. Cornell, Stanford, Vanderbilt, Johns Hopkins, and Carnegie Tech were all founded during the last decades of the nineteenth century.[46] Other families donated buildings and endowed professorships. Religious institutions had increased revenues and founded new universities, often designed to serve particular immigrant communities. These included Manhattan College in 1853, St. Bonaventure in 1858, Boston College in 1863, St. John's University in 1870, Hebrew Union in 1875, and Yeshivat Etz Chaim (later Yeshiva University) in 1886. The revenues of local governments increased fivefold between 1902 and 1922,[47] and some of this money was used to establish universities: Adelphi in 1896, University of California–Los Angeles in 1919, and Long Island University in 1926.

But the greatest growth during the period came at the state level, especially in the Midwest, where "instant" or "people's" universities were created, largely through the land-grant system established by the Morrill Acts of 1862 and 1890. Disparaged as "cow colleges" by the coastal elites, the land-grant universities gained in reputation during the Progressive Era. Writing in the *Saturday Evening Post* in October 1907, John Corbin argued that the University of Michigan's arrival as a "national university" should force eastern elitists to reconsider their attitudes: "From the point of view of the Back Bay and Fifth Avenue, western New York is on the frontier; but from the point of view of the Golden Gate, Chicago lies next the eastern seaboard. Our nomenclature needs revising. The great university of the Old Northwest really lies in the new Middle-East." These new institutions of higher learning might have been remaking the country's geography, but their main goal was to educate the middle class. In a snide 1906 comment that confused individual intelligence with social class, Daniel Coit Gilman, the president of Johns Hopkins, proclaimed, "It is neither for the genius nor for the dunce, but for the great middle class possessing ordinary talents that we build colleges."[48]

Middle-class parents ignored such snobbery and committed themselves to the education of their children. According to Alexandra Oleson and John Voss, "It was the students who came to colleges and universities in expanding numbers [between 1860 and 1920] who formed the principal economic base of American science and scholarship." Middle-class families footed tuition bills and spared their children the responsibility of contributing to the upkeep of the home in order to send them off to college to improve their lot. The number of Americans enrolled in colleges and universities rose from 52,300 in 1870 to 597,000 in 1920, a nearly twelvefold increase in two generations. Then, in the next decade alone, enrollment nearly doubled again, reaching 1.1 million by 1930.[49]

A college education was not the only route to the middle class, however. According to Robert Wiebe, "The main lines of educational development late in the century ran downward from the universities and upward from the primary grades, meeting at the high schools." The high school system lagged behind, and educators recognized the college system could not improve unless the secondary system improved. In 1871 James McCosh, the president of Princeton, described the American education system between the common schools and colleges as a two-story building without a staircase.[50]

During the 1890s, the movement for change began to gather momentum. Parents and teachers pressed universities and the government to help. Local parents' groups convened a national congress to discuss the issues in 1897. Teachers began to organize and joined the parents' groups in calling for an expansion of the secondary system. Between 1890 and 1910 the number of high school teachers and students increased more than fourfold; in the next decade alone, it more than doubled.[51] Over the same period (1890 to 1920) the number of public high schools in America increased from 2,526 to 14,326, and the number of students attending them rose from 202,963 to 1,851,965.[52] By 1920 85.5 percent of all children between the ages of five and seventeen were enrolled in school.[53] Over the next decade improvement was even more dramatic. During the 1920s high school enrollment doubled nationally, from about 2.5 million to 5 million.[54]

Unfortunately, because K–12 education was organized locally, expectations varied enormously among districts. In many rural school districts, for instance, where students were needed during planting and harvest, the school year was only three months long.[55] In some urban districts the mission of schools was mainly custodial. They were meant to keep "bad boys" off the streets while parents worked. Toward the end of the century a reform movement began to advocate for national standards and improved curricula. Parents and teachers spearheaded this movement. Local teacher associations pushed for better pay, improved salary scales, tenure, clear and negotiated procedures for promotion, nonpartisan school boards, and specific professional training requirements for each position in the public schools.[56] Unionized teachers also pressured school boards to diversify the curricula. Increasingly, public high schools offered vocational and commercial tracks that emphasized shorthand, bookkeeping, applied electronics, wood and metal shop, home economics and drafting, as well as a college preparatory track that required English, history, math, science, and often Latin or a modern language.[57] These reforms increased literacy and fueled economic growth, but they also had repercussions for the essay and its status among literary genres.

English as a discipline was a centerpiece of the high school and college curriculum, but that changed after 1890 when the study of literature was separated from writing instruction. Historians of composition studies such as Patricia Bizzell, Bruce Herzberg, Donald McQuade, and Lynn Bloom suggest that the separation of rhetoric from belles lettres can be traced to the work of late-eighteenth-century and early-nineteenth-century theorists such as George Campbell, Hugh Blair, and Samuel Taylor Coleridge who, according to Bizzell and Herzberg, argued for a distinction between "the *active* concerns of rhetoric and the contemplative ones of literature."[58]

During the nineteenth century this theoretical proposition led, first in England and then in the United States, to a breakdown in the historical alliance between rhetoric and literature within secondary and college curricula. The study of classical rhetoric drifted into Latin classes, and within English departments rhetoric combined with composition, creating a new field of writing studies that focused on the essay and employed it for the practical work of teaching students how to write. Literature, on the other hand, focused on poetry, drama, and fiction, which were seen as imaginative and creative genres to be set apart for contemplation and interpretation. Poetry, drama, and fiction were primary genres and meant to be serviced by the essay, a secondary genre that was used to discuss them. According to Bloom, the essay had by 1900 suffered a "fall from canonical status to school genre."[59]

Richard Connors explains that while the teaching of literature was reserved for senior professors, the teaching of writing in "service courses" was turned over to junior faculty, adjuncts, and teaching assistants. Literature courses were more likely to be upper-level electives pursued by English majors, while the basic composition course was (and still is) required of all first-year students. The beginners assigned to teach these classes were given "readers"—textbook anthologies filled with model essays, discussion questions, and exercises designed to walk them through their first teaching experience.[60]

Building on the work of David Olson, John Trimbur has argued that these kinds of texts are "deproductionalized," meaning they remove "traces of authorship and the circumstances of production from essayist prose." In fact, says Trimbur, they paradoxically derive their authority from seeming to be "authorless" and "unwritten": "By appearing to speak for themselves—by ostensibly summarizing and transmitting the current and agreed-upon state of knowledge without reference to the authors or conditions of production— textbooks appear to speak for the culture as a whole." Such authority helps transform the individual essays anthologized in the textbooks from objects of study and interpretation into models for writing and communication; from texts that are imaginative, individual, and difficult into texts that are representative, transparent, and practical; from texts Roland Barthes has identified as writerly into ones that he calls readerly.[61]

The editors of composition textbooks that appeared in America at the turn of the century codified this approach. Their anthologies built on a mode of writing instruction with which their students, who had grown up on McGuffey readers (one hundred twenty-two million of which were sold between 1836 and 1920), would have been familiar.[62] The McGuffey readers, especially the later editions, emphasized secular virtue and national unity and included excerpts from essays by Irving, Lowell, Warner, and Mitchell. The college composition anthologies promoted a similar view of the essay as a genre that was practical and easy to emulate. Maurice Garland Fulton, for example, explained in the preface to his *Expository Writing: Materials for a College Course in Exposition by Analysis and Imitation* (1912) that his goals were fourfold: to teach students writing through the "examination and imitation of good models," to focus on "the kind of writing that is most directly serviceable in practical life," "to draw the selections chiefly from the field of scientific writing," and to pick short selections that could be used along with discussion questions to set up writing "exercises."[63] A look at his selections confirms how thoroughly the new disciple had shifted the study of writing away from literary essays toward practical and scientific articles. Fulton's collection of "specimens" includes the occasional celebration of culture such as Thackeray's "Evening at Theatre," but includes many more pieces along the lines of Charles W. Eliot's "Function of Education in a Democratic Society," Theodore Roosevelt's "Manly Virtues and Practical Politics," Charles Darwin's

"Earth Worms and Their Function," and Thomas Henry Huxley's "Method of Scientific Investigation."

THE SCIENCES, THE HUMANITIES, AND SPECIALIZATION

The separation of English studies into the two subspecialties of literature and composition and the tendency within composition to discard the genteel essay in favor of logical argument and scientific practicality were indicative of broader changes in the way America organized learning and knowledge at the end of the nineteenth century. Prior to the Industrial Revolution, institutions of higher education in the United States had been small liberal arts colleges, usually sponsored by Protestant denominations and devoted to the classical education of well-born young men bound for law, business, medicine, or the clergy. During the late nineteenth century the field of higher education came to be dominated by large publicly funded research universities composed of numerous departments, many of which represented fields of study that had not existed even a few years earlier.

Industrialization, trust in American "know-how," and a new sense of the country's standing motivated these changes. As early as 1848, U.S. Representative Justin Smith Morrill, a Whig from Vermont, argued that American colleges might as well "lop off a portion of the studies established centuries ago as the mark of European scholarship and replace the vacancy— if it is a vacancy—by those of a less antique and more practical value."[64] He soon got his way. Though the humanities and "European scholarship" were not exactly lopped off, the passage of the federal Land Grant Act of 1862 that Morrill sponsored established in every state and territory of the country a land-grant university or college that emphasized the sciences and agriculture.

This trend was contradictory. It reflected not just an anti-intellectual and anti-European bent in American culture but also a desire to emulate European universities, especially the German model. Though leery of Germany's nationalism, rigid class system, and reputation for ponderous rationalism and airy abstraction, American educators admired the German emphasis on patience, science, rigor, and civic responsibility. The German model seemed an antidote to a growing uneasiness in America, particularly among certain leading educators, with the speed and avarice of the Gilded Age. Writing from Germany during this period, William James remarked on the way in which "we Americans are too greedy for *results*" and "think only of means of cutting short the work to reach them sooner."[65]

Key to the German model was its emphasis on science and engineering, and before long the sciences dominated America's new research universities. Older liberal arts colleges felt pressured to move in the same direction. During his forty years as president, a period stretching from 1869 to 1909, Charles W. Eliot completely restructured Harvard, transforming it from a college into a university. To the existing undergraduate program he added a graduate program in arts and sciences and professional schools in law, medicine, and divinity. He increased Harvard's endowment from $2.25 million to more than $20 million, the faculty from sixty to six hundred, and the enrollment from one thousand to four thousand.[66]

The growing prestige of the sciences compelled other disciplines to emulate them. The social sciences emerged as new fields, and even in the humanities more "objective" modes of study such as philology and literary history displaced the classical curriculum. Henry Seidel Canby, the young son of a Wilmington, Delaware, banker who attended Yale and was beginning an academic career in English at this time, recalled this shift in the humanities: "Now the scientific approach became fashionable. Scholars in literature who called themselves scientific began to dominate the graduate schools and extend their influence into the sacred precincts of the undergraduate college. Applying the technique of scientific research to language, they revealed an evolution with laws of its own the discovery of which was a noble extension of knowledge." One might read Canby's use of *sacred* as ironic or merely overblown, but the sarcasm ringing from the word *noble* seems unmistakable. Canby argued that this scientific approach led to dogmatism and nit-picking: "Accuracy in little things was the new virtue, and we were encouraged to believe that the world was more in need of correct texts, exact dates, and knowledge of sources, than of estimates, appreciations, and opinions which, however just, were not scientific because they could not be proved."[67]

The consequences of this scholasticism went beyond the classroom. As the universities trained students in these techniques, more and more readers, whether they were college educated or not, began to read this way. The move toward philology, science, and specialization put tremendous pressures on the personal essay—a genre written by generalists for general readers. Gerard Stanley Lee discussed these changes in a 1903 book entitled *The Lost Art of Reading*. Lee, later a weekly columnist for the *New York World*, wrote, "Literature is getting to be the filling of orders—time-limited orders," and life had turned into "a blur of printed paper." "Society is a crowd of crowds," he said, because we have come to "pride ourselves on educating people in rows and civilising them in bulk." To be a specialist in a crowd, he argued, is anxiety provoking. Overwhelmed and trying to keep up, people now lived their lives "under the domination of the 'Cultured-man-must' theory of education" and had fallen prey to "the industry of being well informed." They had become "specialists" who had lost the "power of reading for principles." The "modern reader," said Lee, was "a skimmer, a starer at pictures," and "a lover of peeks and paragraphs" who was no longer able to think "a whole thought." Specialization was at odds with the tradition of the essayist, who had always been a rambler and generalist. An essayist like Lamb had the gift of "letting go," of digressing and seeing the whole in the part, but the "passing of the essay," said Lee, "at the present time is largely due to the fact that generalisation has been trained out of typical modern minds. We are mobbed with facts."[68]

General readership magazines contained digests, popular science features, and current-events articles that helped individuals develop at least a passing understanding of developments outside their own fields of expertise. They also provided a common set of allusions, understandings, attitudes, and beliefs with which members of the PMC might hail each other. Mass-market magazines, Tom Reynolds has argued, were seen as signaling the arrival of a "new version of democracy" that was based on "the notion that individual success was available to all who worked hard and kept their wits about them" and would replace the old "system of success for the already-wealthy and privileged." Not only did the magazines promote this fundamentally middle-class ideology, claims Reynolds, but they also introduced readers to the often intimidating content of a college education, especially "specialized learning and modern institutional management," as well as the "social side" of college life. Many college students during this era were the first members of their families to attend college, and these magazines helped demystify the college experience. "If the burgeoning college system was going to succeed," Reynolds explains, "it had to make the middle class feel that they belonged in a social arena that had formerly been occupied mostly by the well-to-do."[69]

At the turn of the century, some critics believed that the new magazines had become so adept at preparing their readers for college that they were now, at least for certain people, a kind of substitute for college. By offering ready-made learning and sudden sophistication, these magazines constituted a threat to traditional sources of authority and leadership. Writing in 1907 William James worried that in fifty years Americans might look back and see that "institutions of higher learning had lost all influence over public opinion" to "certain private literary adventures, commonly designated in the market by the affectionate name of ten-cent magazines." Magazines, said James in a 1907 address to a group of female college graduates, were threatening to supplant higher education: "In our essential function of indicating the better men, we now have formidable competitors outside. *McClure's Magazine,* the

American Magazine, Collier's Weekly and, in its fashion, the *World's Work*, constitute together a real popular university along this line."[70]

W. E. B. DU BOIS, THE VOICES OF THE ESSAY, AND PROGRESSIVISM

James was overstating the case, but the new mass magazines were increasing in importance and influence. General readership magazines, according to Canby, were now "as great a literary force as the book in America."[71] These new periodicals did not yet have the prestige or gravitas of the "family house" magazines of the previous century—*Harper's, Scribner's* (later *Century*), *Putnam's*, and the *Atlantic*—but they far surpassed those magazines in circulation and readership and spoke to the new middle class in ways even the print-laden Big Four were beginning to envy and emulate.

The editors of these new magazines were also taking themselves more seriously and had begun to compete with the older magazines for writers and material. Tellingly, James published what would become perhaps his most widely anthologized essay, "The Moral Equivalent of War," three years later in *McClure's*, one of the magazines that he had characterized as a kind of quasi university.

Samuel Sidney McClure had set up the first newspaper syndicate in 1884 and consequently made a fortune serializing books and comic strips. In 1893 he launched his own magazine, which published a popular mix of muckraking and celebrity profiles. He also tried to recruit established literary figures to lend his magazine legitimacy. He wrote to Hamlin Garland, for example, "Drop your *literary* prose and come with us. Use your skill on topics of the day, or stories of big personalities, and you'll make a place for yourself." Garland answered the call. He contributed interviews to McClure's profile feature "Real Conversations," but he always felt that in doing so he had fallen "between two stools"—the "aristocratic" on the one side and the "popular or journalistic" on the other. Garland later admitted, "I wrote for *McClure's*, but I continued to visit *The Century's* literary salon!"[72] McClure assistant Ray Stannard Baker was another example of this kind of multiple-personality disorder. With McClure he helped pioneer idea-driven articles, investigative reporting, a staff system, and the tactic of farming stories out to a stable of freelancers, but under the pseudonym of David Grayson he moonlighted as a genteel essayist, publishing the best-seller *Adventures in Contentment* and its sequel, *Adventures in Friendship*.

The *World's Work*, another of the magazines mentioned by James, also represented the bumpy transition from Gilded Age literary gentility to modern journalism and the consequences that transition would have for the personal essay. The magazine's editor, Walter Hines Page, was a North Carolinian who studied at Randolph-Macon and Johns Hopkins before becoming a reform journalist and moving north to edit the *Forum* (1890–1895) and the *Atlantic* (1896–1899). At the *Forum* he experimented with panels of experts and the commissioning of articles. When he tried to introduce these ideas at the *Atlantic*, however, he ran into resistance. The magazine of Emerson, Lowell, Holmes, and Howells refused to seek out the timely, expecting instead that the timeless would seek out the *Atlantic*. The hushed hallways of the magazine's Back Bay offices still evoked a gentlemen's club, not the noisy brainstorming of a big-city newsroom. When Page founded the *World's Work* with his book-publishing partner, Frank Doubleday, in 1900, he had a freer hand. At Doubleday, Page, and Company (which Doubleday had founded originally with McClure in 1874), the two men spearheaded the search for bestsellers and star authors (even if it meant poaching them) and the practice of first developing a book idea and then finding an author to implement it. Publishers, according to Doubleday, should "invent books which the public really wants, or thinks it wants." The two men ridiculed the way the established houses continued to fetishize the "artistic stuff," as Doubleday put it.[73] Page (the more political of the two) edited their "Illustrated Magazine of National Efficiency and Social Progress" until 1913, when he left to serve as President Wilson's ambassador to England.

In the June 1901 issue of the *World's Work*, Page published an article titled "The Negro as He Really Is" by one of James's former students at Harvard, W. E. B. Du Bois. The piece, which was illustrated by the work of German photographer A. Radclyffe Dugmore, would provide the basis two years later for chapters 7 and 8 of *The Souls of Black Folk*. This collaborative tour of the Black Belt near Albany, Georgia, exposed the crushing burden of poverty and debt on black sharecroppers. It was a kind of forerunner for the work James Agee and Walker Evans would do, when those two men sought to humanize white Alabama tenant farmers in *Let Us Now Praise Famous Men* (1941), a book that began as a 1936 *Fortune* magazine assignment.

A look at Du Bois's Georgia piece and how it made its way into *Souls* reveals some of the difficulties that progressive essayists of the period faced when writing for the new magazines. No one experimented more aggressively with genre or published in a wider range of magazines at the turn of the century than Du Bois. In the six years prior to the publication of *Souls* in 1903, he published essays or articles in a wide range of magazines and journals, including, in addition to the *World's Work*, the *Atlantic*, the *Independent*, *Harper's*, the *Nation*, *New World*, the *Southern Workman*, the *Outlook*, the *Missionary Review*, the *Literary Digest*, the *Dial*, and *Annals of the American Academy of Political and Social Sciences*. Many of these pieces were reworked and incorporated into *Souls*, which is most often remembered and taught as an answer to Booker T. Washington's accommodationist educational policies. Mabie's magazine, the *Outlook*, serialized Washington's ghostwritten autobiography, *Up from Slavery*, between November 1900 and February 1901. Doubleday, Page, and Company published it as a book in March 1901.

It made sense that Du Bois turned to the essay as his form of choice. The essay as a genre offered the range and flexibility he felt he needed to take on a subject as charged and expansive as race in the twentieth century. Du Bois wanted to draw on all his resources—whether intellectual, rhetorical, or emotional. He wanted to bear witness, analyze objectively, and invoke prophecy, and according to Arnold Rampersad, it was the Anglo-American essay of the previous century that gave him the tools to do this. Du Bois studied the formal and elevated tones of Emerson and Carlyle as well as the more familiar and anecdotal approach of Hazlitt and Lamb. According to Rampersad, Du Bois "used the essay to capture the nuances of his amorphous subject, the multiple disciplines of his explication, and the different and sometimes conflicting expressions of his temperament." To do this Du Bois had to bring together into one book a wide variety of pieces that had been published separately and in very different magazines. His first task was to develop a vision of the book as a whole. Rampersad has identified that structure as fundamentally dialectical and composed of three parts—"dealing successively with the history, the sociology, and the spirituality of Afro-America." Other critics have called on Rampersad's tripartite analysis and adapted it to their own readings. For Robert Stepto the book's structure is one of a stasis, immersion, and ascent; for Elaine Wright Newsome, it follows pursuit, captivity, and escape; and for Paul Gilroy, it traces successively the African American struggles against slavery, for citizenship, and for autonomy and community.[74] The chapters of Du Bois's book move across a spectrum of nonfiction genres, ranging from academic article to personal essay, from eulogy to short story, from history to music criticism.

Finding an overall scheme was a necessary first step for Du Bois, but it was not, of itself, sufficient; he still had to reconcile the various types of address he had employed in the original pieces. He rearranged and rewrote the pieces, breaking them up and shuffling and adding to them. He used stanzas from canonical poems and bars from spirituals as paired epigraphs for each of the chapters in order to hold those chapters together. The main glue he used, however, was his own flexible and expansive voice, the range of which he worked to his advantage. Here is the opening of chapter 7, in which Du Bois begins the tour through Georgia: "Out of the North the train thundered, and we woke to see the crimson soil of Georgia stretching away bare and monotonous right and left." The *we* in this sentence could refer to all of the train's passengers, but it could also refer only to Du Bois and his collaborator. A page later, after three paragraphs of description, the narrator says, "But we must hasten on our journey." This sentence hints at direct address, but it is not clear that the reader is a part of this *we*. A few lines further the direct address is made clear: "If you wish to ride with me you must come into the 'Jim Crow Car.'" Du Bois's use of present tense and direct address identifies his reader as white and merges that reader with Dugmore. Narrator and reader will now view the Black Belt not just through Du Bois's prose but also through the German photographer's viewfinder.[75]

This shifting of pronouns, address, and point of view continues throughout the book, affecting both narrator and reader. In an oft-cited essay titled "The Writer's Audience Is Always a Fiction," Walter Ong argues that there are two creators of a writer's audience: first, the author, who "construct[s] in his imagination, clearly or vaguely, an audience cast in some sort of role," and, second, the reader, who, following the cues offered by the author, plays out some version of that role. Certainly, this is the case with *The Souls of Black Folk*. In the book's famous opening lines Du Bois wrote, "Herein lie buried many things which if read with patience may show the strange meaning of being black here in the dawning of the Twentieth Century. This meaning is not without interest to you, Gentle Reader; for the problem of the Twentieth Century is the problem of the color-line." Here again we have direct address, but we also have an audacious claim, made all that much more audacious because it is coming at the "dawning of the Twentieth Century."[76]

Who is this confident narrator? Who is this Gentle Reader? Looking ahead we see that the "forethought" is signed by Du Bois, and so we naturally conclude that the narrator is some version of him. But elsewhere in the forethought the narrator adopts a less audacious, more humble tone: "I pray you, then, receive my little book in all charity, studying my word with me, forgiving mistake and foible for sake of the faith and passion this is in me, and seeking the grain of truth hidden there." Then, further down, we get additional clues as to both narrator and reader: "Leaving, then, the world of the white man, I have stepped within the Veil, raising it that you may view faintly its deeper recesses." The narrator is now marked as African American (or at least as one who is dark enough to cross the color line and be called a Negro); the reader is singled out as white but also sympathetic enough to want to understand black life.

Du Bois changes his mode of address often in the book, sometimes speaking generally of the Negro. In the famous section on double consciousness, for instance, he opts for an impersonal pronoun: "It is a peculiar sensation, this double-consciousness, this sense of always looking at one's self through eyes of others, of measuring one's soul by the tapes of a world that looks on in amused contempt and pity. One ever feels his two-ness,—an American, a Negro; two souls, two thoughts, two unreconciled strivings; two warring ideals in one dark body, whose dogged strength alone keeps it form being torn asunder." Elsewhere, he turns back toward himself and speaks more personally. He closes the forethought with a rhetorical question to his white reader that establishes his own race and states his goal: "And, finally, need I add that I who speak here am bone of the bone and flesh of the flesh of them that live within the Veil?" For Henry Louis Gates Jr. and Terri Hume Oliver, this move to first-person singular is a textual enactment of the point Du Bois is making: "As the reader is greeted by Du Bois in the text, the author comes from behind the veil of the third person to declare both his race and his mission."[77]

In the opening of the book Du Bois employed a familiar convention of Victorian fiction and imagined the Gentle Reader as white, middle-class, genteel, and sympathetic. But in the book's "after-thought," he switched to a soaring Whitmanesque apostrophe and reimagined his reader in a new and surprising way: "Hear my cry, O God the reader; vouchsafe that this my book fall not still-born into the world-wilderness. Let there spring, Gentle One, from out its leaves vigor of thought and thoughtful deed to reap the harvest wonderful."[78]

The cry seems to have been answered. *The Souls of Black Folk* became a history-changing text. It helped overturn the compromise that Washington had negotiated at the Atlanta Exposition in 1895. Two years after *Souls* was published Du Bois and William Monroe Trotter founded the Niagara Movement as a counter to Washington's narrow economism and conciliation, calling instead for full and immediate political equality and "the abolition of all caste distinctions based simply on race and color." A year later the new movement gathered for its second convention at Harper's Ferry, West Virginia, where John Brown had raided the arsenal. There, in his "Address to the Nation," Du Bois spoke boldly on behalf of his race: "We claim for ourselves every single right that belongs to a freeborn American, political, civil and social; and until we get these rights we will never cease to protest and assail the ears of America."[79] In 1909 the Niagara Movement joined with white activists and became the National Association for the Advancement of Colored People (NAACP). A year later, Du Bois, the only African American on the executive board, was named director of publications and editor of the organization's monthly magazine, the *Crisis*, a position he would hold until 1934. Early members of the organization included white essayists and editors such as Jane Addams, William Dean Howells, John Dewey, Lincoln Steffens, and Ray Stannard Baker.

Advocating for equal rights was the right thing to do and addressing the nation was an effective strategy, but the assailing of ears was not a technique that appealed to subsequent generations of American essayists. During the 1920s the young writers of the Harlem Renaissance resisted Du Bois's stentorian tones and high seriousness. In a speech at the NAACP convention in 1926 Du Bois declared, "Art is propaganda and ever must be, despite the wailing of the purists. I stand in utter shamelessness and say that whatever art I have for writing has been used always for propaganda for gaining the right of black folk to love and enjoy. I do not care a damn for any art that is not used for propaganda."[80] As much as they might admire his political commitment, the young writers did not agree with this as an artistic manifesto. For the younger generation, Du Bois might be radical politically, but artistically he was not radical at all. To them, his work reflected best-foot-forward gentility, Victorian prose, and the voice of a supereducated Harvard man. Several of them would write important essays, but Zora Neale Hurston's irreverent humor, Eric Walrond's dry ironies, George Schuyler's Menckenesque satire, and Langston Hughes's not-so-simple Semple stories were all in one way or another attempts to break from Du Bois.

The reaction of the younger African American essayists to the essays of Du Bois was not unlike the reaction of the next generation of white middle-class essayists to the high seriousness of white progressive essayists who dominated the form during the first decade and a half of the twentieth century. Essayists such as William James, Henry Adams, Jane Addams, John Muir, John Burroughs, John Jay Chapman, and Randolph Bourne reflect the earnest expertocracy that was Progressivism. At their best, they used their essays to advance important causes—public education, public health, environmentalism, and immigration reform; at their worst, their earnestness ripened into piety, grandiosity, and elitism.

Either way, they did not found a lasting tradition for the American essay. Like Emerson before them, they were uncomfortable with the first-person singular of the personal essay. *The Education of Henry Adams* (1918), for instance, offers a high-Brahmin version of an autobiography written in the third person. It is a genre that will become unwittingly comic two years later when Edward Bok publishes *The Americanization of Edward Bok* and that Gertrude Stein will soon turn inside out with *The Autobiography of Alice B. Toklas*. Du Bois turned various modes of address to his advantage, but other essayists of the period had less success. Listen, for instance, to the discomfort as Bourne shifts among pronouns—the first person continually trying to insert itself—in

his 1913 *cri de coeur*, "The Handicapped—by One of Them," published anony-
mously in the Atlantic:

> If he [the Handicapped] has to go out for himself to look for work, with-
> out fortune, training, or influence, as I personally did, his way will indeed
> be rugged. His disability will work against him for any position where
> he must be much in the eyes of men, and his general insignificance has a
> subtle influence in convincing those to whom he applies that he is unfitted
> for any kind of work. As I have suggested, his keen sensitiveness to other
> people's impressions of him make him more than unusually timid and
> unable to counteract that fatal first impression by any display of personal
> force and will. He cannot get his personality over across that barrier. The
> cards seem stacked against him from the start. With training and influence
> something might be done, but alone and unaided his case is almost hope-
> less. At least, this was my own experience.[81]

Bourne's anonymity, his concern lest it appear he is asking for pity, and his
desire to make a general statement leave his own personality unable to get
across the barrier that is the third person. Even in this passage, the cards seem
stacked against him.

Chapman's earnest and poetic antilynching essay "Coatesville" (1912)
offers another case in point. On the first anniversary of a lynching in a small
town in Pennsylvania, Chapman hired a hall and traveled to the town to
speak before a public prayer meeting. "We are met," he began, "to commemo-
rate the anniversary of one of the most dreadful crimes in history—not for the
purpose of condemning it, but to repent our share in it." When Lincoln com-
memorated the dead at Gettysburg, he said, "We can not dedicate—we can
not consecrate—we can not hallow—this ground," and the *we* was the people
gathered there as well as the nation for which Lincoln as president and commander in chief spoke. Chapman was a Harvard-educated New Yorker, son of
the president of the New York Stock Exchange, ancestor and namesake of the
nation's first chief justice. He was not from Coatesville. Two people attended
the prayer meeting. The intentions are good, but when he says of the lynching,
"We are involved in it. We are still looking on," the *we* is without antecedent,
and the essay tends toward an antiracist posture.[82]

Bourne and Addams would begin to recognize how humor could help them
make a point. In the last months of his short life, Bourne argued for the possibilities of the humorous light essay. Addams explored the ironies of myth and rumor
in her essay "The Devil Baby at Hull-House" (1916). Even though she was at the
center of the "scandal" that is her subject, Addams is herself largely absent from
the essay. In many ways the progressive essayists are the sons and daughters

of Emerson. As Lopate said of Emerson (and Bacon), they may make "flickering references to an 'I,'" but they are mainly concerned with the "expression of impersonal wisdom and authority." They mean to think big thoughts. They mean to change the world. So, we have James writing "The Moral Equivalent of War" (1910) or Burroughs "The Gospel of Nature" (1912). Even "Stickeen," Muir's small anecdote about getting lost while walking his dog on an Alaskan ice field, grows into a parable about nature and immortality. Discovering the universal in the particular is certainly in the tradition of Montaigne, but when Muir is finally able to coax his little dog across a crevasse, both punctuation and prose swell almost out of control: "And now came a scene! 'Well done, well done, little boy! Brave boy!; I cried, trying to catch and caress him; but he would not be caught. Never before or since have I seen anything like so passionate a revulsion from the depths of despair to exultant, triumphant, uncontrollable joy."[83]

Even Twain seemed to be carrying the weight of the world during the Progressive Era. He wrote a satiric critique of imperialism ("To the Person Sitting in Darkness" [1901]), a dialogue on determinism ("What Is Man?" [1906]), and several pieces about God's cruelty. His dark turn could be explained by the fact that he was facing his own death, had lost his wife and daughters, and was battling bankruptcy, but the work of his last years also seems representative of the time.

Twain's humor inoculated him against pomposity. Others were less lucky. The mantle of Emerson, with all its seriousness and impersonality, was too much to don. In 1899, on the occasion of the publication of Chapman's *Emerson, and Other Essays*, Mary Winsor published a piece titled "John Jay Chapman, Essayist" in which she wrote:

> We are in great want of exhortations to moral courage, to unshaken individuality, to personal integrity. The world can never outgrow Emerson's teachings or the teachings of his disciples, and we, in this country, at this hour, stand more than ever in need of his purifying and bracing influence as, day by day, the promotion of rapid transit and the consequent facility of communication, the diffusion of a homogeneous and mediocre education, the pressure of corruption weighing alike on rich and poor, the real or fancied necessity of catering politically to the lower elements of the populace, the similarity of interests and opinions required for the stability of democracy—as all these things tend more and more to obliterate distinctions between individuals and to establish throughout the United States that deadly monotony of which foreigners complain so volubly.[84]

It is too much to ask of Emerson. It is certainly too much to ask of Chapman. One can hear Progressivism collapsing under its own heavy weight.

THE "DEATH" OF THE ESSAY, 1900–1920

Too much was also being asked of the genteel essay that had been a main-stay of family house magazines. The move to take up reformist causes, to muckrake, and to enter the new mass magazines was putting tremendous pressure on the essay as the late Victorians had conceived it. The essay's via-bility became again a heated topic of debate. Between 1900 and 1920 more than thirty articles about the essay appeared in both old-school journals such as *Harper's* and the *Outlook* and in modern mass magazines such as *Munsey's* and *Ladies' Home Journal.*

As we have seen, in the last years of the old century, writers had begun to complain that the essay was old-fashioned and in need of renewal, though there was little agreement about what renewal might mean. Now, it seemed that might be changing. An anonymous reviewer surveyed several recent collections of essays in the December 3, 1904, issue of the *Outlook.* The reviewer could well have been Mabie, who edited the magazine and had a long interest in the essay. Whoever it was opened the piece with the complaint that in recent years it had been hard to find collections of "true essays," which he defined as "opinions pleasantly offered on subjects to which every cultivated reader might bring a predisposition and a taste." But, the reviewer announced, nine collections released that fall suggested some positive changes. In a collection by Bliss Perry, for instance, one essay "recalls the college professor of the old school," while another "speculates upon the pressure of modern life into the professor's thought." Dated techniques per-sisted—especially in the work of Repplier and Felix E. Schelling—but H. W. Boynton's collection *Journalism and Literature* struck a more contemporary chord. Boynton, wrote the reviewer, admirably "combines something of the fullness of the well-read man with the readiness of the timely one." To some extent, Boynton's prose style could "be characterized as being of the street." Perhaps, suggested the writer, the essay "should be more familiar with arts and letters than is the lecture-room, as clubbable as the club, and no less conscious of a spirit of the times than is the marketplace itself."[85] There was something new here. The *Outlook*'s reviewer did not share Howells's fear of the debasement of taste by the new reading public or the older man's con-cern that literature and journalism were being confused. Instead, he argued for an essay that might seek a broader readership and be willing to engage with the marketplace and the street.

A year later an anonymous writer in the *Outlook* (again, quite possibly Mabie) declared that the "art of essay writing has been revived," though revival seemed to consist of one step forward and two steps back. The author expressed a concern that the new essayist be "vigorous and effective" and avoid the "atmosphere which sometimes exudes from college walls, as disease used to exude from the walls of the old-fashioned solidly built hospitals," but also argued that essays were "preeminently the product of meditation, leisure, and the ripening of the quiet life," and should be "wholesome and genial." Lamb and Elia were invoked as models.[86]

These two surveys from the *Outlook* and a third that appeared there in 1907 mentioned approvingly the work of Brander Matthews. The anonymous 1907 reviewer claimed that among essayists, "we have no more expert craftsman" than Matthews, who, though an academic, "has a journalist's instinct for the subject of the hour and a journalist's courage in putting the contemporary view without evasion or apology."[87]

Matthews was an important presence in turn-of-the-century literature and politics. As president of the Modern Language Association and the National Institute of Arts and Letters, professor at Columbia, founder of the Authors Club, New York journalist, and editor of fifteen collections of poetry, biography, essays, and criticism, he worked especially hard to bring American literature into the college curriculum and literary canon. He was also an essayist who wrote extensively on the history and form of the essay, published surveys of the essay in a wide variety of magazines, and edited the important *Oxford Book of American Essays* (1914).

Matthews was a contradictory and transitional figure, caught between the Genteel Tradition and literary modernism. He was a clubby member of the old New York literary establishment, who also promoted modern writers such as Twain and James Weldon Johnson; a noted academic, who wrote regularly for newspapers and magazines; and a member of the Authors League of America, who, when 60 percent of its members voted to affiliate with the American Federation of Labor, organized the remaining 40 percent to threaten to resign and blocked the move to unionize. Finally, he was the only son of a millionaire whose father lost everything in the panic of 1873. Fortunately for the family, his mother had money of her own, and an inheritance from her enabled him to live beyond his professor's salary, residing in a tony West Side neighborhood and summering in Europe or at Shinglenook, his home in Narragansett.[88]

Just as the essay was caught between literature and journalism, so was Matthews caught between his view of the author as amateur gentleman and his life as a working professional. It was a tension he felt deeply. The *Outlook* celebrated Matthews as an essayist with a journalist's instinct, but he suspected that journalism and literature were "incompatible." The journalist, he claimed, tried to work "for the day only" and the literary artist "for all time," but he allowed that intention was not everything. Sometimes the work of the journalist "survives longer than its allotted twenty-four hours; and, more often than not, what the man of letters does fails of immortality." Magazine editors might claim that their monthlies were more literary than the daily paper or a weekly magazine, but Matthews found such distinctions "without a difference, and altogether misleading." Journalism may be "a craft" and literature "an art," but the work of the professional writer contains elements of both: "Yet this [attempt at art] which was wrought in secret and with delicious travail, the artist must vend in open market, in competition with his fellow-craftsmen; putting it up to be knocked down by the highest bidder, huckstering his heart's blood, and receiving for it whatever the variable temper of the public may deem it be worth at the moment."[89]

The moment in which Matthews wrote was a turbulent one, and he engaged it. He intervened early and adamantly in favor of an International Copyright Agreement,[90] and like Mabie and Bok he was a friend and active supporter of Theodore Roosevelt. As Lawrence J. Oliver has shown, Matthews and Roosevelt began campaigning together for "literary Americanism" as early as 1888. Both men were prolific essayists who employed the form to promote an ideology of "true Americanism"—a "manly" conception of the nation that shunned the "colonial" worship of England and Europe while simultaneously celebrating the Anglo-Saxon race and Manifest Destiny. Roosevelt advanced this view in popular essays such as "The Strenuous Life" (1900) and "Race Decadence" (1911). For his part, Matthews argued that "warlike temper," "aggressiveness," "imperialistic sentiment," and even "shopkeeping" were "in our blood."[91]

Among genteel essayists Matthews praised the "cosmopolitan" Curtis, whose "mellow note" could be "heard distinctly" even in New York, "where strident voices fill the market-place." However, he turned sharply against Repplier, who he decided was "very clever and very colonial." He found her penchant for second-rate British essayists while failing to quote Hawthorne or Lowell "inexplicable."

His problem, however, was not only with Repplier's Anglophilia, or "colonialism," but also with her gender. "In literature as in some other things," Matthews pronounced, "a woman's opinion is often personal and accidental; it depends on the way the book happens to strike her." Roosevelt's dismissal of Repplier was even more overtly sexist. In a letter to Matthews he called her a "female idiot" and a "sporadic she-fool." In public print he was more careful. Of a piece she had written about the relationship between literature and war, he wrote that she "delights only in battles that are won by the expenditure of nothing more violent than rose water."[92]

Matthews allowed that Repplier was a good writer, but his disgust with her "colonialism" kept him from elaborating on her abilities as an essayist. He did, however, write about the form of the essay elsewhere. In 1913 he discussed the state of the genre in *Munsey's Magazine*. Some "despondent critics," he wrote, might believe that the "invention of the telegraph and the telephone" was threatening the art of essay; he did not. Those critics might complain that "nobody nowadays sits before his own hearth, and is thereupon moved to write about 'A Wood Fire,'" and, he acknowledged, "in this hurrying twentieth century, in the busy New World, we do not often find in our magazines papers on 'Wood Fires,'" but he did not see this as a terrible loss. Perhaps a great writer could elevate that subject, said Matthews, but it is likely that such an essay would be too cozy and confined. In a passage reminiscent of Lowell, he suggested an alternative view:

> The essential quality of a good essay is not to be sought in the writer's making something out of nothing, but in the commingled wit and wisdom, humor and good humor, with which he chats to us, his unknown friends, with all the freedom of the good talk whose flavor goes up the chimney. We ought to feel, as we read his paragraphs, that the essayist was writing from a full mind, and that we are enjoying the privilege of listening to a gentleman and a scholar—to employ the good old phrase so vitally significant. We ought to feel the he has something to say to us which he enjoys saying, and which he trusts we shall enjoy hearing. He is expressing himself and distilling the results of his observations and reflections on life, on men and women, on manners, and on books. He is giving us the seemingly spontaneous opinions of a man of the world, illustrating his precepts from his own practise and from his own reading.[93]

For Matthews the site of the essay is significant, but as site, not as subject. It is not the fire itself that is important, but the intimacy, spontaneity, and fullness of mind it allows. The hearth offers a respite from the hurry of the day and the noise of the street. It promotes a particular relationship between the essayist and his reader, a relationship in which the essayist is able to express and be himself. But, as Matthews feels compelled to admit, his essayist is still "a gentleman and scholar," and the talk of the essay can be as ephemeral as chimney smoke.

The years prior to World War I saw several writers grappling with the same problems Matthews had identified: the tension between literature and journalism, the goal of permanence, America's troubled relationship with England and Europe, the role of audience, and the sources of style and voice. Most of these writers were more pessimistic and conservative than Matthews.

They praised Repplier, claimed style was everything, espoused a more exclusive kind of essay, and longed for an older, cozier, Ik Marvel–like fireside.

A writer in the May 17, 1913, issue of *Harper's*, for example, sniffed that "one way to dislike books is to like newspapers," mourned the "passing of literature," ridiculed "what might be called the 'reading public," and concluded that there was little hope for "the poor contemplative essayist." But even this finicky correspondent grudgingly accepted the current turn to modernism: "But perhaps, too, the contemplative essayist must conquer new realms. Perhaps only when the aeroplane is in full flight and new data for abstraction is [sic] given can he sit down again and write with impunity of the untracked paths of lonely abstraction."[94]

The next spring, in April 1914, Richard Burton published an influential piece in the *New York Times Book Review*, in which he was much more distrustful of the marketplace than Matthews had been. Burton, who had worried publicly about the state of the essay as early as 1894 and decreed in 1902 that the essay was essentially a function of "mood and form," now added that the essayist is "the aristocrat of letters," who writes only for "the 'dear,' the 'gentle' reader" and not for the "Philistine." The essayist, he wrote, "finds his audience among those readers who have the taste to recognize his quality. It is before the open fire or under the evening lamp that his magnetized victim sits a-smiling and dreams away the hours in the best of companionship." How, Burton asked, might the essayist separate himself from that "group of pseudo-essayists who peddle out facts"? The answer, he proposed, was to ignore content and embrace style, for "like a flower, [the essay] blooms for blooming's sake, since beauty is its only excuse for being." He cited some familiar names as examples of those who bloomed for blooming's sake: "In the United States, writers like Holmes, Warner, Ik Marvel, and in our own more immediate day Miss Repplier, Dr. Crothers, and Mr. Lee, remind us that the line has not perished and that suchlike authors are not to be confused with the excellent souls ostensibly out to instruct and guide."[95]

Later that year in the introduction to his widely adopted essay anthology for secondary schools, Claude Fuess quoted Burton twice and echoed many of his sentiments. "Our current magazines," wrote Fuess, ". . . are enlivened with short treatises on such diverse matters as the Panama Canal, the importance of vivisection, and the evils of monopoly." But these, he explained, are "frankly ephemeral in their purpose, and make no pretense of being permanent literature. Such treatises, which are better classified as 'articles,' plainly do not belong in the same category with the genuine Essay. The true Essay, on the other hand, has a distinct literary aim. Its object is not primarily to spread knowledge, but to delight and stimulate its readers." The sarcasm behind "enlivened," the dismissal of "articles," and the attempt to sacralize the essay by capitalizing the word reveal Fuess as out to do more than just distinguish one genre from another. He is doing battle with mass culture. Like Howells, he fears the debasement of taste, and like Matthews, he is concerned about the permanence of literature. But, unlike either of them, he believes the essayist's goal should be to make something out of nothing. In this he agrees with Burton, whom he quotes: "An essayist without style is a contradiction in terms." For Fuess the essay is an "artificial product," and its "best examples" have "an aristocratic flavor." When he then asserts that it is experiencing "a wholesome revival," he is whistling in the dark. His examples give him away. He lists nine contemporary essayists: five are British, and to Burton's list of three Americans—Crothers, Lee, and Repplier—he adds Burton himself.[96]

Washington Irving, biographer of Columbus and Washington, U.S. ambassador to Spain, and as author of *The Sketch Book of Geoffrey Crayon, Gent.* (1820), America's first great essayist. Portrait by Alonzo Chappel from Evert A. Duykinck, *A Portrait of Eminent Men and Women of Europe and America, with Biographies* (New York: Johnson, Wilson, and Company, 1873). Reprinted by permission of the James Smith Noel Collection at Louisiana State University in Shreveport.

Sara Payson Parton (pictured here about 1866) re-created herself as
Fanny Fern and became one of America's most popular columnists.
Her first collection, *Fern Leaves from Fanny's Portfolio,* appeared in
1853 and sold seventy thousand copies within a year. Photo from
the Library of Congress, Prints and Photographs Division.

William Dean Howells was a novelist, Lincoln's biographer, Twain's friend, defender of the Haymarket martyrs, and editor of the *Atlantic* and *Harper's*. He feared that sometime during the magazine revolution of the 1890s, "the essay began to confuse itself with the article." Photo courtesy of the Photography Collection, Miriam and Ira D. Wallach Division of Art, Prints, and Photographs, the New York Public Library, Astor, Lenox, and Tilden Foundations.

Donald Grant Mitchell, about 1880. Mitchell's *Reveries of a Bachelor* (1850), narrated by the quintessential fireside bachelor, "Ik Marvell," sold more than a million copies and led Scribner's list for more than fifty years. Photo courtesy the Photography Collection, Miriam and Ira D. Wallach Division of Art, Prints, and Photographs, the New York Public Library, Astor, Lenox, and Tilden Foundations.

George Ade (seated) and John T. McCutcheon in their Chicago apartment around 1894 or 1895. The two men, who became friends while members of the Sigma Chi house at Purdue, collaborated on a column for the *Chicago Record* called "Stories of the Streets and of the Town"—Ade writing, McCutcheon illustrating. The two were also regulars (along with Chicago columnists Bert Leston Taylor, Eugene Field, and Finley Peter Dunne) at the Whitechapel Club, which, according to Ade, was "a little group of thirsty intellectuals who were opposed to everything." Photo courtesy of the Miriam and Ira D. Wallach Division of Art, Prints and Photographs, New York Public Library, from a photo donated by Frederick Richardson.

In her "happy half century" as an essayist, Agnes Repplier (pictured here about 1910) produced fifteen volumes of essays on subjects ranging from dogs and ale to Christianity and war. She was an active participant in the debate over the "death" of the essay. In 1894, she wrote, "The essay may die but just now it possesses a lively and encouraging vitality." By 1918 she was less sanguine: "The personal essay, the little bit of sentiment or observation, the lightly offered commentary which aims to appear the artless thing it isn't,—this exotic, of which Lamb was a rare exponent, has withered in the blasts of war." Photo from the George Grantham Bain Collection of the Library of Congress.

Rhodes scholar, editor of the *Ladies' Home Journal,* Book-of-the-Month Club judge, and conductor of the column "The Bowling Green," Christopher Morley was perhaps America's best-known essayist. Photo by Charles H. Davis from the 1918 edition of Morley's *Shandygaff: A Number of Most Agreeable Inquirendoes upon Life and Letters, Interspersed with Short Stories and Skits, the Whole Most Diverting to the Reader (1918).*

Columnist, Algonquin Circle wit, Book-of-the-Month Club judge, founder of the American Newspaper Guild, and Socialist Party candidate for Congress, Heywood Broun urges guild members to join the Congress of Industrial Organizations at a 1937 convention in Cleveland. Photo © Bettmann/CORBIS.

Harold Ross grew up in Salt Lake City and always felt like a rube from the provinces. Katherine White called him a "a natural literary man" who "spent his whole life reading to catch up." When he founded the *New Yorker* in 1925, he famously promised it would not be "for the old lady in Dubuque." By 1932 half the magazine's subscribers lived outside the metropolitan New York area. Photo by Nickolas Murray (1926), Jane Grant Photograph Collection, University of Oregon Library Special Collections.

In an influential 1933 piece, "A Little Old Lady Passes Away," John Waters announced the death of the genteel essay, "that lavender-scented little old lady of literature." Illustration for John Waters, "A Little Old Lady Passes Away," *Forum and Century* (July 1933).

Franklin and Eleanor Roosevelt in the president's study in 1933, their first year in the White House, the year of FDR's first fireside chat, and one in which they each published a book, prompting E. B. White to write, "Both President and Mrs. Roosevelt, to name only two other literary people, have published a book in the past year; and to realize that they, who are really busy, can do it, while we, who seldom have anything pressing on hand, cannot, is extremely discouraging." Photo courtesy of the Franklin D. Roosevelt Presidential Library and Museum, Hyde Park, New York.

E. B. White referred to his childhood home at 101 Summit Avenue in the Chester Hill neighborhood of Mt. Vernon, New York, as his "castle": "From it I emerged to do battle and into it I retreated when I was frightened or in trouble. The house even had the appearance of a fortress, with its octagonal tower room for sighting the enemy and its second-story porches for gun emplacements." Photo by permission of the White Literary LLC and from the E. B. White Collection, Division of Rare and Manuscript Collections, Cornell University Library.

E. B. White and James Thurber on the steps of the Angells'
rented summer house at Sneden's Landing in the Hudson
River Valley, 1929. At the end of the next decade when
White was "disenchanted" with himself and in the middle of his "abdication," Thurber scolded him in a letter,
"You are not the writer who should think that he is not
a writer." Photo by permission of the White Literary LLC
and from the E. B. White Collection, Division of Rare and
Manuscript Collections, Cornell University Library.

A 1942 meeting of the Book-of-the-Month-Club judges and officers *(clockwise from left):* Christopher Morley, Meredith Wood (vice president), Harry Scherman (founder and president), Henry Seidel Canby, and Dorothy Canfield Fisher. Morley and Canby were also editors of the *Saturday Review of Literature.* Photo by Herbert Gehr/Time Life Pictures/Getty Images.

Katharine and E. B. White with one of their dachshunds (probably Minnie) sometime in the early 1940s near their saltwater farm in North Brooklin, Maine. Photo by permission of the White Literary LLC and courtesy of *Bangor Metro*.

New York, New York

The Arrival of the Colyumnists

T he carnage and dislocations of the First World War shook, and
perhaps ended, the Progressive dream of a country being led
forward by trained and rational experts. At the same time, the
arrival of airplanes, the Model T, motion pictures, and radio acceler-
ated an already rapid rate of modernization to a speed that, to many
Americans, felt breakneck. New York, where the soldiers had shipped
out and then demobilized, was the center of this change. It had become
the capital of the modern world and of mass culture—a focus for those
who feared modernization and those who felt drawn to it. The city for its
part, especially Greenwich Village, saw itself at odds with the small-town
Middle American culture associated with the old middle class. During
the 1920s, however, New York's colyumnists, as they called themselves,
stepped into the breach and began to mediate between Manhattan and
the rest of the country. Through syndication, writers like Franklin Pierce
Adams, Heywood Broun, Don Marquis, and Christopher Morley developed nationwide readerships.

These new essayists benefited from the simultaneous emergence of a
cadre of cultural critics, entrepreneurs, publishers, editors, and impre-
sarios who celebrated their work. In the midtwenties a series of important articles by Canby, Carl Van Doren, Stuart Pratt Sherman, and Burton
Rascoe identified the colyumnists as real writers who were helping revital-
ize the American essay.

LEAVING THE ACADEMY, BECOMING MIDDLEBROW

Middlebrow culture grew out of a deep dissatisfaction with specialization. The tension between specialists and generalists manifested itself within the university in the uneasy marriage of the arts and sciences, but beyond the academy other Americans were also concerned about the problem of "over-specialization" and the rise of "technocracy." Americans worried that too many decisions were being left to the experts, that specialization narrowed us as a people, and that our search for the "new" was leading us to forget the past. Most wanted to be successful and practical, but not if it also meant being boring, standardized, and soulless. They appreciated the time-saving devices that science provided them, but wondered where the time had gone.

Liberal arts advocates resisted the new emphasis on science, technology, and specialization within the university, and some of them left the academy in search of a larger audience. Stuart Pratt Sherman, writing in the *Nation* in 1908, assailed the "pseudo-scientific specialists" for driving from the university the very students who had "real taste and literary power," though he also cautioned that "we need more generalizers" but "not flimsy generalizers." That same year John Erskine called for college English departments to drop the historical-philological approach and its cultivation of professors as experts in esoteric specialties and subspecialties. He proposed instead that English instructors teach a wide range of "great books" in small discussion groups where the instructors were "not to lecture or in any way behave like professors."[1]

Trends, however, were against them. Within most university English departments, the philologists won out. In his 1936 memoir of college life during the late Victorian era, Canby recalled that the period between 1870 and 1910 marked "the triumph of applied science" and "the defeat of the classics in American education." It was the time of what Gerald Graff has called the "failure of the generalists."[2]

At the time of the war, Canby began to consider whether general education might best take place outside the university. In 1918, while still a young professor at Yale, he was invited to a Cambridge University symposium, "The America of Today." There he argued that the future of American culture might lie in the "slowly mounting level of the vast bourgeois literature that fills not excellently, but certainly not discreditably our books and magazines." Two years later, in a collection titled *Everyday Americans*, he decided that America's "destiny will be among the middle class." And this new day felt imminent. "Economic conditions," he wrote, pointed toward the "triumph of the bourgeoisie," for America seemed "to be entering a period when a vastly greater number of men and women will have reasonable security of moderate income." This would mean, he believed, that the "aristocracy" (both "land-holding" and "moneyed") and the "proletariat" would be "captured" at least intellectually "by the dominant class," the "everyday American," the "middle class."[3]

Canby's terms are muddled—he conflates "middle class" and "bourgeoisie," hides them both behind the meaningless phrase "everyday American," and seems to confuse "bourgeoisie" with "aristocracy"—but clearly he was placing his stock in the idea of an expanding middle class. This can be explained by the fact that he was writing during a period of income compression, the first of only two sustained periods during the twentieth century when inequality decreased and the middle class grew.[4] But he was overly optimistic. Income compression would not be sustained, America was not about to do away with inequality, and the middle class might have seemed ubiquitous, but it would not become dominant. But his optimism soon enabled him to leave Yale and become, in the words of Gordon Hutner, "the middlebrow cultural authority par excellence" and "perhaps the most influential book critic that twentieth-century literary journalism ever produced."[5]

THE WAR AND THE ESSAY

At the same time Canby was making his case for the middle-class reader, other critics were restarting the debate over the essay.

Agnes Repplier had recently met Roosevelt and been won over to his aggressive Americanism. In a series of articles in the *Atlantic,* she joined him in attacking President Wilson's neutrality and warned of the security threat posed by unassimilated immigrants. These pieces were fiercely polemical, though Repplier was generally opposed to the idea of the essay as engagé. Soon after America joined the Allied effort in April 1917, she expressed concern about the effects the war was having on the essay. In the 1890s Repplier had argued that her version of the essay would survive the challenges of modernity. Now she was less sanguine. In a 1918 piece titled "The American Essay in Wartime," she wrote, "The personal essay, the little bit of sentiment or observation, the lightly offered commentary which aims to appear the artless thing it isn't,—this exotic, of which Lamb was a rare exponent, has withered in the blasts of war."[6]

Not everyone agreed with her—about the war or the essay. Randolph Bourne opposed the war and argued with Repplier in the *Atlantic,* where he proposed that cultural pride among immigrants and the "failure of the 'melting-pot'" should lead Americans to take up "an investigation of what Americanism may rightly mean." Americanism to him meant an America that was "cosmopolitan," not Anglo-Saxon. Bourne had a deformed face and was barely five feet tall and hunchbacked, and he wrote movingly about alterity, most notably in his 1911 essay "The Handicapped." Unlike Repplier, he thought the essay needed to take on subjects as large and as personal as war, disability, and ethnicity. A student of Matthews and John Dewey at Columbia, Bourne broke with them and their wing of Progressivism over the war. In the pages of the *New Republic, Seven Arts,* and the *Dial,* he critiqued Dewey's pragmatism and dismissed Matthews as a writer "to whom literature was a gesture of gentility and not a comprehension of life."[7]

In November 1918 Bourne published a critique of the "light essay," warning that the "light essay is a truly perilous thing," easily placed in the magazines and often seducing the best young American writers, some of whom "found whole careers on it." It may have been unfair, he admitted, to see the light essay as mere "journalism dressed up, as it were, for a literary party," but too often the form had served as "an illegitimate method of securing the literary sensation without doing the genuine literary work." Just now, he wrote, other forms—"novels, verse, drama"—seemed to be doing the heavy lifting. In the light essay, "you always feel something lacking, even in the piquant petulance of Miss Repplier." There were, however, light essays that amounted to something more, and, he argued, "the good essay does not go stale."

For Bourne the best of the contemporary essayists was Robert Cortes Holliday. With Holliday, wrote Bourne, you sometimes "wish he had endowed his papers occasionally with more mind," but he did give you the real New York. He "loiters on upper Broadway," "delights in the thunder of the trucks on Hudson Street," and values the voices of "scrubwomen," "bartenders," and "policemen." Bourne wrote of Holliday, "He is neither a gentleman nor a preacher nor a maiden lady nor even a playgoer, as most American essayists are," yet "with all his informality of language and mood he always manages to escape both cheapness and self-consciousness."[8] Unfortunately, Bourne did not live to participate in the revival of the essay that Holliday's emergence suggested. He died in the flu epidemic of December 1918, a month after his piece on the light essay appeared in the *Dial.*

Creation myths are just that—myths. But if any one writer was there when the first of the new essayists walked in the door of a New York newspaper office, it was Holliday. Like many of these new writers, Holliday came to New York from the provinces—in his case from Indiana at the age of nineteen for art school. He loved New York but could never forget where he came from. Morley would later write of his friend Holliday, "He used to complain that he never could sleep on the train between New York and Tarkingtonapolis. Both towns meant so much to him, he was torn between two anxieties." Holliday described the replenishing effect one of these train rides had on his language. Just back from a few months in England, he took the train from New York to Indianapolis, reading a New York paper, an Indianapolis paper, and three national magazines en route. There, in the smoking car, he was "struck very forcibly by the vast number of Americanisms, by the richness of our popular speech, by the 'punch' it has, and by the place it holds in the printed page," and in a fever he listed the Americanisms that jumped off those pages: "nothing doing, hot stuff, Right O! strong-arm work, some celebration, has 'em all skinned, mad at him, this got him bad, scared of, skiddoo, beat it, a peach of a place, get away with the job, been stung by the party, got by on his bluff, sore at that fact, and always on the job."[9]

In 1917 Morley helped Holliday land the job as editor of the *Bookman*. The magazine had long been a center for discussion of the essay, and over the next five years, while Holliday was there, it would publish four more such pieces, including one by Holliday himself in 1919. Writing under the New York pseudonym of "Murray Hill," Holliday cheekily challenged a number of old saws. He questioned the "ancient convention" that one "should have an *idea* to write an essay," claiming instead that what the essayist needs to do is "make a noise like an idea." He dismissed the fear of confusing the essay and article that dated back to Howells, declaring that the essay is "what is now commonly called an article." Slyly and lest Bourne's warnings about the lightness of the light essay go unheeded, he added that "to write the best sort of essay, which is about nothing much, you really need any number of ideas." Look at Montaigne, he said, whose essays were made of nothing but ideas and digressions.

He claimed fellow colyumnist Don Marquis was an heir to Montaigne because when Marquis writes about "the Ten Commandments [he] begins quite naturally with a disquisition upon the importance of the good shape of the human ear." But immediately, Holliday recognized he had misstepped and put a curse on Marquis. Whenever a new writer "essays to write an essay," he ends up smothered under the "mantle of the illustrious dead," the "old clothes of Charles Lamb (Oh, Elia, of course!), or 'R. L. S.,' of the author of 'The Reveries of a Bachelor," etc., etc., etc." So, adds Holliday, "if I had inadvertently given the impression of winding the mantle of Montaigne about Mr. Marquis I make all possible haste to unsheathe him. For in his own habit he is quite as he should be." The reduction of Stevenson to initials, the pardon-me reversal on Elia, the elision of Ik Marvel's name, the punning on the word *habit*, and the many etceteras in themselves signal a break from the past. To the genteel essayists, such a swipe at Lamb was blasphemy, but as Morley would note, Holliday was "probably more like Hazlitt in temper and touch and experience than any other journalist of our time," and a shift from Lamb to Hazlitt marked a shift from old to new, from sweet to wicked.[10]

In his quicksilver moves from Montaigne to Marquis, Holliday exhibited an improvisational digressiveness that he believed the modern essay should pursue and that he likened to modern music: "Peculiar thing about newspapers. That is, about their 'book pages' and 'literary supplements.' Lately, more or less lately, there have been popping up here and there about the country, at any rate in the two principal cities, pages and supplements of a good deal of brightness, affairs of something of a rollicking nature, things with some dash and go to them, with a *flair* for the cheer-o. In fine, with jazz."[11]

THE CHICAGO COLYUMNISTS AND THEIR "ROBIN'S EGG RENAISSANCE"

In 1890 Chicago (Holliday's second principal city) passed the one million mark and became the nation's second-largest city. During the next decade, it grew in population by 54 percent, pioneered the skyscraper, and hosted the Columbian Exposition, where Frederick Jackson Turner read his paper on the closing of the frontier. By 1917 Mencken was calling Chicago America's "most civilized city" and its "literary capital."[12] The *Dial* had been published there since 1880, Harriet Monroe's *Poetry* since 1912. Louis Sullivan and Frank Lloyd Wright had made it the center of American architecture. Mencken, however, always employed hyperbole, and he loved to tweak New York. Sherwood Anderson was probably more accurate when he described Chicago's literary movement as a "robin's egg renaissance." "It fell out of the nest," he explained, because its progenitors always left too soon, usually for New York.[13]

In 1918 Alexander Stoddart published a piece in the *Independent* titled "Journalism's Radium: The Colyumn." Colyumning (as it would be called for the next decade) was a new phenomenon—glowing and powerful. The form suddenly seemed to be everywhere, appearing in newspapers from New York to Bismarck. Stoddart defined it as a "mélange of paragraphs, jokes, verse, reprint, contributions, letters and even illustrations" that appeared "in the same place every day." It was also, he added, a "separate and distinct art" that few practiced well. There were good colyumnists in cities such as San Francisco (Ambrose Bierce) and Detroit (Edgar Guest), but it was Chicago that really "took to colyumning," and Eugene Field and Bert Leston Taylor of that city were the originators.[14]

More specifically, one might even trace the point of origin to the White-chapel Club, some rented rooms behind Henry Kosters's saloon at the corner of LaSalle and Calhoun. Here, a group of irreverent young newspapermen met, drank, and played during the 1890s. Named after Jack the Ripper's London haunt, the place was done up with skulls, weapons, nooses, and a coffin-shaped bar. George Ade (an early member along with Field and Taylor) described this dark precursor of the Algonquin Round Table as "a little group of thirsty intellectuals who were opposed to everything." The macabre decorations, like the club's name, reflected the group's ironic view of their own ambulance chasing. Ade, for instance, had gotten his first big break when the freighter *Tioga* exploded on the Chicago River and he happened to be the only reporter in the newsroom. The group viewed themselves as littérateurs forced to write for a living, outsiders forced inside by circumstances. They were part of a generation of journalists, who, according to Lazar Ziff, "insisted on talking to one another about the hypocrisy of the social system even while they were being paid to explain it away, whose faith in the big scoop was not entirely alien to a faith in the power of prose, and who read everything they could lay their hands on and fanned each other's literary aspirations."[15]

Whitechapel formed itself in opposition to the Press Club of Chicago (though a few individuals held joint memberships). They pitted straight talk against go-along professionalism, logrolling, and the cheap sentimentalism of do-gooders. In 1891 they ran their "treasurer" (there were no dues), Frederick "Grizzly" Adams, for mayor of Chicago on a platform that opposed "all Turkish baths and other sweatshops."[16] They mistreated clubhouse guests ranging from Teddy Roosevelt to John L. Sullivan, and their escapades climaxed in the cremation at the Indiana Dunes of the body of an associate who had committed suicide.

As colyumnists, these writers injected their prose with this same dark humor. They thrived in the no-man's-land between news and opinion, and introduced urban working-class characters and personae to the American essay. Like their readers, they enjoyed *and* distrusted consumer society. Their éminence grise was Field, whose "Sharps and Flats" ran in two different Chicago papers between 1883 and his death in 1895. Theodore Dreiser recalled how Field's columns remade the city for him: "These trenchant bits on local street scenes, institutions, characters, functions all moved me as nothing hitherto had. For to me Chicago at this time had a peculiarly literary or artistic atmosphere."[17]

Other prominent Whitechapel columnists included Ade and Finley Peter Dunne. Dunne spoke in his column through the heavy brogue of Mr. Dooley, a first-generation Irishman and bachelor pub keeper on the South Side. He used this persona to lampoon imperialism, machine politics, and the wealthy. Mr. Dooley's ethnic critique of Roosevelt's "true Americanism" proved so popular that "Tiddy" himself felt compelled to read the columns aloud at cabinet meetings and strike up a correspondence with Dunne.[18]

Dunne spoke almost exclusively through Mr. Dooley, but Ade used both the dialect of his characters and his own Standard English. His column, "Stories of the Streets and of the Town," appeared on the same page of the *Chicago Record* as Field's "Sharps and Flats." Ade alternated his own unpretentious, middle-class Hoosier voice with that of characters such as Artie, the brash office boy; Doc Horne, the lovable liar; and Pink Marsh, the savvy African American shoeshine boy. Illustrated by Ade's friend, roommate, and Purdue fraternity brother, John T. McCutcheon, the pieces evolved into what Ade called "fables in slang." Roosevelt may have admired Mr. Dooley, but Kansas newspaper editor William Allen White said, "I would rather have written *Fables in Slang* than be President."[19]

Bert Leston Taylor's innovations emphasized content and organization over voice and dialect. B. L. T., as he signed himself, reversed the regular migration route of the colyumnists. He grew up in Manhattan and wrote for papers in Vermont, New Hampshire, and Duluth before coming to Chicago in 1899 to take over a column of news briefs at the *Chicago Journal*. When he added light verse to his humorous takes on the news, the column took off. Its popularity led the *Tribune* to hire him away, and there he applied his technique to a new column called "A Line o' Type or Two." He moved back to New York for a few years, but the *Tribune* lured him back to Chicago, where he stayed until his death in 1921.

Taylor's return to Chicago was an exception. More Chicago colyumnists moved to New York and stayed, though with mixed results. After sixteen years with six different Chicago papers, Dunne went to New York in 1901 to write for magazines. He tried to maintain his syndicated column and keep Mr. Dooley in his South Side pub. It didn't work, so he began to edit, first for the *Morning Telegraph*, then *Collier's*. Finally, with the help of some wealthy patrons, he became part owner of the *American Magazine*, presided over its slide (after 1915) from muckraking progressivism to inspirational boosterism, retired comfortably to Long Island, and gave up writing altogether. Ade's experience was similar. In 1900 he left Chicago to write for Broadway (writing 7 plays in three years) and Hollywood (writing 114 movies, directing 10). He made a lot of money, bought a twenty-four hundred–acre estate near his Indiana hometown, and wintered in Miami. Yet he never fulfilled the hopes writers such as Howells and Twain had for him, or that he had for himself. The term *middlebrow* would not make its first appearance for another five years, but it was the taint of middlebrow to which Ade was alluding in a 1920 reminiscence titled "They Simply Wouldn't Let Me Be a High-Brow," in which he admitted, "I was almost an author." The early days of colyumning, he recalled, were "not all lavender." He had to compete with "the double-leaded editorial and the kidnapping mystery" for space, but in time he developed his characters, his column was syndicated, and he was offered book deals. He also turned his fables into Broadway shows, one of which, *The College Widow*, grossed two million dollars. His plan was to "grab a lot of this careless money" and return to the Midwest to write "the great American novel," but soon found himself golfing a lot and turning into a "Professional Slangster" who received "messages of commendation from nearly everyone except Mr. Howells."[20]

Ade's ambivalence reflected the tension between not just cornpone humor and suave sophistication, or modest and immodest success, but also the Midwest and New York. The 1870 census had been the first to show farmers as less than half of the workforce; the 1920 census would be the first in which America's population was more urban than rural. Having come to Chicago from small towns, many of the Chicago columnists were equipped to connect cracker-barrel philosophy and big-city street smarts, but as Ade suggests, the job was a tricky one.

A second wave of Chicago writers, most of whom made their names in New York after the war, seemed to negotiate the move to New York and into mass culture more successfully than Ade's generation had. Franklin Pierce Adams, a Chicago native, was born a decade and a half after Ade, Taylor, and Dunne. A disciple of B. L. T., he signed his columns F. P. A., and began his career at the *Chicago Journal*, then headed to New York in 1904, where he developed new tricks for easing the daily grind of colyumning. He gossiped, corrected bad grammar in other columns, offered a weekly diary in the manner of Samuel Pepys, and, like B. L. T., accepted a lot of verse and other (unpaid) contributions from his readers. One commentator likened this last technique to Tom Sawyer's whitewashing the fence.[21] Adams became best known for "The Conning Tower," which ran in the *New York Tribune* and *New York World* throughout the 1920s and 1930s. Marquis, Robert Benchley, Ring Lardner, Dorothy Parker, and James Thurber all started in F. P. A.'s column; so did E. B. White, who sent his future wife, Katharine, poems via "The Conning Tower" while they were courting. In short order, a posse of colyumnists followed Adams from Chicago to New York, including Marquis, Will Cuppy, Burton Rascoe, and Ring Lardner.

The Chicago columnists showed that essays belonged in newspapers. Their columns made peace with the medium's space constrictions, relentless deadlines, profligate illustrations, and new readers. They learned that to compete for the attention of the busy readers, they needed good openings, hooks, or what B. L. T. called "platforms." Earlier generations had seen the ads and general busyness of newspapers and magazines as corrupting, but the columnists enjoyed experimenting with typography and layout. Marquis stuck to lowercase, ostensibly because his alter ego, Archy the cockroach, could not hold the shift key down at the same time he hit a letter key, but the format also proved eye-catching, as did the snippets of light verse Adams and others reprinted. Some of the colyumnists had worked in advertising; others began as illustrators. Holliday started out as a cartoonist. Later, E. B. White made his office mate, James Thurber, into a cartoonist by fishing his stuff out of their wastebasket and giving it to Harold Ross, their editor at the *New Yorker*. Morley and others collaborated with John Alan Maxwell, whose drawings of flappers in cloche hats drinking martinis and tweedy men browsing bookstalls became iconic. New magazines such as *Punch, Vanity Fair,* and the *New Yorker* would become as well known for their cartoons, photography, caricatures, and design as they did for their writing.

Some old-school critics said the colyumnists were not essayists at all but mere journalists who "retailed" New York. These critics longed for a return to the genteel essay. Mary Terrill, for instance, asserted in 1920 that the essay was "the delightful art of literary rambling" and "the natural matrix of the sensitive, the *raffiné*," and she was sure it was "coming back again." It was bound to be resurrected by a "decadent" or "dilettante" adept at putting a "ribbon around the bouquet" of a genial viewpoint. Two years later Charles Brooks argued that an essay "cannot be written hurriedly upon the knee" or by one whose hands are "red with revolt against the world," but must be the work of a man with a desk and a library who sits "snug at home, content with little sights," writing an essay of "small circumstance and agreeable gossip." F. E. Schelling agreed that an essay should not "argue" or "preach," for it is "the daintiest, the purest and the most delightful of all the forms of literature," "a delicacy for the aristocrat, the Brahmin among readers." He reiterated the old emphasis on personality, but added that "mere personality is not enough." Dr. Johnson, for instance, had plenty of personality, but it was a prickly, show-offy, domineering personality. Schelling preferred the quiet voice of E. V. Lucas, Lamb's biographer and the closest thing to Lamb the age could offer. Lucas had been so "inconspicuously the gentleman" when he had met him a few months earlier that Schelling now could not "remember a single one of his many happy remarks." Apparently untroubled by such evanescence, Schelling went on to assert, "An exhibition of pyrotechnics is all very fine; but a chat by a wood fire with a friend who can listen, as well as talk, who can even sit with you by the hour in congenial silence—this is better."[22]

Such genial voices were now on the defensive. Most critics called for an essay that was tough, funny, and engaged, not dainty or pure. "Lamenting for lost arts is, and ever has been one of the favorite indoor sports of those choice souls—self-chosen—who hold literature is a 'precious, precious thing' and deplore any tendency on its part to play with the rough, common boys of Popularity and Commercialism," wrote Berton Braley in the August 1920 issue of the *Bookman*. The "elect" who declare the essay dead are out of touch, claimed Braley, for "the great bulk of us . . . meet the essay in the daily paper, in the weekly magazine, in the popular monthly, in advertising pages, on cards in the stationer's shop, and heaped high on the best-seller counter of the bookstores."

Braley believed the self-defeating snobbery of this literary elect had its sources in Anglophilia, and he joined Bourne and Holliday in criticizing the Annunciation of Lamb. The elect see "the essay as a sacrosanct possession of Lamb, Addison, and a few others who are dead," and so regard it "as dead. In other words, if it isn't Lamb it isn't an essay." America fought in the war to save Britain and had emerged a world power, emboldening these critics to call for a new American essayist, just as Emerson had called in 1844 for an American poet. In 1920 Colby attacked English gentlemen's reviews as reinforcing class distinctions and national chauvinism. Such magazines are "written by persons of the better sort for persons of the better sort," and exist "to tell coal-heavers and other outside creatures they are low." He explained that by "outside creatures," he meant "almost everybody," or at least everyone in the Western Hemisphere, who supposedly had "the worst possible taste," being as it was "notoriously external to the British Isles." Echoing Matthews and Roosevelt, he called on "the American literary class" who had succumbed to this "unfortunate colonialism" to break with it.[23]

Two years later, in 1922, Rascoe declared literary independence in familiar language: "For I hold these truths to be self-evident: that in the field of essay-writing contemporary Americans are incomparably superior to the modern Englishmen; that our essayists hold their own with the essayists of all other countries; and that it is intimidated deference to assume the contrary."[24]

Canby agreed, with some qualifications. "The new epoch of the American essay is well underway," he wrote, but it will flower only when we "scrap a mass of fine writing about nothing in particular" and dispense with the "dilettantes" who engage in the "merely literary." Historically, claimed Canby, there had been two strains of American essayists: those like Emerson and Thoreau who assailed their readers with "hard-hitting statement, straight out of intense feeling or labored thought," and others like Twain and Josh Billings who engaged in "easy-going comment on life, often slangy or colloquial and frequently so undignified as not to seem literature." Contemporary essayists were stuck between these two poles, but tending toward the latter. As Malcolm Cowley put it, "In those days [the twenties] hardly anyone read Emerson, but we all admired Thoreau in a distant sort of way." Canby hoped that the new essayists would draw from both traditions. The change could come from either direction. On the one hand, "the moralists and reformers and critics of American life [might] learn to mature and perfect their thought until what they write is as good as their intentions." On the other hand, the "easy-going humorist, often nowadays a column conductor, or a contributor to the *Saturday Evening Post*" might slow down and take "time to deepen his observation and to say it with real words instead of worn symbols."[25]

COLYUMNISM

In 1923 Mary Ellis Opdycke elaborated on the connection between the new American essay and the colyumn, a form she thought was "rapidly becoming the pillar of American literature." In a *New Republic* piece provocatively titled "Colyumnism," Opdycke proposed semiseriously that America was held together more by the colyumn's popularity than by any political doctrine. Its topicality, ubiquity, and celebration of the individual personality made the colyumn "our national brand." The colyumnist "has united several hundred thousand readers into one happy family." Young, diverse, scattered, and hungry "for common understanding" and "the fusion of a hundred different races," the nation was turning to the colyumnists for advice about what to eat, drink, say, and read. If a "sinister hint of their power as advertising agents hangs about their attractiveness," said Opdycke, it works both ways, for (as Braley had also suggested) "coluymnistic methods have sifted into advertising. Everything the New York colyumnist does becomes his copy."[26]

Opdycke faded from the scene, but her thoughts about the significance of the colyumn were soon reinforced and expanded upon by two literary critics who would become major figures in middlebrow culture. The first of these, Stuart Pratt Sherman, was a prodigy—a full professor at the University of Illinois at the age of twenty-six and by thirty department chair and author of more than 150 publications, including poetry and short stories as well as editions, textbooks, anthologies, literary criticism, and dozens of book reviews in the *Nation* and the *New York Evening Post*. Sherman was a transitional figure, caught between an Arnoldian desire to defend standards and a modernist sensibility that said literature must be made new. This tension expressed itself in his early work as a reviewer and essayist. Rubin points to a pep talk he gave himself in his journals, in which he urged himself to use a more familiar, modern, even consumerist language in his own essays: "As you widen your audience you omit your parentheses; you eliminate dependent clauses; you reduce subordination . . . ; you reduce allusion; you erase shades; you don't soften lines; you remember you are advertising—a 'Poster' not an etching."[27]

Sherman's prominence helped him carve out a position at Illinois as resident generalist and insulate himself from the drift toward philology, but in 1924 he (like Canby) left to edit a new middlebrow journal—in his case, *Books*, the literary supplement to the *New York Herald Tribune*. According to Rubin, when he was first being courted for this position, the *Herald*'s art critic urged his editor to treat Sherman as one "would popular columnists like Mark Sullivan, Don Marquis, or the authors of sports and radio features—that is, to invest money in his salary, shower him with publicity, and 'make him comfortable.'"[28] The negotiations led to Sherman's being given an assistant and a weekly column that would be printed on the first page of *Books*.

The assistant was Irita Van Doren, the wife of his protégée Carl Van Doren. Carl and his brother Mark had been Sherman's students at Illinois before moving to Columbia for graduate work. Mark served in the first cadre of instructors in Erskine's Great Books course. Carl and Irita worked with Sherman and Erskine on the *Cambridge History of American Literature*, a counterpart to the *Literary History of the United States* that Canby helped edit for Macmillan. (The editors barely credited Irita's work.)[29]

Opdycke had suggested that the colyumnists were creating a national brand and combining writing with advertising; Sherman and Van Doren proposed that these new writers were advertising two products in particular: New York and their own personalities. New York in the 1920s was, as Ann Douglas has put it, a "mongrel"—enormous and exotic, its streets brimming with immigrants, unimaginable wealth, awful poverty, and new ideas. Van Doren admitted that colyumning had begun in Chicago, but declared, "In New York, to which so many things are drawn by its sheer magnitude, the column has at present its greatest prestige and influence." For most Americans the city's magnitude was as intimidating as it was magnetic. Van Doren proposed that the colyumnists made New York less terrifying because they were able to "retail the gossip, promulgate the jests, discuss the personalities, [and] represent the manners of New York." New media made this possible. Syndication and big-circulation magazines meant that their work might best "be compared to radio instruments designed to broadcast them over a good part of the continent." Paradoxically, what they broadcast was intimacy, or as Opdycke declared, "The Pacific coast knows what the colyumnist likes for breakfast, almost before he has ordered his supper. His secret sins are syndicated from Texas to Maine."[30]

The colyumnists also had literary precursors and models. They were, Van Doren offered, "town wits, as Addison and Steele were in their merry London, as Irving and [James Kirke] Paulding were in the New York of a hundred years ago," and like them they made New York accessible by being "topical" and "local" in their writing.[31] Sherman agreed. The colyumnists were giving New York "a more genial and kindly air than it has had since the days of Diedrich Knickerbocker," and he described the "affectionate familiarity" that made this possible:

> Like the periodical essayists of Queen Anne's time, with their Scandal Clubs and Tatlers and Spectator Clubs, they undertake to meet their readers where they are, and they know that to do so their writing must sound like an extension of familiar conversation. It must introduce no topic that can't be made current. It must be light enough to be digested with coffee and rolls. It must be pointed enough to wake up the man from New Jersey crossing the ferry in the cool, sleepy-eyed morning. It must be amusing enough to relax the tension of the tired business man and make him forget, when he goes up to bed, to mourn for his lost night cap.[32]

The colyumnists made New York seem genial, claimed Sherman, by being genial themselves. The idea was not entirely new. The popularity of the column had already led to the appearance of how-to books on the subject, one of them titled *The Gentle Art of Columning: A Treatise on Comic Journalism* (1920).[33] But Sherman pressed the argument, claiming that the colyumnists' geniality was rooted in the essay tradition. They came by this "tolerant smiling skepticism" naturally, he wrote, for "the true essayist since Montaigne's time has been a man of even, easy, adaptable temper."

This wry and friendly worldview appealed to the new middle class in a way the avant-garde approaches being pursued by other artists did not. Sherman compared the colyumnists with the modernist poets whose revolution had become "so comprehensive that there was no public left to view the procession" and (in a nod to Sinclair Lewis) the "truth-telling novelists [who had] started a parade down Main Street," and concluded that the "essay lends itself better to a balanced representation of life than either free verse or the current realistic novel." These new essayists rescued their genre from the academicism and gentility in which it had become mired, returning it to its roots in Renaissance humanism and bourgeois individualism. Sherman differentiated colyumnists like Holliday, Morley, Broun, and Benchley from their immediate predecessors—"clergymen, professors, novelists and literary ladies" such as Crothers, Matthews, Repplier, and Henry Van Dyke. The day's "busy newspaper men" wrote with "a quicker tempo" and more "joy."

In Sherman's search for "true" essayists and long traditions, one hears a man who is trying too hard. Sherman was himself a moderate, and it was the tendency of the essayists to "recoil from the violence of partisanship" and "the fatigue of 'strained attitudes'" that appealed to him. He was looking for someone to help him mediate the culture wars. The colyumnist—as long as his taste was middlebrow, his politics middle of the road, and his personality even tempered—fitted the bill. When he called up Montaigne's "mild but universal skepticism" as the perfect antidote for the troubles of his New Jersey commuter, when he suggested that both essayist and modern man should "recoil from the violence of partisanship" and seek respite in amiability, when he invoked Arnold to say that the colyumnists are to the "'serious' editorial writer and the savage critic" as bees are to "wasps and hornets" because they produce not stings but "wax and honey—'sources of sweetness and light,'" and when he invoked Carlyle to argue that colyumnists "are beginning to create a literary atmosphere with 'organic filaments' of civility," Sherman seemed to push his insights too far, asking the colyumnists to save a whole culture without really trying.

Often, however, Sherman grew so aware of his hyperbole that he flip-flopped. He turned his irony back on himself and then his quips overreached, as when he suggested "to a young woman seeking advice, 'Flirt with a poet, engage yourself to a novelist, but marry an essayist,'" or that Morley's excessive Anglo geniality made him imagine Morley leading a band of carolers in a round of "God rest you, merry bourgeoisie, let nothing you dismay." These jokes are humorous enough, but they turn the modern essayist (and, by implication, his reader) into a kind of Pangloss of the suburbs. Sherman had ratcheted his expectations down so far as to make the colyumnists not just genial but complacent. He concluded approvingly that they "are not doing any 'big constructive thinking.' They refuse to accept responsibility for the universe. These journalistic humanists are modest; they do not even attempt to reform the world. They are occupied rather in discovering how many likable things there are in the world as it is, and they seem satisfied if they make it no worse." Such faith in the power of amiability leads, not surprisingly, back to Lamb and a tired anecdote: "Of all the sorts of their fellow men they [the colyumnists] say, as Charles Lamb said of a certain not very prepossessing person: 'How can we hate them? We know them.'"[34]

Actually, the colyumnists were not so universally cheerful, and even when funny, they could be dark. One can almost hear Marquis mocking Sherman's version of sunny-side up, for instance, in this anarchic riff from one of his classic pieces, "The Almost Perfect State": "No matter how nearly perfect an Almost Perfect State may be, it is not nearly enough perfect unless the individuals who compose it can, somewhere between death and birth, have a perfectly corking time for a few years. The most wonderful governmental system in the world does not attract us, as a system; we are after a system that scarcely knows it is a system; the great thing is to have the largest number of individuals as happy as may be, for a little while at least, some time before they die."[35]

Canby believed a true bourgeois writer could take America to its exceptional destiny, and Sherman again seems more moderate—perhaps the nation's citizens can get along and see the world as a likable place. Like Canby, he saw these new essayists as introducing literature to the newspapers and mass magazines and middle-class readers to literature. The New York colyumnists, he wrote, were "busy newspaper men" who had "blazed their way out to the new public" that was "truly democratic," the "wide circle composed of every man and woman who reads a newspaper."[36]

One of these readers was E. B. White. More than twenty years later White could recall the excitement he felt when he "squander[ed] a nickel on the early edition" of the *World* or the *Sun* in order to read Adams or Marquis: "I think the new generation of newspaper readers is missing a lot that we used to have, and I am deeply sensible of what it meant to be a young man when Archy was at the top of his form and when Marquis was discussing the Almost Perfect State in the daily paper. Buying a paper then was quietly exciting, in a way that it has ceased to be."[37]

White's appreciation of both Adams and Marquis testifies to his own wide tastes and to the diversity among the colyumnists. Adams channeled Pepys, and Marquis pretended to be a cockroach, but they shared distaste for the affectations of middlebrow matrons. In his column, Marquis featured a character named Hermione who met regularly with a "little group of serious thinkers." Her thirst for presentable knowledge was unquenchable:

> I'm taking up Bergson this week.
> Next week I'm going to take up Etruscan
> Vases and the Montessori system.
> Oh, no, I haven't lost my interest in sociology.
> Only the other night we went down in the auto
> and watched the bread line.
> Of course, one can take up *too many* things.[38]

It was Hermione whom Braley had in mind when he called the self-chosen elect who lament over the lost art of the essay a "little group of serious thinkers."[39]

THE PERSONALITIES OF THE COLYUMNISTS

Broun and Morley, colleagues with Canby on the Book-of-the-Month Club's first board of judges, constituted another pair of writers whose differences suggest the range of the colyumnists.

In their books on middlebrow culture Janice Radway and Joan Shelley Rubin discuss these two writers at length, and while they acknowledge the differences between them, they focus on their shared celebrity and the way in which it served the interests of Harry Scherman and his modern "selling machine" for books.[40] For Rubin, Morley "personifies the conflation of culture with performance that formed a dominant motif in Book-of-the-Month Club advertising," and Broun's "demonstration of personality made him an enormous asset as part of a marketing strategy based on apprehension about the survival of self." Radway opts for the term *consumer subject* rather than *personality*, believing it better captures the "fundamental interplay between culture and economy," but is in fundamental agreement with Rubin. "Together," says Radway, "Heywood Broun and Christopher Morley functioned for the Book-of-the-Month Club as specifically literary exemplars of a new, more modern subject." They represented "the invention of a magnified subject, an egregiously idiosyncratic individual" and "exhibited, in embodied form, the categorical similarity—the fungibility—of virtually all cultural materials."[41]

It is true that eccentricity sold, and both men were eccentric, and the emphasis by Radway and Rubin on performance and personality does get at the constructedness of cultural value, but in conceiving of them primarily as pitchmen for the Book-of-the-Month Club, they tend to lose track of them as writers. Thus, Radway states, "The considerable fame of both Heywood Broun and Christopher Morley, in fact, had little to do with what they did and everything to do with who they were."[42] Who they were, however, emerged not just from ad copy, promotional campaigns, and radio appearances, but also and especially from what they wrote.

The confusion may have to do, at least in part, with the fact that both men were essayists. If they had been novelists, they would not have been mistaken for their narrators, but as essayists, they were. Woolf used Beerbohm to get at this ontological problem:

> He has brought personality into literature, not unconsciously and impurely,
> but so consciously and purely that we do not know whether there is any

relation between Max the essayist and Mr. Beerbohm the man. We only know that the spirit of personality permeates every word that he writes. The triumph is the triumph of style. For it is only by knowing how to write that you can make use in literature of your self; that self which, while it is essential to literature, is also its most dangerous antagonist. Never to be yourself and yet always—that is the problem.[43]

Triumph is a big word, but certainly the accomplishment of Broun's and Morley's essays resulted from the self they created in their essays and the literary style they used to create that self. Radway argues, however, that what Broun offered was "not style in the usual literary sense of highly crafted idiom" but rather "the spectacle of style," style as the display of a particular set of tastes and opinions. Rubin claims, "Broun pushed Morley's personal approach to the point where it displaced literature almost entirely," adding that "Broun staked his authority not on his ability to supply rarefied percep- tions that came from specialized training but instead on his flair for com- municating the down-to-earth observations that anyone might make." Both critics disparage Morley's writing style as overwrought and "anachronistic." Rubin's authority here is Canby, who said that Morley "came dangerously close to flaunting archaic style at the expense of substance."[44] They have caught the two essayists in an impossible either-or. Broun is portrayed as having no style and doing what anyone could have done, Morley as being all style and little else.

In actuality Broun was more formally adventurous than either Rubin or Radway gives him credit for being. His prose was wry, clear, and convinc- ing, and he experimented with fables, essays written in the third person, mock prefaces, and a new kind of ironic sportswriting that juxtaposed press-box vernacular with classical allusions. Nor was Morley's own irony as fluffy and old-fashioned as Rubin and Radway claim. Of the two, Morley's interests were more thoroughly literary and specialized—Lamb, ghosts, and mystery stories; Broun's were more modern, extraliterary, and political. Rubin accuses Broun of filling his columns with "observations that anyone might make," but in fact he took brave positions on issues not many were willing to touch—lynching, Harvard's refusal to pay its maids a living wage, Eugene Debs, Emma Goldman, the Red Scare, capital punishment, free speech, the evils of Fordism (in both the United States and the Soviet Union), the general strike in San Francisco, and the Scottsboro Boys. His defense of Sacco and Vanzetti cost him his job at the *World*. He helped found the Newspaper Guild and ran for Congress as a socialist.

That Morley, a Lamb-like would-be Elizabethan who loved his library, and Broun, a Hazlitt-like political radical who loved going to the fights, were friends suggests the range of New York colyumn writing during the 1920s. The period was busy, transitional, and fraught with tensions. In Adams's retrieval of Pepys or Morley's return to the hearth, one senses an anxious desire for tradition and ballast; Broun and Lardner, on the other hand, were after a more modern American voice. The colyumnists were drawn to gossip, movies, and radio, but also prided themselves on the classical educations they had acquired, sometimes at the nation's most prestigious universities. Broun, Benchley, and Robert Sherwood all attended Harvard, where the last two were presidents of the *Lampoon*. Morley was a Rhodes scholar. Clarence Day went to Yale. Rascoe attended the University of Chicago. Colby taught at Columbia and New York University. Yet, as E. B. White remarked of Marquis, they were "never quite certified by intellectuals and serious critics of *belles lettres*."[45] Genteel critics considered them hopelessly plebeian (as, in time, would New York's public intellectuals), but the colyumnists chose popularity. They wanted to write for and educate a broad readership, but they understood that their choice came with certain trade-offs. Writing under deadline for a mass audience meant they could not usually write in the leisurely, elevated style of the literary quarterlies.

BENCHLEY AND "BROW-ELEVATION"

This tension is especially evident in the work and life of Robert Benchley. At once sophisticated and absurd, learned and goofy, Benchley helped establish a persona that would become influential and immensely popular—the Little Man. The Little Man was a well-meaning middle-class suburbanite who, though modern, felt out of step with his time. He was a literate new professional—educated, but not overeducated—who usually found himself a step behind his fast-talking kids and stylish wife, and always at the mercy of a tyrannical boss, merciless bureaucracy, and never-ending stream of new and mystifying gadgets.

Benchley's older brother, Edmund, was killed in the Spanish-American War, and Robert attended Exeter and Harvard on scholarships provided by his brother's wealthy fiancée. Later F. P. A. rescued him from a job at Curtis Publishing and helped him land a position at the *New York Tribune*'s magazine. When it folded, Benchley freelanced and gave government work a try before returning to the *Tribune,* where he worked during the Great War with his old Harvard classmate Ernest Gruening. The two were in charge of a regular pictorial spread, but when they printed photo essays that featured African American troops in Europe and exposed lynching in the South, management worried that the paper might be charged with sedition. Gruening was fired, and Benchley resigned in protest. It was a pattern he repeated two years later when he and another Harvard friend, Robert Sherwood, walked out of their jobs at *Vanity Fair* in support of Dorothy Parker—the magazine's drama critic, whom they believed had been fired for correctly panning Billie Burke, the actress wife of powerful producer Florenz Ziegfeld. Benchley needed the job. He was married with two small children at the time. Parker would call his resignation "the greatest act of friendship I'd known."[46]

Like Benchley, the Little Man spoke truth to power, but he did so quietly, individually, almost inadvertently. Norris Yates has claimed that the Little Man, "even in his most deteriorated condition, represents the closest we can get to the ideal, rational citizen," but for others that was not close enough. C. Wright Mills claimed that his book *White Collar* was "about the new little man in the big world of the 20th century," and so was "everybody's book." Mills wanted to sympathize with the Little Man and admitted he had "been writing *White Collar* since I was ten years old, and watched my white-collared father getting ready for another sales trip," but for him, the Little Man was finally "the hero as victim" and a "privatized man." He was "not radical, not liberal, not conservative, not reactionary," but "inactionary" and "out of it." Dwight Macdonald was even more unforgiving. To him the Little Man was "a self-confessed ninny and know-nothing" who embodied "the humor of the inadequate."[47]

The Little Man presented a cultural as well as political problem. Like the new middle class to whom they spoke, the colyumnists were uneasy about their relationship to high culture. They were possessed of a deep ambivalence—the "simultaneous idealization and abjection of 'culture'" that Jonathan Freedman calls "the defining mark of the middlebrow." They were caught between two sets of literary models and two self-images, between high and low culture. As Mills put it, "In serious literature white-collar images are often subjects for lamentation; in popular writing they are often targets of aspiration."[48]

Benchley tried to put a positive spin on the problem in a 1922 piece titled "The Brow-Elevation in Humor." The word *middlebrow* with all its pejorative connotations would not appear for three more years, but *middlebrow* seems to be exactly what Benchley (like George Ade before him) had in mind. In this essay he contrasts his contemporaries with the cornpone humorists of an earlier generation and finds the present trend toward sophisticated, urban humor encouraging. His test cases are Mark Twain and Franklin Adams. "In the days when Mark Twain was writing," wrote Benchley, "it was considered good form to spoof not only the classics but surplus learning of any kind."

There is nothing really wrong with such humor, said Benchley, and it is still practiced, but there is also "an increasing large section of the reading public who, while they may not be expert in Latin composition, nevertheless do not think that a Latin word in itself is a cause for laughter." Twain, he believed, would be astounded to learn that F. P. A. ran a famous "daily newspaper column in New York" based often on "translations of the 'Odes of Horace' into the vernacular," translations that even James Russell Lowell would have seen as "terrifically high-brow." But times had changed, said Benchley, for now "thousands of American business men quote F. P. A. to thousands of other American business men every morning." It is, he concluded, a change for the better: "Can it be said that the American people are not so low-brow as they like to pretend? . . . If the truth were known, we are all a great deal better educated than we will admit, and the derisive laughter with which we greet signs of culture is sometimes very hollow. In F. P. A. we find a combination which makes it possible for us to admit our learning and still be held honorable men. It is a good sign that his following is increasing."[49]

Even in this rosy conclusion, however, there are clues that this middle way is bumpy and that Adams's "combination" of high and low might be hard to maintain. The hyperbole in "admit" and "honorable" itself admits of urgency and high stakes, and Benchley's standard spelling of *column* suggests his need to separate from the colyumnists and even that their era was coming to an end. The Algonquin wisecracks would be less funny after the Crash of 1929.

In the end Benchley's career proved cautionary. He professed to be lazy, but was not. By the end of the decade he would be writing three columns (the old spelling was back in effect) a week while simultaneously reviewing plays for the *New Yorker*, appearing in a weekly radio show, and writing, producing, and starring in dozens of Hollywood shorts. His busy schedule seems to have been a way to keep the contradictions at bay. Certainly, it must have been wearing to commute daily from Scarsdale, to match wits over lunch every day at the Algonquin, to wear constantly what Yates calls the Little Man's "mask of befuddlement," and to drink one's way through evening after evening of first nights. Benchley meant to elevate American humor— not as Adams did, by translating Horace or pretending to be Samuel Pepys, but through an exhausting show of sophistication. It was an act he pulled off for years, though he seems to have been terrified by the knowledge that his shtick could easily slide into snobbery or silliness.

In her discussion of the Algonquin wits, Nina Miller suggests, "the Round Table shared the pervasive fantasy that a national culture had replaced class difference with democratizing style—of which sophistication was the premier expression," but at the same time, "sophistication and wit were promoted as mainstream cultural values even as they served to mark the elite."[50] Sophistication, she argues, was inherently contradictory. Benchley and friends knew the tourists were ogling them from the other side of the rope, and the more famous the Algonquinites became, the harder it was to keep the performance "spontaneous" and "fun." The conceit held that anyone could put on the mantle of sophistication, but in reality anyone, at any time, could be found out.

Benchley in particular tried hard to be a university wit, but his own Harvard degree was delayed when he failed French and economics. He also presented himself as a family man—Gertrude, his grade-school sweetheart, and the kids at home in Westchester—but he had affairs with actresses, prostitutes, store clerks, a teenage showgirl, and the wife of an associate. He stood with Gruening against racism and with Parker against censorship, marched for Sacco and Vanzetti, and supported the Loyalists in Spain, but considered himself as nothing but a "confused liberal" who registered Republican and voted Democratic. He sniffed out the subtle manipulations of advertisers who used direct address to personalize their appeals or the use of phony stereotypes to shame people into buying Dr. Eliot's Five-Foot Shelf, but he essentially quit writing when he went to Hollywood. He died an alcoholic at the age of fifty-six.

There were other indications in Benchley's work that all was not well in the ranks of the middlebrow publishers. In the same volume in which his essay about brow elevation was collected Benchley also savaged the schizophrenia and false modesty in *Ladies' Home Journal* editor Edward Bok's silly use of the third person in his autobiography: "The only connection between Edward Bok the editor and Edward Bok the autobiographer seems to be that Editor Bok allows Author Bok to have a checking account in his bank under their common name."[51] That this comes from someone who himself worked for Curtis Publishing is a reminder how small the world of New York publishing was and how easily one could slide up or down a rung. It was becoming clear that middlebrow was not a peaceful gathering of honorable men, but more like a no-man's-land ringing with potshots and divided by desperate distinctions.

GREENWICH VILLAGE VERSUS THE *SATURDAY EVENING POST*

Benchley's attempts to elevate humor's brow and distance himself from Bok and Curtis were indicative of a widening cultural gulf. The mid-1920s brought the arrival of not just the colyumnists but other purveyors of middlebrow culture as well—the Book-of-the-Month Club, the Literary Guild, the *New York Herald Tribune Books*, the *Saturday Review of Literature, Time*, the *New Yorker*, and E. Haldeman-Julius's "little blue books."

The critics who claimed the colyumnists were ushering in a new American essay—Canby, Sherman, and Carl Van Doren—were heavily involved in most of these developments. All three men left academic appointments during this period so they could speak more directly to a general readership, guide busy middle-class people to the books they thought they should read (or at least be familiar with), promote the essay as an essential genre, and build the central institutions of middlebrow culture. After leaving Columbia, Van Doren served as chairman of the first selection committee of the Literary Guild and worked as literary editor of the *Nation*, where he wrote a book column titled "In the Driftway."[52] In 1920, at the same time Irita Van Doren and Sherman were starting the *New York Herald Tribune Books*, Canby, Morley, Amy Loveman, and William Rose Benét developed the *Literary Review*, a book review supplement published by the *New York Evening Post*. In February 1926 Canby joined Broun, Morley, and Dorothy Canfield Fisher on the first board of judges for Book-of-the-Month Club. Sherman's promising career as an editor and essayist was cut short that August when he died of a heart attack at the age of forty-four while on vacation when his canoe overturned in Lake Michigan.

After Sherman's death, Irita Van Doren succeeded him as editor of *Books*. Irita, who like her husband, Carl, and his brother Mark had worked as a literary editor at the *Nation*, would edit *Books* for the next thirty-seven years, until her retirement in 1963. As its editor she provided regular columns and reviewing opportunities to many important essayists, including Virginia Woolf, Joseph Wood Krutch, Irwin Edwin, Malcolm Cowley, Constance Rourke, and Ellen Glasgow.[53]

This fever of middlebrow activity in the midtwenties was part of a movement to fill the gap between a "high" art and mass culture. Looking back on that time, Cowley characterized it as a period of "a private war between Greenwich Village and the *Saturday Evening Post*." The modernist artists centered in the Village saw mass culture, as represented by the *Post*, as a tar baby to be avoided at all costs. The *Post*, for its part, published articles and cartoons about the Village, calling it a "haunt of affectation," a bohemian ghetto populated by "long-haired men and short-haired women." Here, said Cowley, "was a symbolic struggle: on the one side, the great megaphone of middle-class America; on the other, the American disciplines of art and artistic living." But the irony, Cowley continued, was that the "New York bohemians, the Greenwich Villagers, came from exactly the same class as the readers of the *Saturday Evening Post*. Their political opinions were vague and by no means dangers to Ford Motor Company. . . . They were trying to get ahead, and the proletariat be damned. Their economic standards were those of the small businessman."[54]

Andreas Huyssen's trope for this apparent breach between modernist and mass culture, between these two fractions of the middle class, is the Great Divide.[55] He argues that the gap seems wider in retrospect, because the high modernists whose work would become canonical were so successful at promulgating the view that their work was "purer," more difficult, and uncontaminated by mass culture. In actuality, relations between modernism and middlebrow were messier and more entangled than they have usually been characterized.

Take, for instance, Ezra Pound's dealings with the emerging middlebrow institutions. Pound is usually considered the highest of high modernists. He certainly argued for a difficult art for the elevated few, but even in the early 1910s he recognized that group of readers as a niche market to be carefully exploited. He apparently thought *imagisme*, for example, was more exotic and therefore appealing than *imagism*, perhaps even worth copyrighting.[56] In time Pound tried to win a larger audience for modernism, which meant publishing in mainstream journals. As early as 1921 he placed an article titled "Parisian Literature" in Canby's *Literary Review*. His *How to Read, or Why* (1931), an only slightly ironic version of the how-to books on which middlebrow culture thrived, was published by Irita Van Doren in *Herald Tribune Books* in three installments in January 1929. It was the first of a series of testy little primers that Pound, the village explainer, turned out over the next decade, including *ABC of Economics* (1933), *ABC of Reading* (1934), and *Guide to Kulchur* (1938). In 1928, intrigued by the success of the Book-of-the-Month Club, he even proposed in a letter to Louis Zukofsky (laced with his usual mock-American Poundisms) that they "decide on six or ten or 12 books that are FIT to print, and fer us to constitoot ourselves a bloody sight BETTER book of the month, or quarter, better 'book of the quarter.'" Pound was dead serious about this project, which he saw as a "paying proposition," and he deputized Zukofsky to talk to publishers such as Clifton Fadiman and to possible contributors such as William Carlos Williams and Marianne Moore.[57] The plan did not pan out (though something quite like it, the Readers' Subscription Book Club, did appear in 1951).

Pound proposed collaborations with middlebrow figures, trying always to keep the upper hand. In another letter to Zukofsky he imitated a movie

Nazi in stipulating the conditions under which he might write for the *New York Sun*'s review page: "Eef dhey vill be meek & 'omble like Canby . . . , I vill write for 'em." Irita Van Doren was apparently not 'omble enough, for soon after she serialized *How to Read, or Why*, Pound withdrew as "visiting critic" for *Herald Tribune Books* and lambasted her in a letter: "You know perfectly well that I consider BOOKS like every other god damn American advertising medium, IS engaged in retarding the entrance into America of any and every live thought. . . . You are NOT as stupid as the groveling bugs on some of the other papers, and for that reason you are all the more RESPONSIBLE for the impossibility (wherein most americans live) of keeping in touch with what is BEING thought." Shortly thereafter he scolded Williams for catering to the Van Dorens: "WE have never had enough influence with the sons of bitches who run the N. Y. pubing/ houses. And you cant wait for the VanDoren fambly to sanction yr/ activity."[58]

Later, his rhetoric got even hotter. James Laughlin recalled the morning in 1935 when he and Pound hatched a plan to start their own publishing house (the now famous New Directions). They had been looking over some of Laughlin's poems, and Pound, exasperated at the heavy editing he thought they required, finally told Laughlin he would never be a real poet and should "do something useful" instead. Laughlin asked what that might be, and Pound shot back, "Why dontcher assessernate Henry Seidel Canby?" Laughlin replied that he was not smart enough to get away with that, to which Pound said he should become a publisher, because he was smart enough for that.[59]

Canby and his associates were not pushovers, however, and occasionally issued their own cagey overtures. Realizing that the modernists harbored crossover dreams, middlebrow deal makers decided to strike their own kinds of bargains. Canby worked with Bennett Cerf to devise a successful ad campaign in the *Saturday Review* for Joyce's *Ulysses*, and when Harcourt Brace published Stein's *Autobiography of Alice B. Toklas*, the publisher enlisted Carl Van Doren to reassure readers in the ad copy that the book was "lucid and direct." Pound may have seen Canby as 'omble, but he seems actually to have been very patient. For his part, Canby referred to Pound and Eliot as "wild men," and recalled that although Pound "offered to do some prophesying" for his magazine, Canby could not use what the wild man sent him because they were only "comments about a local and not important art show" and, worse, Pound "was abusive when not paid twice our rates."[60]

These kinds of tense negotiations went on behind the scenes, but Cowley was right about the public attitude New York's bohemian modernists took regarding the mass magazines such as the *Post*. Between 1917 and 1928, the

Post's circulation increased 50 percent (from 1.9 million to 2.8 million), and its ad revenues increased 300 percent (from $16 million to $48 million).[61] Curtis Publishing as a whole enjoyed similar growth. Every year from 1918 to 1930, between 38 percent and 43 percent of all national advertising revenue in general magazines went to Curtis magazines.[62]

Modernist critics feared Curtis's publishing empire was standardizing magazines in the way Ford had standardized automobiles, and indeed, the two commercial giants developed a close and symbiotic relationship. Ford began to use the pages of the *Post* to advertise his products and promote his worldview. During 1924 and 1925 he introduced his Michigan complex to America in a series of twice-monthly double-page ads in the magazine. In a 1926 "as told to" story in the *Post*, Ford trumpeted his theories of capitalist development. Prosperity, said Ford, was based on his system of increasing production in order to increase consumption.[63]

Ford's assembly line required the standardization of parts. Everything from bolts to pistons had to be identical and interchangeable. Every Model T also seemed to carry Fordism out the door of the Highland Park plant and across the country. Not only was the process of production standardized, but so also were the product and, it was feared, the consumer. Some Americans began to worry that if all their countrymen bought and drove the same black Model T, and read the same *Saturday Evening Post*, the country would lose the rugged individualism that had made it exceptional.

At the same time, middle-class Americans from the Midwest thirsted for news from the big city, and ambitious Greenwich Village writers were drawn to the possibility of reaching a new and broader audience. The relationship between the two was an uneasy one. Midwesterners were shocked by what they heard from Manhattan and felt threatened by urban life; Greenwich Villagers worried their voices and art would be homogenized and flattened by mass culture. There was fear in both Greenwich Village *and* the Midwest that Fordism, standardization, and centralization would come with a tremendous downside. As Cowley put it, "Publishing, like finance and the theater, was becoming centralized after 1900. Regional traditions were dying out; all regions were being transformed into a great unified market for motorcars and Ivory soap and ready-to-wear clothes."[64]

Once again, it was Canby who stepped into the breach. He believed that centralization and standardization were here to stay and that writers, editors, and publishers must find a way to use the new systems and technologies, or be used by them: "Standardization—whether in machinery or *mores*—is a means to an end. If the means extinguish the end, good-by to literature—and civilization. But though dangerous in a community such as America is now, and Europe will soon become, this means is indispensable; it exists; it must be handled, not denied." Standardization could generate new income, raise the standard of living, increase leisure, and create a new class, whose members, said Canby, would be "determined to eat better, dress better, read better, live better, and even to think better." The essay could play an important role in this process. He believed that if these new readers,

> who have not read beyond the newspapers, if there, begin to crave fiction, essays, the magazines that supply them successfully will have to be standardized—have been, as a matter of fact, as successfully standardized as the Ford car, with all the advantages, as well as all the disabilities, of standardization. What can go in such a magazine, and what cannot go, are both rigorously defined. It cannot be a medium for literature, though literature may slip into it; it must serve its need, and that need is real and not to be cancelled by idle criticism. The America that is learning to keep its teeth clean, read pretty good books, preserve reasonably good manners, eat properly prepared food, is the America of *The Saturday Evening Post, The Ladies' Home Journal,* the America of public schools and advertisements. Given a general condition of uplift, and such standardization is inevitable. You cannot begin to civilize all of the people all of the time except by broad methods broadly applied.[65]

Canby was a practical visionary. He knew how to raise money and deal with media moguls. In 1920 he had been able to launch the book section of the *Evening Post* largely because the paper's owner, Thomas Lamont, believed in the project. The paper itself, however, bled money, and so in 1924 Lamont put it up for sale, and it "was swallowed," wrote Canby, "in one expensive gulp by the Curtis family organization." But, because the *Literary Review* had developed a national readership of its own, Lamont separated it from the *Post* in the sale and agreed to let Canby try to keep it afloat. Canby went looking for money and soon found it. Two of his wealthy former Yale students, Henry Luce and Britton Hadden, had just launched *Time,* and he interested them in his book review. With some additional capital from Lamont, Time, Inc., agreed to publish the review, which was rechristened the *Saturday Review of Literature.* August 1924 was, Canby recalled, "the right time for a corporate literary personality to be born." In fact, he saw it as the dawn of the age of middlebrow: "The real end of the nineteenth century was close at hand. . . . I had shaken off some pedantic ideas and no longer yearned to publish articles that only scholars could understand, and which no one, not even scholars, read."[66]

ROSS'S PROSPECTUS AND THE ARRIVAL OF
THE *NEW YORKER*

Canby may have shaken off some pedantic ideas, but the *Saturday Review* would always maintain an air of stodginess and pedantry. In the very first issue, Canby announced that the magazine would "be like a modern university." He would acknowledge that he felt driven by a "Jeffersonian belief in the necessity of education for a successful democracy" and wanted "criticism to be first of all a teaching job."[67] Some middle-class readers found his curriculum too dry, but others enrolled. The magazine's circulation grew throughout the 1930s, and though it never climbed above 28,500, its subscribers were wealthy and influential. Studies showed that its readership eventually led that of all weekly magazines in income, education, professional occupations, book-club membership, foreign travel, book purchases, and investments.[68]

Canby's new magazine also served as the main forum for the debates over the state of the essay, featuring ten major articles, reviews, or essays on the essay during its first fifteen years. But while Canby's magazine was discussing the essay, Harold Ross was recruiting his Algonquin friends to write essays for his new magazine, the *New Yorker*.

A high school dropout from Salt Lake City, Ross possessed neither Canby's education nor his penchant for uplift. He enjoyed reference books and was a stickler for clarity, but claimed reading literature was a chore. Katharine White found this claim disingenuous. She recalled him as "a natural literary man" who "spent his whole life reading to catch up."[69] Ross played the rube as a way of keeping New York's expectations of him low. A founding member of the Algonquin Round Table, he was neither witty nor sophisticated, but his magazine was.

At the age of eighteen Ross decided to work his way to New York as a tramp reporter. Two years later, in 1913, having held twenty-three jobs along the way, he finally got there. He scrambled for a while in the city but could not find permanent employment, so he limped back home to work in his father's salvage business. After a dismal year there, he headed west, literally covering the waterfront for the *San Francisco Call* before enlisting in the army and shipping out to France. He finagled a job as the managing editor of the *Stars and Stripes*, the army's paper for enlisted men. Its staff included Adams, sportswriter Grantland Rice, *New York Times* drama critic Alexander Woollcott, and future Roosevelt press secretary Stephen Early, with Broun and Lardner as informal stringers and drinking buddies. At the end of the war Woollcott introduced him to Jane Grant, an old friend of his from the *New York Times* now working in France for the YMCA. She had come east from Kansas to New York the same time as Ross. They quickly fell in love and married. She convinced him to give Manhattan another chance.

Back in New York Ross helped edit a veterans' magazine, then briefly a humor magazine called *Judge,* but he wanted to start his own magazine. Like Canby, he sensed an opening in the still largely unexplored territory that existed between mass magazines like the *Saturday Evening Post* and highbrow little magazines like the *Dial.*

He would use as his model the sophisticated humor magazines that were popular at the time. Besides *Judge,* which had a circulation of two hundred thousand, these included *Vanity Fair, Life,* and *College Humor. Life* (where Sherwood, Parker, and Benchley had moved after the *Vanity Fair* walkout) was the oldest and most popular, having been founded in 1883 and boasting a circulation of five hundred thousand. These magazines evolved from nineteenth-century college humor magazines such as the *Harvard Lampoon* and *Yale Record.* College enrollment tripled between 1900 and 1930, and a generation of middle-class youth grew up on these two kinds of magazines. The mix of witty allusions, inside dope, and cartoons in the New York–based humor magazines helped alums keep in touch with a college sensibility, but it also helped the undegreed and uninitiated learn about modern urban life. Paula Fass suggests that the popularity of these magazines was symptomatic of a larger trend in American culture away from a family-based culture toward a peer-based one, or what she calls "peer society." As we have seen, central heating, electric lights, and a precisely marketed mass culture had scattered families from the joint activity of the parlor to their own rooms and activities. Fass argues that children and young adults were also spending more time among peers. In the past they had worked alongside adults in shops and factories, or on farms, but the rise of public education threw them together with each other in a new world of school and extracurricular activities.[70]

Mass magazines like *Collier's* and the *Post* had begun to feature writers like Fitzgerald, Hemingway, Lewis, and Dos Passos, and the urban humor magazines followed suit, also publishing writers who would come to be seen as literary or modernist. Mencken was the regular drama critic at *Judge;* Edmund Wilson was the book reviewer at *Vanity Fair.* A single issue of *Vanity Fair* (July 1923) included work by T. S. Eliot, Aldous Huxley, Gertrude Stein, and Djuna Barnes.[71]

This was the context into which Ross launched his new magazine about New York. In August 1924, the same month the first issue of the *Saturday Review* appeared, Ross had lunch with Raoul Fleischmann, a wealthy heir in a family of bakers and yeast manufacturers. He pitched his idea to Fleischmann, who liked it and agreed to put in twenty-five thousand dollars, a sum Ross and Grant were to match. Fleischmann stipulated that Ross must get some of the colyumnists on board. He promptly signed Parker, Woollcott, and Broun to the "Board of Advisory Editors" and appended the list to a prospectus, which he began to circulate. The response from prospective backers and advertising agencies was good, and the first issue of the *New Yorker* appeared in February 1925.

Ross's now famous 517-word prospectus placed his product in the middle-brow moment and the world of the colyumnists.[72] "*The New Yorker*," he began, "will be a reflection in word and picture of metropolitan life." It would promote New York by featuring a list of each week's "amusement offerings" and notes of what was happening in the "smart gathering places—the clubs, hotels, cafes, supper clubs, cabarets and other resorts." Like the Book-of-the-Month Club, it would offer "a list of the season's books which it considers worth reading." Like the colyumnists it featured, it would make Manhattan manageable, "jotting down in the small-town newspaper style of the comings, goings and doings in the village of New York." This "talk of the town" would come (or seem to come) from a Mr. Von Bibber III (an Irving-like persona who, in a few months, gave way to the Regency dandy Eustace Tilley).

In a nod to the cornpone the Chicago colyumnists had brought with them, Ross promised that the magazine's jottings would "contain some josh," though "some news value" as well. So as to separate the *New Yorker* from the humor magazines, Ross's prospectus promised honesty, accessibility, and good reporting as well as wit. Almost every paragraph of the prospectus asserted that the magazine would be funny but not too funny. There was, the prospectus reassured, a middle road between reporting and opinion, or, in Ross's words, the "stenographic" and the "interpretive." He promised, "*The New Yorker* will present the truth and the whole truth without fear and without favor but will not be iconoclastic." Ross's dream of objectivity was (White would later write) a "simple dream," a belief that his magazine could always be "good," "funny," and "fair," and such a dream was meant to appeal to the American middle class's conception of itself as exceptional, personable, and always above the fray.[73]

Ross's evenhandedness and smoothing over belied the fact that he was elbowing his way into a crowded market. When his second sentence says simply, "It will be human," Ross seems to be characterizing his as the most general of general interest magazines. Richard Ohmann has explained how the term *general* as descriptive of magazines erased a number of differences: "'General,' despite its apparent inclusiveness, was a term of limitation, of negation. It erased, from its conception of audience, their existence as farmers, as engineers, as housewives, Methodists, Democrats and so forth, and so on. The 'general' magazine addressed readers around or above categories of occupation, party, religious faith, and gender."[74]

Ross's real agenda soon came into focus, for the rest of his lead paragraph was a cascade of anaphora and declarations meant to separate the *New Yorker* from its competition: "Its general tone will be one of gaiety, wit and satire, but it will be more than a jester. It will not be what is commonly called radical or highbrow. It will be what is commonly called sophisticated, in that it will assume a reasonable degree of enlightenment on the part of its readers. It will hate bunk." Ross's careful tacking between *human* and *sophisticated* suggests *Vanity Fair* but with fewer in-jokes and less pretension.

The niche marketing continues in Ross's declaration that the magazine will not be "radical or highbrow." As with all negative definitions—*nonfiction*, for instance—these negations might seem to leave the field wide open, but they do not. In the code of the market, Ross is distinguishing the *New Yorker* from specific magazines. By not being radical, it will not have an ax to grind in the manner of the *Liberator*, or even the *New Republic*; by not being highbrow, it will not be as dry or expect as much of its readers as the *Atlantic*, or even the *Saturday Review*. Trysh Travis calls this niche "high middlebrow."[75]

Ross's final assertion that his magazine will "hate bunk" also had special resonance in 1924. Eight years earlier Henry Ford had famously said, "History is more or less bunk," and at the moment when Ross was circulating his prospectus, the best-seller lists featured William Woodward's novel *Bunk*, a satiric fantasy about advertising and celebrity culture that introduced the word *debunk* to the American lexicon.[76]

Woodward was a former advertising copywriter who, with his friend Sinclair Lewis, founded the *Publishers' Newspaper Syndicate*, a middlebrow book-marketing supplement that mixed ads and reviews. Michael Webb, his novel's protagonist, ran into trouble when his bunk-detecting device began to find the stuff everywhere. Carl Van Doren gave the book a favorable review in the *Nation*, calling Woodward's background as an adman the "happiest possible" for the task. He described Webb as "a pricker of bubbles, a devastating intellect among contented morons."[77]

In the real world, debunking proved just as tricky. In an essay titled "The Virtues and Limitations of Debunking," Kenneth Burke argued that the debunker falls into a dilemma because "in order to combat a *bad* argument, he develops a position so thorough that it would combat *all* arguments," including his own. Burke saw debunking as growing out of the muckraking tradition and as "interwoven with the history of liberalism." The liberal as debunker had good instincts and, like Ross, reveled in irony, but he was unsystematic and fell into the habit of taking indiscriminate potshots.[78]

The avid, continuous, and hyperspecific positioning of Ross's prospectus went beyond marketing. Ross was fighting for a strategic location in the literary field. This field, as defined by Bourdieu, is "neither a vague social background nor even a *milieu artistique*" but "a veritable social universe where . . . there accumulates a particular form of capital and where relations of force of a particular type are exerted." It is, in short, a battlefield, marked by "universal competition."[79] The largest of Ross's competitors was Curtis Publishing, and Ross devised a most ingenuous way to separate the *New Yorker* from Curtis's magazines and to lure readers from them. He did it with the most famous line of his famous document: "*The New Yorker* will be a magazine which is not edited for the old lady in Dubuque."

Ross did not invent this little old lady. She appeared first at the turn of the century in Taylor's Chicago column "A Line o' Type or Two," when that city was working overtime to distinguish itself from the hinterlands. She represented an audience of small-town librarians, spinsters, and schoolmarms who had been blamed at least since Twain for "civilizing" America's boys and men. In 1924 New Yorkers like Ross saw her as working hand in hand with Curtis to control American culture through the *Ladies' Home Journal* and *Saturday Evening Post*.

They also blamed her for the decline of the American essay. She was Hermione and her little group of serious thinkers. She was Lewis's Thanatopsis Club. She was the liberal Protestantism Hamilton Mabie peddled in the *Journal*. She was the leader of Braley's self-chosen elect who had lamented the lost art of the essay and saddled the essay with a "Fauntleroy complex."[80]

In less than a decade the era of the little old lady would be over. John Waters published an influential piece in 1933 titled "A Little Old Lady Passes Away," in which he announced the death of the genteel essay, "that lavender-scented little old lady of literature." He pegged her demise quite specifically on Christopher Morley, whom he referred to as "the little old lady's favorite American nephew." By taking a swipe at Morley, Waters was also criticizing Canby and the *Saturday Review,* which featured Morley's column, "The Bowling Green." Waters blamed Morley and his ilk for "carrying familiarity too far." In Morley, the qualities that had made the genteel essay popular—its "intimacy, reverie, [and] whimsy"—had ripened into cuteness, affectation, and irrelevance.

Essayists like Morley, said Waters, now assumed one of three poses. They portrayed themselves as "quaint old fuss-budgets" out to win the gushing approval of their "sisters, wives, and maiden aunts," as prematurely aged "Anglophiles" lost in "bookish archaisms," or as "coy writers" who teased their mothers, flirted shamelessly with "schoolmarms from Brookline, Mass.," and "delighted in tickling the risqué with the feather end of their pens." Unfortunately, said Waters, "the high schools, with well-meaning but pitifully misdirected affection, took to teaching" these corrupted versions of the essay "to their fuzzy-lipped brats," with the result that "whole herds of pubescent illiterates" and "inglorious" would-be "Morleys" were being loosed on the culture.

In the end, however, even Waters dissolved into nostalgia. He decided America still needed the little old lady. "A new and dizzyingly complex world," he wrote, has "roared across the quiet hearth," and "the loud talk of collectivism and social trends and economic determinism" has drowned out the old conversation. Soon, "the hard young sociologists" with "their cock-sure -*ologies*" may "have her pages [in the magazines] all to themselves." But, wrote Waters, "I hope not." The editors of the *Saturday Review* recognized Waters's essential unity with their own position on the essay and showed they could take a joke. In July 1934 they titled a review of an essay anthology in their pages "The Demise of a Little Old Lady."[81]

Ironically, Ross was also divided about the little old lady and the gentility she represented—a no-nonsense outsider from Colorado, he picked the monocle-wearing, butterfly-sniffing dandy Eustace Tilley as his magazine's mascot. Such contradictions grew from his having recognized that the little old lady was changing and that gentle teasing was a good way to market his magazine to her (as well as to sophisticated New Yorkers). Having taken this swipe at her in the prospectus, he quickly added, "This is not meant as disrespect, but *The New Yorker* is a magazine published for a metropolitan audience and thereby will escape an influence which hampers most national magazines. It expects a considerable national audience, but this will come from persons who have a metropolitan interest."

The first task, then, was to find and consolidate a readership in the New York area. Ads and copy emphasized that the magazine was Manhattan based. Ross's first accounts came from friends and acquaintances. The first issue included advertisements for Broadway shows and New York publishers, including Boni and Liveright, whose editorial director, Beatrice Kaufman, was the wife of advisory editor George Kaufman, and Haldeman-Julius, with whom Ross played poker. Ross knew there were a lot of old ladies in Dubuque who would read the magazine's ads and restaurant listings with longing, its cartoons to test their own sense of humor, and its profiles in order to know who was who. He said he would not edit with her in mind, but he did, and his plan worked. By 1930 subscribers outside the metropolitan New York area made up 30 percent of its circulation; two years later the figure had risen to 50 percent.[82]

And not all ladies from Dubuque were old. Some were young single women or housewives with new and expanded consumer power, intent on staying up-to-date. While still in Dubuque, the lady could not reserve a table at 21 or buy a ticket to a Broadway show (as much as she might want to), but she could order a book for herself or a Hathaway shirt for her husband. Ross knew Middle America was essential to his middlebrow project, and he planned to access the region through its women, using provocation and reverse psychology to do so. His remark seemed tactless at first, but he was never known for being politic. In fact, his avoidance of politics sometimes made him that much more impolitic. He was an editor and entrepreneur, not a writer or politician.

Heywood Broun, on the other hand, was a writer and thoroughly political. And unlike his friend Ross, he had grown up in Manhattan. As a socialist and trade union organizer, Broun was also concerned with building alliances and tearing down stereotypes. He was a New York wit and advisory editor to the *New Yorker,* but he was less cynical and more progressive than most of the new essayists. By the 1930s his *New York Telegram* column (*colyumn* having drifted from use by then), "It Seems to Me," had become, according to Michael Denning, a "mainstay of the Popular Front."[83]

In October 1930 Broun devoted an installment of that column to the question of New York's relation to the provinces. He claimed to have received a letter from a Miss V. M. of Fargo, North Dakota, who wrote:

> Can you tell someone who's never been to New York, and maybe never will be, how to be a New Yorker? I work out here in an office from 9 to 5, and I don't get much chance to read, but I do get *The American Mercury* and *The New Yorker.* And the radio at night makes me feel more in touch with the East. I listen, and I'm trying to develop a classical taste in music. Recently I ordered a dress from a New York store that I saw in an advertisement and a set of bridge cards from a shop on Fifth Avenue. Maybe you could tell me if I'm on the right track to becoming a New Yorker.

This cluster of middle-class desires—New York fashions, classical music, middlebrow magazines and radio shows—feels so overdetermined as to be suspect, but whether the letter is genuine or not, it could have been, and in his answer Broun treated it as such. He tried to avoid being patronizing but could not fail to see the lady's earnest attempt as futile. He understood New York's draw. Everyone is intrigued by life in the Big City, he wrote, and always has been. Even in ancient times, people undoubtedly wanted to "get away from this one-horse town and go to Babylon or Carthage or Rome."

But he cautioned against such grass-is-always-greener thinking, offering that "it's a good thing to be a New Yorker—when you are in New York—but in Fargo I'd be a Fargoian or a Fargoite, or whatever you call it."

All of which is not to say that he did not love New York. He did. As wonderful as New York was, he tells the lady, it was not *that* wonderful, assuring her (and reminding himself) that "life can be just as humdrum in this magical city as in Dubuque or Fargo." Not that New York was ordinary—it was not, he said, but neither was it the "Utopia" that some of the "journalists" who write "syndicate stuff" would have us think it is. Its streets were not "paved with gold," nor was it populated exclusively by "opera singers and motion picture stars and novelists," people who talk like "George Jean Nathan or H. L. Mencken." But neither was it the "inferno," the "'foreign city'" that its nativist detractors would have us believe it to be. He signed off with a defense of New York's immigrant population, especially the city's Jews, arguing that not only were "Jewish families . . . among our oldest settlers," but also that it was "silly to make a reproach" of the fact that there are "millions of Jews in New York." All this talk of "'foreigners'" and "100 percent Americans," he concluded, was not "in accord with our traditions."[84]

Broun's column appeared five days before election day in 1930, when Broun, running as a Socialist Party candidate in the first election since the Crash, came in third in the race for Congress from New York's Seventeenth District. In the previous three years, he had twice been fired from the *World*, first for his defense of Sacco and Vanzetti, and later for a piece in the *Nation* in which he called the *World* a "pseudo-liberal paper." During the next three years, he would found the Newspaper Guild and be kicked out of the Socialist Party for speaking at a Communist Party rally.

Ross and Broun approached politics differently but were friends. Their wives, Jane Grant and Ruth Hale, were founding members of the Lucy Stone League, and though both couples divorced, all four stayed close. Ross described himself as "a liberal, though, by instinct" and claimed to be "incapable of having partisan politics." The tensions between the two men are predictive of the contradictory role that the *New Yorker* would play in the development of the essay in the coming decade. According to his successor, William Shawn, Ross's reverence for facts and hatred of propaganda made him "suspicious of 'thinking'—his magazine was not to publish either essays or what are called articles of opinion."[85] This narrow definition of the term negates the role the magazine's reviews, "Notes and Comment," "letters," "casuals," humor pieces, and profiles would play in the development of the American essay during Ross's tenure.

Shawn was right, however, in suggesting that Ross's political and editorial inclinations kept a certain kind of essay from developing in the magazine. Ross's editorial conventions, such as his preference for "paragraphs" in "Notes and Comment," adherence to an anonymous editorial "we," and refusal to use bylines or contributors' notes, worked against the inclusion of longer, more personal essays in the magazine. But the political pressures of the 1930s—criticism from the Left, the rise of the Popular Front, and the growing fascist threat—did tug the *New Yorker* away from the persona of the Little Man and his liberal debunking. It would take a dispute between Ross and his main editorial writer, E. B. White, and the subsequent loss of White to a rival magazine to shake Ross loose from some of his hobbyhorses and finally open the *New Yorker* to politics and personal essays.

5

STARTING OUT AT THE *NEW YORKER*

B orn in 1899, E. B. White was the youngest of Samuel and Jessie White's six children by five years. He grew up in the family's big Queen Anne house at 101 Summit Avenue in Mt. Vernon, New York, America's first subdivided suburb.

In 1850 a group of skilled artisans who wanted to escape the "ruinous rents" and the "rapacity of landlords" in New York City set out to create Mt. Vernon. They organized themselves as Industrial Home Owners Society Number One, purchased 367 acres from five Westchester farmers, laid out quarter-acre plots on a grid, put in streets, established a commercial center at the railway station (in White's youth the town was a twenty-five-minute train ride from Grand Central Station), and in a few years built more than three hundred homes. Covenants were weak, however, and during the downturns of the next decade, many of Mount Vernon's lower-middle-class residents sold out to wealthy newcomers who joined lots and built bigger houses, including the one at 101 Summit Avenue in Mt. Vernon's exclusive Chester Hill neighborhood.[1] White referred to the house as his castle: "From it I emerged to do battle and into it I retreated when I was frightened or in trouble. The house even had the appearance of a fortress, with its octagonal tower room for sighting the enemy and its second-story porches for gun emplacements."[2]

White's family had followed his mother's parents from Brooklyn to Mt. Vernon in 1891. William Hart, Jessie's father, was a well-known painter, member of the Hudson River School's second generation, and founding president of the Brooklyn Academy of Design. The tensions between fractions of the middle class that were evident in Mt. Vernon's history worked their way into White's family, for Jessie was proud of her father's status and often referred to him as "an Academician." Samuel was successful in his own right, but

White recalled that his mother "pulled rank on him, now and then, by pulling William Hart on him. After all, Father was just a businessman, son of a carpenter. Her father was an artist."[3]

Samuel had to drop out of school at the age of thirteen when his father's alcoholism left the family destitute. To help support his mother and four siblings, Samuel took a job as a "bundle boy," wrapping boxes for a Manhattan piano manufacturer, Horace Waters and Company. He stuck with the firm and learned everything he could, from keeping books to tuning pianos, and he moved up. By the time he was forty-five and his last child was born, he had become the firm's vice president and general manager.

This success was not enough for his wife, but her sniping was a kind of dissatisfaction with which he was familiar already. His own mother had come from English "landed gentry" but lost her inheritance when she married a tradesman. The tenuousness of success and the divisions of class seem to have moved with the family to the house on Summit Avenue. White assumed that his grandfather, the "Academician," had suggested, or perhaps required, his parents to move to Mt. Vernon because it was "tonier" and "better for their children" than Brooklyn.[4]

Samuel White was fortunate to have landed a job with Horace Waters and Company when he did. Pianos were a growth industry at the turn of the century when family sings were middle-class after-dinner rituals. Richard Ohmann points out that a piano cost about two hundred dollars, a third of a working-class family's annual income in the late 1880s, making it quite definitely a middle-class commodity. The arrival of the professional-managerial class meant the piano business boomed. Between 1890 and 1910 the number of pianos in use in the United States increased six times faster than the country's population, the total number growing from eight hundred thousand to four million. By 1910 one in every five American households possessed one.[5] According to Ohmann, "The great majority of middle and upper middle class families must have decided that their way of life entailed the possession, and doubtless use, of a piano."[6]

Certainly, White's family did. "One of the fringe benefits of being the son of a piano man," White recalled, "was that our parlor at 101 Summit Avenue was well supplied with musical instruments: a Waters grand, a reed organ with phony pipes, and, at one period, a Waters player piano called an 'Autola.'" White and his five siblings constituted "practically a ready-made band. All we lacked was talent." But despite that impediment, they "sang, composed, harmonized, and . . . [even] . . . took lessons for brief spells in an attempt to raise the general tone of the commotion."[7] The informality of the White parlor is striking for the time. Their rambunctiousness suggests that even inside their sprawling Queen Anne, the Whites were more modern and less genteel than many of their contemporaries—more *Life with Father* or *Cheaper by the Dozen* than *The Five Little Peppers* or *Christian Parlor Magazine.*

The Whites' parlor was not, however, completely devoid of Christian piety and Victorian decorum. White recalled his father's cultural positions as conservative "in a rather sensible and large-spirited way." Samuel White was a Democrat drawn to Wilson's Christian Progressivism, and Henry Ward Beecher was a strong and early influence. In Brooklyn, Samuel White and his family had been among the twenty-five hundred who regularly attended Beecher's famous Plymouth Congregational Church where total annual pew rentals topped sixty thousand dollars.[8]

Samuel was self-conscious about that fact that he was self-educated, so he valued formal education, provided books for his children, and ensured that they went to good schools. For himself, however, reading was a practical and private endeavor. A copy of Beecher's sermons was about the only book his son recalled seeing his father read. It is not clear whether the elder White was more enamored of Beecher's progressive politics (antislavery, protemperance, suffragist, Darwinian) or the minister's aphoristic blend of Christianity and practical advice. Certainly, Beecher's *Proverbs from the Plymouth Pulpit* (1887) advanced the kind of rags-to-riches pep talk that must have rung especially true to Samuel White, whose rise from "bundle boy" could hardly have been more Alger-like.

White recalled that as a boy he could hardly wait for the next issue of the *American Boy* or *St. Nicholas Magazine,* wholesome children's magazines full of animal stories and Victorian values. The magazines' writing contests promoted a new kind of achievement or, as White put it, a "boy's dream for premiums," a "youth's dream of recognition." He was especially proud when he placed a story or poem and received one of the premiums—"the pictures of pony carts and magic lanterns tortured my grasping little heart with life's not impossible fulfillment."[9]

He continued to write, working on his high school newspaper and then editing the *Cornell Daily Sun.* At Cornell he also wrote for the literary magazine and acquired the lifelong nickname of Andy, after the university's first president, Andrew D. White. He also became a member of the Manuscript Club, a kind of informal writers' workshop that met monthly at the home of Professor Martin Sampson. There, and at the weekly "Monday nights" at Professor Bristow Adams's house, White participated in wide-ranging fireside chats about everything from "the ethics of newspaper work to the oppression of Korea by the Japanese."[10] Adams was an illustrator, forester, and journalist, who had edited the Stanford humor magazine as an undergraduate and worked for the U.S. Department of Conservation. His ready wit, environmental commitment, and progressive politics appealed to White, who felt more at home there than at 101 Summit.

White graduated from Cornell in 1921 and promptly took off across country with a college friend in a Model T they called Hotspur. They meandered west, bunking in fraternity houses, while White made money by writing term papers for students or stories for local papers. When they arrived in Seattle that fall his friend went home. But White landed a job at the *Seattle Times*. At first he covered local news; it was not a good fit. Shy by nature, he did not enjoy Rotary and Chamber lunches. The problem was accentuated by the fact that he was, as he would recall later, "under the influence of Mencken and Lewis, and felt proud disdain for business and businessmen." His stories about the doings of the Kiwanis and the Elks were too often late, uninspired, or even, apparently, sarcastic. The editor recognized talent, however, and moved him to features, even giving him for a time free rein to conduct a column of witticisms and light verse. It was more to his liking, but in retrospect he decided he took himself and the opportunity too seriously:

> My [diary] entry for June 15, 1923, begins: "A man must have something
> to cling to. Without that he is a pea vine sprawling in search of a trellis."
> Obviously, I was all asprawl, clinging to Beauty, which is a very restless
> trellis. My prose style at this time was a stomach-twisting blend of the
> Bible, Carl Sandburg, H. L. Mencken, Jeffrey Farnol, Christopher Morley,
> Samuel Pepys, and Franklin Pierce Adams imitating Samuel Pepys. I was
> quite apt to throw in a "bless the mark" at any spot, and to begin a sentence with "Lord" comma.[11]

White would not assimilate these influences and really make them his own for almost two decades, and even then it would take the shock of fascism's rise to help him do it. For now, he remained too cute, and his Seattle editor finally let him go. White decided to take a steamer to Alaska but had only enough in savings for a one-way ticket. Seemingly stuck in Skagway, he lucked into a job working the bar on the same ship and was able to get back to Seattle. His parents decided enough was enough, and he took the train home to launch himself on New York City, writing copy and doing layout for various Manhattan advertising agencies, including the Frank Seaman Agency. But, like others who were writing ad copy at the time, including F. Scott Fitzgerald, Dorothy Parker, and Hart Crane, his heart was not in it. Living in his parents' house compounded his feeling that he was floundering. He wrote later, "I found it impossible to get out of bed in the morning. . . . I was little help to Frank Seaman, who expected me to bring myself to a slow boil in behalf of Mentholatum, Du Pont Tontine Window Shades, Du Pont Cellophane, and other items on his list."[12]

But Seaman's was a day job. White spent his evenings writing humorous pieces and tried to send at least one "noble nubbin of poetry" each week to Morley or F. P. A. He would "squander a nickel on the early edition" of the *World* to see if one of his poems had made it into "The Conning Tower." Adams, wrote White, "gave a young writer three precious gifts: discipline, a sense of gaiety, and a brief moment in the sun." Twenty-five years later, he remembered those years: "I burned with a low steady fever because I was on the same island with Don Marquis, Heywood Broun, Christopher Morley, Franklin P. Adams, Robert C. Benchley, Frank Sullivan, Dorothy Parker, Alexander Woollcott, Ring Lardner and Stephen Vincent Benét. . . . New York hardly gave me a living at that period, but it sustained me. I used to walk quickly past the house on West 13th Street between Sixth and Seventh where F. P. A. lived."[13]

In the summer of 1925, after two years at Seaman's, White decided to leave. About the same time, he moved from his parents' house into an apartment on West Thirteenth Street (on the same block as F. P. A.) with three fraternity brothers from Cornell. He would limp along on his savings for a while and freelance full-time.

Providentially, this was the moment Harold Ross was launching the *New Yorker.* The first issue had appeared that February. White bought a copy for fifteen cents at the newsstand in Grand Central Station on a tip from a friend that it might be a good place to submit some writing. It was a good tip. He placed a piece in the magazine's ninth issue. It was, not surprisingly, a parody of advertising—a series of brief ads on behalf of the season of spring:

> *New Beauty of Tone in 1925 Song Sparrow*
> Into every one of this season's song sparrows has been built the famous
> VERNAL tone. Look for the distinguishing white mark on the breast.[14]

Over the next few months, White placed more pieces in the *New Yorker*—a defense of the skuzzy Bronx River and some Little Man pieces about a good-natured drunk on a commuter train and a magnanimous fellow whose waitress spills milk on him. He was finding his feet at the same time the magazine was. After good newsstand sales of the first issues, circulation sank during the summer to 1,500, but by the end of the next year it rose to 46,446.[15] White continued to place work in the magazine, and in the fall of 1926 Ross and his new assistant editor, Katharine Sergeant Angell, hired him as a part-time staffer. During the next year he switched to full-time, and soon he was writing more of the magazine than anyone: the opening "Notes and Comment," newsbreaks (column-filling quips about a headline or news story in the manner of B. L. T.), light verse, even cartoon captions. In the spring and summer of 1927, he did a series of one-page mock advertisements that satirized ad copy and sold subscriptions to the magazine. In each ad, a clueless young clerk named Sterling Finny and his equally dim wife, Flora, confronted a social faux pas that could be remedied only by a weekly dose of the *New Yorker*. The opening of the April 23 ad has Sterling telling his wife he must move away for the sake of their son, lest the boy "come under the influence" of a father who is "not interesting":

> Only the week before, a neighbour had said to Mr. Finny, "I hear that the American wing of the Metropolitan Museum of Art is very entertaining." And all Sterling could answer was: "I, too, hear that the American wing of the Metropolitan Museum of Art is very entertaining."
> The neighbour moved away.
> . . . Perhaps you too have a dear baby who will soon be old enough to know what an ass his father is! Are you going to leave home, or will you take the simple measures to get bright? *The New Yorker* is written entirely by fathers and mothers whose children are proud to know them. Browse for a few minutes between its covers each week—you will quickly acquire so much culture that even your children will be glad to have you around the house![16]

Each ad included a photograph of store mannequins done up as the Finny family and a tear-off subscription form. The series poked fun at the way advertising played on the pretension and anxieties of middlebrow customers. The Book-of-the-Month Club, for instance, had launched the year before with the tagline "Why is it you disappoint yourself so frequently in this way?"[17] But the Finny campaign also struck close to home. In the same April 23 issue in which Sterling had to leave home, an ad for the Arthur Murray Dance Studios explained "why good dancers are popular": "There are plenty of people who can dance just good enough to 'get by'—but very, very few who are really good dancers. That is why the man or woman who *is* the exceptional dancer is always admired, always sought after, always sure of a good time."[18]

The *New Yorker*'s advertising director expressed displeasure with the campaign, but readers and advertisers seemed to appreciate its visual and verbal ironies (though the mannequins probably got more laughs than "neighbour," the slightly pretentious Anglicism being a departure from house style that was essentially an in-joke). The Finny pieces were popular enough to be collected in a pamphlet titled *Less than Nothing; or, The Life and Times of Sterling Finny* (1927), and circulation by the end of the year had grown to more than sixty-one thousand.[19]

Understanding and alluding to the equal-opportunity satire of the *New Yorker* showed you were in the know. The magazine's irony could, it seemed, inoculate the highbrow against snobbery and the middlebrow against pretension, just as it could save the Little Old Lady in Dubuque from being a hick. Touring the headquarters of the Book-of-the-Month Club years later, Radway noticed "framed prints of several *New Yorker* cartoons gently gibing the club and its social-climbing members," which she took as markers of the club's "institutional awareness of its history and position."[20]

But in another sense, the *New Yorker* was not all that different from the Book-of-the-Month Club. It was offering a version of the same kind of product but with irony. The Finny ads did, after all, include a subscription form. The *New Yorker* had broken more fully with the Victorian dream of uplift and so was more modern, but in actuality it was offering a hipper, more urbane form of the *Good Housekeeping* seal of approval. If the *New Yorker* said something was au courant, it was. Sterling Finny might whimper, "I am not *au courant*" (which, he explains to Flora, means "not tidy"), but the reader need not worry, for as the ad assured, "Do you know it is just as easy to be *au courant* as it is to be a Baptist?"[21] The *New Yorker* was selling New York and modernism in a way the colyumnists had only dreamed of.

Roland Marchand has argued that the early 1920s marked a turning point in American advertising when ads became more personalized and consumer centered (as opposed to product centered). Products now helped solve a consumer's problems. Marchand calls advertisers at this time "apostles" and "mediators" of modernity. As apostles they peddled the latest; as mediators they attuned themselves to consumer resistance to the modern. "Their role," notes Marchand, "was, indeed, ambiguous. They served their clients as intelligence agents, yet their intelligence-gathering lay in their success in presenting products in the words and images that consumers most cherished." And in fact, he continues, "what made advertising 'modern' was, ironically, the discovery by these 'apostles of modernity' of techniques for empathizing with the public's imperfect acceptance of modernity, with its resistance to the perfect rationalization and bureaucratization of life."[22]

Advertisers were emblematic of the PMC as a whole in that they were called upon to mediate the struggle between labor and capital. The attempt by White and the *New Yorker* to stand aside and comment on the role of advertising did not exempt them from advertising and its effects. The *New Yorker* might joke about it, but it was selling self-improvement and middle-class instruction just as much as the Book-of-the-Month Club was. Slicing and dicing middlebrow culture made the magazine high middlebrow, but high middlebrow was nonetheless middlebrow.

Though irony did not exempt the magazine from contradictions of being middlebrow, Harold Ross seems to have believed that it did. From the outset, he argued that the *New Yorker* would stand outside the tawdriness of commerce. His prospectus declared that the magazine would not be "radical," but would "hate bunk"; would be comical, but "more than a jester." In fact, he was arguing for an impossibly high-minded goal of objectivity. According to his successor, William Shawn, Ross believed the magazine must never "publish anything for a hidden reason" or anything written from "an ulterior motive, however worthy." Ross did not exactly mean for his magazine to be above the fray—in a sense, everything was fair game—nor did he mean that the *New Yorker* did not publish anything that might be called an "essay," but he did mean that the magazine was not (supposedly) to publish pieces that took sides. That, he believed, would make it "sectarian." He tried always to draw a distinction between satire and polemic, between opinion and advocacy, between editorials and comment.

Ross wanted White to be funny and apolitical, and prior to the Crash, that goal seemed possible. What it meant in practice was that White, once he took over "Notes and Comment" in late 1926, could make fun of President Coolidge or the Bureau of Internal Revenue, of publicity-hungry authors or misbehaving conventioneers, but on the Sacco and Vanzetti case (which cost Broun his job at the *New York World*), he had to stay silent, claiming ignorance of the facts. The Scopes trial was an opportunity to poke fun at the South; the Lindbergh crossing was an opportunity to criticize commercialism. This latter was the biggest story of the year, and it overwhelmed many columnists. Even Broun celebrated the triumph of man over nature, and others touted science and good old American know-how in purple prose. White, on the other hand, saw the advertisers flying wing with Lindy and cautioned the new hero about the future:

> We noted that the *Spirit of St. Louis* had not left the ground ten minutes before it was joined by the Spirit of Me Too. A certain oil was lubricating the engine, a certain brand of tires was the cause of the safe take-off. When the flyer landed in Paris every newspaper was "first to have a correspondent at the plane." . . . [W]e were made uneasy by the volume of vaudeville contracts, testimonial writing and other offers, made by the alchemists who transmute glory into gold. We settled down to the hope that the youthful hero will capitalize himself for only as much money as he reasonably needs.[23]

The passage is quintessential *New Yorker*, quintessential White. He is after bunk, in the form of the hard sell, but his own technique is the soft sell. He is not criticizing Lindbergh; he is giving him advice.

White was adept at this gentle irony, but not always comfortable with it. He was already growing impatient with light humor and short paragraphs, and by 1928 he also was falling in love with Ross's assistant, Katharine Angell. The affair was barely secret. White sent her several love poems through F. P. A.'s column, "The Conning Tower." She was falling for him as well but was married and the mother of two young children. The two coworkers resisted, tried to be discreet, cut things off, and started up again. Part of the dance involved White deciding to leave the *New Yorker* and Katharine trying to keep him there. In 1929, when she finally left for Reno to get a divorce, White, uncertain, about to turn thirty, and perhaps wanting to give her the time and room she needed, wrote that he might resign. She replied:

> If you do keep on the New Yorker job, why not limit yourself definitely to, say, three days in the office,—and give yourself a real break in writing something your want to the rest of the time—or not writing at all if you don't want to. . . . Perhaps you won't be a Heifetz, perhaps you will, I can't say—Perhaps you won't be Willa Cather, but there's a good chance you may be (she, by the way, never wrote a book anyone noticed till she was almost forty—she worked on magazines). . . . Oh, stop preaching, Katharine.[24]

White stayed at the magazine, the divorce was finalized, and the next year they married.

"MAKING FRIENDS WITH THE ESSAY": FRANKLIN ROOSEVELT, COLYUMNIST

The 1920s were also a time of reassessment and some floundering for Franklin Roosevelt, who spent most of the decade away from politics. He had been the vice presidential candidate on the Democrats' losing ticket in 1920, but in 1921 he contracted polio and withdrew from public life. He did not reenter politics until he made the torturous walk to the podium at the 1924 Democratic National Convention in order to nominate Al Smith (a walk that would become the famous climax of *Sunrise at Campobello*), and he would not hold public office again until 1928, when he was elected governor of New York. At two points during this period of reassessment, he wrote newspaper colyumns. He was drawn to the form's friendly tone, its popularity among the broad middle class, the opportunity it afforded him to test the political waters, and the synergy it shared with radio.

Other politicians had lately written op-ed pieces and essays—most notably Franklin's uncle Teddy, who, as we have seen, was an active and widely read essayist. Teddy had demonstrated that an essay or article could provide a way to reinvent oneself. When he arrived in the New York State Assembly in 1881, he was, at twenty-three, the youngest representative ever. With his squeaky voice, Saville suit, pince-nez on a black ribbon, and hair parted in the middle, Teddy was practically laughed out of the statehouse. It was a scene reminiscent of that one just four years earlier when Roscoe Conkling attacked George William Curtis at the Republican State Convention as a "man-milliner" and "dilettante." The same Tammany politicians and New York City Democratic papers now called Teddy a "dude," "Nancy boy," "Jane-Dandy," "his Lordship," "little man," and "Oscar Wilde."[25] Roosevelt rode across the Dakotas and up San Juan Hill in order to counter this characterization and stake out a political career, but his plan also had him write dozens of essays promoting the strenuous life, trust busting, literary Americanism, and other manly pursuits so as to overturn the tradition of bachelor effeminacy that was haunting him and that had haunted the genteel essay since the days of Irving and Ik Marvel.

Other politicians of the era, such as Henry Cabot Lodge and Woodrow Wilson, also wrote essays. It was not surprising, then, to see references to their work in the literary discussions of the 1920s. Sherman's 1924 defense of the colyumnists, for instance, closed with a claim for the essay's personal touch as an antidote to the anxieties and alienation of modern life. For Sherman (as for Opdyke, Canby, and others), the colyumnists were the great uniters, humanizers, and erasers of difference because they offered an appeal from one personality to another:

> They tend to make the stranger at home in the world, and the lonely and insignificant man in town or country, who talks with no one in the morning, noon or night, feel yet, as he opens his paper, that he is not the only one of his kind, but that he is neighboured on all sides by his kindred and that in farmhouse and town mansion and White House there are millions of other strangers, essentially as lonely and insignificant as he. This is, perhaps, as near to a homelike feeling as a man can expect to come in this world.[26]

Franklin Roosevelt's political ambition could not have let him see the occupant of the White House as being as insignificant as anyone else, but the potency of its personal appeal would not have been lost on him.

A 1927 article by Samuel McChord Crothers, "Making Friends with the Essay," made much the same argument. Crothers, biographer of Holmes and champion of the gentle reader, was one of the last of the genteel essayists. His collections of essays included *By the Christmas Fire* (1908) and *Among Friends* (1910). A Unitarian minister and firm believer in the ability of the essay to transcend the page and speak personally, he seemed sometimes to confuse realms. He call his biography of Holmes *Oliver Wendell Holmes, the Autocrat and His Fellow Borders* (1909), and his book on Emerson was titled *Ralph Waldo Emerson: How to Know Him* (1921). Crothers died in 1927, so this article was one of his last pieces. The article, which is mainly a reading of Theodore Roosevelt and Wilson as essayists, argues, as Sherman had, for the power of friendship and, like Ross, for the necessity of nonpartisanship. Because the essay "is not a sermon," wrote Crothers, and because the essayist "is really quite indifferent whether his reader agrees with him or not" and "has no desire to convert," but only "to share what is in his mind," the reader will find it easy to "make friends" with him. He claims both presidents were "accomplished essayists," but he prefers Roosevelt to Wilson. Wilson's essays are admirable, but a bit too "academic" and "delicately wrought." Roosevelt's *Strenuous Life* and *History as Literature, and Other Essays,* on the other hand, offer a balanced approach to both literature and life, one that is "without pedantry" and is therefore capable of "breaking down the barriers" between the "dignified" and the "undesirable."[27]

Franklin Roosevelt also had a background in journalism. As president, he loved to remind the reporters at his almost weekly press conferences that he had been editor of the *Harvard Crimson* and that twice during the 1920s he had written columns for local newspapers. His two forays into colyumn writing were important preparation for the writing and delivering of the fireside chats. His first stint as a columnist occurred during April and May 1925, while he was convalescing from polio in Warm Springs, Georgia. He substituted for his friend Tom Loyless, who was ill and unable to write his column for the *Macon Daily Telegraph.* Loyless, a liberal newspaperman and fellow investor in the clinic and resort at Warm Springs, was dying of cancer, though neither man knew it at the time. Three days a week in a column called "Roosevelt Says," Roosevelt mixed anecdotes and policy. He told stories about life at Warm Springs, joked about how his friend Loyless had foisted this job on him so that he could go pick wildflowers, and held forth on issues such as the importance of immigration to the continued development of America and the need for civil service reform.

Three years later, during the late summer and early fall of 1928, Roosevelt wrote a second column. This one, titled "Between Friends," he wrote in order to help his friends Morgan Hoyt and Ed Hayden revive their sagging weekly, the *Standard* of Duchess County, New York. The column did increase circulation, but it also provided Roosevelt with a place to promote Smith's run for president and pave the way for his own run for governor of New York later that fall. Roosevelt claimed to enjoy writing these columns and prided himself on the fact that he wrote them himself. He opened his first piece for the *Standard* by saying, "I am glad to have a chance to be an occasional 'colyumnist' . . . this summer and autumn," and then added with some, but perhaps not complete, irony that "Will Rogers, Heywood Broun and F. P. A." had better "look out."[28]

TALKING ON THE "RADDIO": THE CREATION OF THE FIRESIDE CHATS

In 1924 Roosevelt's mentor, Al Smith, lost his presidential bid in large part because he was so bad on the radio. He nervously touched the microphones (which he referred to as "pie plates") and sometimes wandered away from them completely. His pronunciation of radio as "raddio" became a national joke.

Radio had arrived hard on the heels of the bungalow revolution during the century's early decades. The first radio station began broadcasting from Detroit in 1920. By the end of 1922, there were six hundred stations, and in 1924, when Roosevelt nominated Smith for president at the Democratic National Convention, about fourteen hundred stations broadcast the speech to approximately 3 million sets. By 1928 the number of American radio sets was up to 8.5 million; by 1932, 18 million; and by 1936, 36 million.[29] At first radios were novelties—crystal sets constructed from kits by mostly male ham operators who tinkered with them in their dens or backyard sheds. By the end of the decade, however, large, easy-to-operate console models had made their way into most living rooms, especially those of the aspiring middle class. White remembered getting enough money together when living with his college friends on West Thirteenth Street to buy a radio-with-loudspeaker, which was a step up from a radio-with-headphones. They listened to the first Dempsey-Tunney fight on it in 1926.

Bruce Barton recognized immediately the potential of the new medium to sell candidates as well as goods, but he also understood that most candidates would need to be repackaged. Barton, a former magazine editor, creator of "Betty Crocker," and marketer of Dr. Eliot's Five-Foot Shelf of Harvard Classics, served as an unpaid public relations adviser to the Republican

National Committee during the 1924 campaign. He told them that President Coolidge needed to move away from rallies and into America's living rooms:

> It would be a great and impressive thing, if,—say every second Monday night, beginning October first,—the President of the United States would talk to his employers, the people, about the way in which their work has been handled. Let the subject be interestingly stated and announced in advance. Let the President tell me, a salaried man, why I am paying 25 percent less taxes this year. . . .
>
> In other words the radio has made possible an entirely new type of campaign. It enables the President to sit by every fireside and talk in terms of that home's interest and prosperity. La Follette will roar and the Democrat will pound his stuffed shirt. But if the President will only talk to the folks (not address them) he will re-elect himself.[30]

Coolidge ignored the advice but won anyway.

By 1928 the entire Republican Convention was broadcast, and together the two parties spent ten times more money on radio spots than they spent on print ads. As secretary of commerce, Herbert Hoover had overseen the incredible early growth of the broadcasting industry. The radio, he said, "has brought . . . political discussion to almost every fireside."[31] But Hoover's theoretical understanding of the new medium did not always translate into successful practice. On the air he was nervous and spoke in a monotone but, like Coolidge, was able to beat Smith.

The Crash was more than enough to unseat Hoover four years later, but he was also defeated by Roosevelt's smooth, confident radio voice. Roosevelt had honed that voice by speaking on the radio three or four times a month as governor of New York. He was the first president to grow up with radio—he was fifteen when Marconi took out his patent for a "wireless telegraph"—and during his presidency the medium matured. The National Broadcasting Company (NBC) and the Columbia Broadcasting System (CBS) were networking stations at the time of his inauguration; the Mutual Broadcasting System and American Broadcasting Company (ABC) were organized soon after. A 1939 survey had the average American listening to the radio more than twenty hours each week.[32] When he addressed the nation about the banking crisis on the evening of March 12, 1933, in his first "fireside chat," Roosevelt spoke via 150 stations to sixty million people in twenty million homes. By 1940 he was reaching one hundred million listeners, three-quarters of the American population.

Roosevelt recognized early on that radio not only allowed him to conceal his infirmity and to travel without traveling but also gave him access to the living rooms of a vast and heterogeneous audience. In 1929 he told the *New York Times*, "Whereas five years ago ninety-nine out of one hundred people took their arguments from the editorial and news columns of the daily press, today at least half of the voters sitting at their own firesides listen to the actual words of the political leaders on both sides and make their decision on what they hear rather than what they read."[33] Two things are telling about this quotation. The first is the implication that the speech of politicians—this politician anyway—should be valued over the writing of newspapermen. The second is the invocation of the fireside as a place where you will not be manipulated by group pressure. Roosevelt's advocacy of this new and direct relationship was an argument for radio exceptionalism and radio citizenship.

Harry M. Butcher of the Washington bureau of CBS, in a May 7, 1933, press release, was the first to use the term *fireside chat* in reference to Roosevelt's radio talks.[34] The president and his speechwriters quickly picked up on the way the phrase resonated with the public and began using it themselves, reserving it for a particular type of address. Of his more than three hundred radio addresses as president, no more than thirty-one were fireside chats.[35] He worried about overusing the chats, lest they "lose their effectiveness," and rarely gave more than three in a year.[36] Roosevelt and his advisers understood they were selling a man as well as his policies, and they tried to make that man seem as trustworthy and familiar as possible. He would be learned but straight shooting, genteel but down-to-earth. He may have grown up in libraries and drawing rooms, but he understood that he needed to be at home in the living rooms of the families to whom he was speaking. Most of the fireside chats opened with Roosevelt addressing his listeners as "my friends."[37] This choice echoes not only the title of his 1928 column "Between Friends" but also the traditional characterization of the essayist as friend.

Roosevelt's chats were written, but they were meant to sound spoken. He used short words, American idioms, and common analogies to make his remarks feel familiar and fatherly. According to Samuel Rosenman, his head speechwriter, Roosevelt read revision after revision aloud in order to find the "words that he would use in informal conversation with one or two of his friends." While he talked, said Francis Perkins, "his head would nod and his hands would move in simple, natural, comfortable gestures," as if "he were actually sitting on the front porch" with his listeners. No detail was overlooked. Alerted to the fact that a separation between his front two lower teeth caused a slight whistle over the air, he had a removable bridge made, which he kept in a silver box next to his bed. More than once an aide had to run to get it just before airtime. Roosevelt also ad-libbed during almost every fireside chat. To create the atmosphere of intimacy he felt he needed, he delivered the chats not from the Oval Office but from the small Diplomatic Cloak Room on the first floor of the White House with just a few friends and family sitting nearby on folding chairs. It worked. Journalist Henry Fairlie recalled, "Radio sets were not then very powerful, and there was always static. Families had to sit near the set, with someone always fiddling with the knobs. It was like sitting round a hearth, with someone poking the fire; and to that hearth came the crackling voices of Winston Churchill, or George Burns and Gracie Allen, and of FDR. . . . It was not FDR who was at his fireside . . . , it was we who were at our firesides." Or as *New Republic* columnist (and White collaborator) Richard Strout put it, "You felt he was talking to you, not to 50 million others but to you personally."[38]

Roosevelt and his aides pitched the chats as informative and educational rather than political. This distinction allowed the networks to classify them as public service announcements and thereby donate free airtime. It also gave the president the rhetorical license to portray them as "commonsensical." As he said of his first chat about the banking crisis, "It was my endeavor to explain these things in a non-political language, so that the great mass of our citizens who had little or no experience with the technicalities of banking would be relieved of their anxiety as to whether they would ever see their money again."[39] For middle-class listeners, this "non-political" language raised Roosevelt above mere partisanship and appealed to their view of themselves as nonideological. Having convinced the networks and the Federal Communications Commission that the chats were "nonpartisan" and "educational" explanations of government policy, the administration got free airtime during prime time and an exemption from equal-time rules. The chats were generally kept to thirty minutes or less so they could fit between regularly scheduled shows.

Like the work of the colyumnists, the tone of fireside chats tapped into America's cornpone tradition. In an early chat, Roosevelt said, "When Andrew Jackson, 'Old Hickory,' died, someone asked, 'Will he go to heaven?' and the answer was, 'He will if he wants to.' If I am asked whether the American people will pull themselves out of this depression, I answer, 'They will if they want to.'"[40] And like the newspaper columns, the chats used direct address, irony, street talk, and put-downs, sometimes all at once:

> The next time anyone says to you that this war is "in the bag," or says, "It's all over but the shouting," you should ask him these questions:
> "Are you working full time on your job?
> "Are you growing all the food you can?
> "Are you buying your limit of war bonds? . . .

"Because—if your answer is no—then the war is going to last a lot longer than you think."

The plans we made for the knocking out of Mussolini and his gang have largely succeeded. But we still need to knock out Hitler and his gang, and Tojo and his gang. No one of us pretends that this will be an easy matter.[41]

THE *NEW YORKER* DURING THE 1930s

In the spring of 1933 White wrote a letter to Gus Lobrano, a college friend and former roommate in the Village who would later join him at the *New Yorker,* about the day of Roosevelt's inauguration. "All through the campaign," wrote White, "I thought Mr. R. was something of a pain; but the pain is gone. . . . You talk about stirring times: you should have been in New York that crazy March 4." He described being caught in a traffic jam caused by a demonstration by radical groups: "Driving my capitalistic limousine through the town, I felt like a noble in the French revolution, and expected at any minute to run down a child and have to use my whip on the rabble." After this ironic self-lashing he wrote to Lobrano how stirred he felt standing on a corner of Lexington Avenue and reading Roosevelt's "fear itself" address. "It was a great day," confided White, "and I won't forget it." As exciting as the city was, that day at least, White felt compelled to confide, "Kay and I are seriously thinking of taking to the land: we cut out farm ads."[42] The letter introduces the political discomfort and ambivalence toward city life that would haunt White throughout the 1930s.

It was not that White did not love New York. He did, and by 1933 he had done more than any other writer to make the *New Yorker* the voice of Manhattan. The magazine, which opened each week with his "Notes and Comment," had taken over the job of identifying trends, showcasing the city, and infusing middlebrow culture with irony. By the mid-1930s its circulation passed 125,000, advertising income was more than two million dollars, and annual profits exceeded six hundred thousand dollars. In 1934 the *New Yorker* contained more advertising pages than any magazine in the country.[43]

Katharine and E. B. White were integral to creating the style and format of the *New Yorker,* and they benefited financially from its success. Estimates put her 1934 salary at eleven thousand dollars and his earnings from the writing for the magazine that year at nearly twenty thousand dollars—this when a fifth of American workers were unemployed and annual household income was less than two thousand dollars.[44] As an editor, Katharine also received stock options. By 1937 she owned 350 shares, or nearly 5 percent, of the magazine's parent company, F-R [Fleischmann-Ross] Publishing Corporation. The company was privately held, so the value of the stock is hard to guess, but her biographer estimates that at the time it was worth at least thirty-five thousand dollars and perhaps as much as sixty thousand.[45]

The Whites lived very comfortably. Though they were married just a month after the Crash in 1929, they enlarged and remodeled their Greenwich Village apartment twice during their first years together, a period during which they also rented cottages and chartered sailboats for a month each summer in Maine. Later in 1933, the same year he had revealed to Lobrano the idea of moving to the country, they bought a twelve-room farmhouse in North Brooklin, Maine, with forty acres, outbuildings, and views across the bay of Mt. Desert Island. Two years later, they added a thirty-foot sailboat, and, feeling their Eighth Avenue apartment to be small despite the remodeling, they moved uptown to a rented house with servants' quarters in Turtle Bay Gardens on Manhattan's East Side.

The irony inherent in the fact that his own fortunes were rising as those of the nation were sinking was not lost on White. Years later, writing to a friend who had published a memoir of life at the *New Yorker* during the 1930s, he admitted, "Your description of the depression was quite enchanting, and also disturbing to me, because I have lived all my life with a guilty feeling about the depressed years. The *New Yorker* was, of course, a child of the depression and when everybody else was foundering we were running free, and I still feel that I escaped the hard times undeservedly and will always go unacquainted with the facts of life."[46]

At the time, however, White tried to stave off guilt with humor, exactly the job Ross paid him to do. In one piece he joked that the *New Yorker* took only one unequivocal stand during this period: firm opposition to moving the information booth in Pennsylvania Station.[47] In another, he spoofed the grave expectations of others:

> I have been asked to interpret the recent tailspin of pig iron. In a technocracy such as ours, one must go behind the facts. . . . It is marvelous back here behind the facts—just like being backstage at the theatre. Walter Lippmann is here, and George Soule, and Stuart Chase, and Howard Scott, and John Maynard Keynes; in short, all the big people of the depression. . . . Hundreds of facts have been piled together to form a curtain, and all of us are busy writing. It is warm here, and comfortable, and I wish I had found this place a lot sooner.[48]

But throughout, the tone is that of a man who doth protest too much, a man who knows Rome is burning.

At the same time White kept was keeping cozy behind the facts, Franklin Roosevelt was publishing a collection of his campaign speeches, and his wife, Eleanor, signed to do a series of articles for the Hearst syndicate and the North American Newspaper Alliance (NANA) as well as several radio shows. Conservatives created a stir, arguing such advocacy was inappropriate for a first lady. Eleanor had wide support, including that of Heywood Broun (who was in the midst of organizing the Newspaper Guild), but backed off at first. By late spring the controversy had died down, and she signed contracts to write monthly columns for NANA and *Women's Home Companion*. That fall she published *It's Up to the Women*, a collection of some of her earlier speeches and articles.

White admitted in a "Notes and Comment" piece that he was distressed at the "paucity of [his] literary output," which amounted to nothing more than a "few rather precise little paragraphs" for his "funny little magazine." Half jokingly, he added, "Both President and Mrs. Roosevelt, to name only two other literary people, have published a book in the past year; and to realize that they, who are really busy, can do it, while we, who seldom have anything pressing on hand, cannot, is extremely discouraging."[49]

White's discontent became even more apparent the following year when he published a collection of his *New Yorker* "casuals" titled *Every Day Is Saturday*, in which he revealed for the first time that he was the writer of the magazine's unsigned "Notes and Comment." The success of the book, the relief at having broken his anonymity, and his desire to write something more lasting and substantial than the "few rather precise little paragraphs" that made up "Notes and Comment" each week led him to ask Ross if he could write a signed column instead in the front of the magazine. Ross refused, arguing that it would disrupt the magazine and that the prestige of the magazine resided in its use of the editorial "we," a conceit that he said lent White's paragraphs more weight than they would have as the spouting of an individual. The only concessions White was able to win were the promise of a masthead (on which Ross never delivered) and the right to pick the order in which his anonymous paragraphs appeared. This latter did allow White to occasionally assemble a kind of miniessay made up of loosely connected, but self-standing, paragraphs.[50]

White did not like the strictures Ross was enforcing, and he shared his feelings in a letter to Lobrano that fall: "It is almost impossible to write anything decent using the editorial 'we,' unless you are the Dionne family. Anonymity, plus the 'we,' gives a writer a cloak of dishonesty, and he finds himself going around, like a masked reveler at a ball, kissing all the pretty girls."[51]

Another costume he donned was that of Eustace Tilley, the imaginary Regency dandy in top hat and monocle who graced the *New Yorker*'s first cover (and has continued to appear there every year on Valentine's Day, the magazine's anniversary).[52] That February White's conflicted feelings toward the magazine were evident in the eighth anniversary issue: "What the changing times will do to Comrade Tilley's rather formal hat, for which he still feels a sentimental though embarrassed attachment, is a matter of conjecture. Already it shows the dents of rioting."[53] This kind of irony did not satisfy Ralph Ingersoll, an old friend and former colleague of White's at the *New Yorker*, who, in August 1934, published a twenty-page exposé of the *New Yorker* in *Fortune*, the Luce business magazine he was then editing.

In 1929 Ingersoll had left the *New Yorker*, where he had been Ross's managing editor, to help his Yale friend Henry Luce launch *Fortune*. He pulled together a staff of liberal Ivy Leaguers that included Archibald MacLeish, James Agee, and Dwight Macdonald. The first issue of *Fortune* appeared in February 1930, four months after Wall Street had crashed. It would seem an inauspicious time to debut a magazine focused on American business, but Luce and Ingersoll soon found a successful formula. *Fortune* offered a mix of muckraking and hagiography that in the end celebrated corporate liberalism. The magazine criticized both Hoover and Roosevelt, spiced respectful profiles of business leaders with critiques of their businesses, and wrapped it all in a distinctive set of heroic, sentimental illustrations and photographs that several critics have dubbed *capitalist realism*.[54] Of *Fortune* photographer Margaret Bourke-White, Macdonald said, "She made even machines look sexy." As Macdonald later put it, "Luce was divided between his pro-business convictions and his journalistic instinct which told him the CIO was news and that the wonders of American Cyanamid Co. weren't. He compromised (as did we) and for a few years *Fortune* was a pastiche of mildly liberal articles on 'social' themes and reluctantly written 'corporation pieces.'"[55]

Ingersoll's critique of the *New Yorker* was among the mildly liberal articles to which Macdonald refers and served as a model for a more rigorous piece Macdonald published three years later in the *Partisan Review*. Ingersoll's piece honed in on important issues White had already begun to mull but was also personal, petty, inconsistent, and sometimes hypocritical. Ingersoll was himself from society—a product of Hotchkiss and Yale. His family had been producing ambassadors and governors for a century, but he was a relative newcomer to leftist politics, though about to begin an affair with Lillian Hellman who would lead him toward the Communist Party. He had helped create the *New Yorker*'s

"Talk of the Town" section, but now he criticized the Whites for the magazine's fuzzy politics: "If you complain that *The New Yorker* has become gentler and gentler, more nebulous, less real, it is the Whites' doing: Andy's gossamer writing—in his increasingly important 'Notes and Comment,' in his flavoring of the whole magazine with captions and fillers—Katharine's buying and editing, her steady civilizing influence on Ross himself." The backhanded compliments continued when Ingersoll declared, "Thurber and White are the soul of *The New Yorker*," but "the White whimsey is barbed rather than soppy. No fairy slapping of the wrists, he is a Fidel La Barba punching beautiful little blows."[56] La Barba may have been world champion, but he was a flyweight; White may be barbed and beautiful (though not homosexual), but he is merely whimsical.

White had his own doubts about the lightness of the blows Ingersoll was landing. What angered him was the fact that Ingersoll, so instrumental himself in creating the *New Yorker*, exposed him as the writer of "Notes and Comment" (*Every Day Is Saturday* would not be out for two more months) in an unsigned article and that Ingersoll, himself a silk-stocking proletarian, should speculate so publicly about the salaries and stock options of the magazine's editors and staff.[57]

Ingersoll's piece prompted a feud between Ross and Luce that went on for years. It included a famous 1936 *New Yorker* profile by Wolcott Gibbs in which he savaged Luce and his magazines, using "Timespeak" to do it. He mocked *Time*'s penchant for epithets and "maddening coagulations" such as "beady-eyed," "snaggle-toothed," "cinemaddict," and "radiorator," and especially its use of inversion: "Backward ran sentences until reeled the mind. . . . Where it all will end, knows God!" But, as noted, Ross had his own quirks—his dogmatic adherence to the editorial "we" and an inordinate love of the comma, serial and otherwise, both of which White found irritating. As he put it later in an interview with the *Paris Review*, "Commas in *The New Yorker* fall with the precision of knives in a circus act, outlining the victim."[58]

Luce responded to the Gibbs profile by commissioning caricaturist Al Hirschfeld to draw the mustachioed Ross as Joseph Stalin. White, however, entered the fray only to land a single-sentence punch. A "gossip note" in his August 18 "Notes and Comment" asserted, "The editor of *Fortune Magazine* makes thirty dollars a week and carfare."[59]

A PLEBISCITE ON THE ESSAY

While White was lying low, the decades-old debate over the essay was heating up again. In December, Canby and the editors of the *Saturday Review* published an uncompromising defense of the genteel essay that prompted a tremendous backlash. Oddly, they picked Katharine Fullerton Gerould to make the case. Gerould was an accomplished short story writer and essayist, but politically and culturally she was intensely conservative. As early as 1920 she had blamed the "extirpation of culture" in America on "the increased hold of the democratic fallacy on the public mind" and on immigration policies that had led to an "influx of a racially and socially inferior population." In 1926 she published an article in *Harper's* titled "The Plight of the Genteel" in which she linked the continued existence of genteel culture with the very preservation of "civilization."[60] Such positions were widely challenged even in the twenties, but by 1934, with the advent of the Popular Front, they were becoming anathema.

In the *Review*'s year-end issue, Gerould reiterated some old arguments. She quoted *Saturday Review* assistant editor Amy Loveman, who in 1930 had echoed Woolf echoing Stephen: "The pace of the time is too swift for the essayist, and the temper of the public too impatient." The new writing, Gerould worried, "is so much of and for the moment that it cannot hope to be valid for more than a moment." Indirectly, she blamed Roosevelt for the public's flagging interest in Lamb, arguing, "The epoch of the New Deal is not an epoch in which people are lured by . . . dissertations on roast pig." The "average reader," she sniffed, craved the inside "dope" and wanted "facts, figures, propaganda, and counter propaganda about" such things as "hogs in Kansas."

Gerould's East Coast snobbishness can be faintly heard in this dismissal of the concerns of Kansas farmers, but it rings louder when she mentions having rented "a cottage from friends, [in which] we found the walls of the study lined with large volumes—bound files of the *Atlantic, Harper's, Scribner's,* and the *Century*" that provided "ample reading for the whole summer." These old magazines possessed "style, quality, [and] literary virtue." To her, the contrast was so stark that "1900 is readable" and "1930 is not." She bemoaned "our new planetary self-consciousness" and asserted that while English magazines make many of the same mistakes as American magazines, their mistakes were "less annoying . . . because the English write better than we do." In an apparent reference to British aestheticism, she added, "We are all hedonists, I suspect; and what I resent is having (outside of bound volumes) nothing but newspapers to read." She closed by calling for a "plebiscite" on the essay, asking her readers if they wanted mere "articles" or the high art of the "essay," if they wanted "news" or the "truth."[61]

She had misjudged her readers. In 1934 most Americans, even the middle-class readers of the *Saturday Review,* did not consider themselves hedonists, were not able to stay a whole summer in a cottage, and could not ignore the news. A few readers agreed with her, but even they acknowledged that the times were against them. Most were outraged. One recalled Gerould's 1920 piece on the extirpation of culture as a reminder of how long she had been indulging in "nostalgia for the good old days" and concluded, "Mrs. Gerould is complacent, slightly irritating. My plebeian vote is in favor of the present and the future against the past." Another wrote, "Middle-class people are going hungry," and "Hitler and his horrors represent something far more pressing, more insistent than the themes which engross Mrs. Gerould." Alfred Dashiell, the managing editor of *Scribner's*, wrote to inform Gerould that "this is not an age of polite letters, and writing has ceased to be the province of the cultured." He had polled his own readers, he said, and only 3 percent of them wanted to return to her kind of essay.[62]

In January and February 1935, the debate filled the letters column of the *Saturday Review*. Then, in the next issue, Canby intervened by publishing an opinion piece of his own as well as a measured historical survey of the essay by literary critic Elizabeth Drew. Drew examined the long history of the essay in order to establish its resilience and identify its essence. That essence, she wrote, lay in the essayist's use of "creative egotism" to "communicate personality." Drew generally stuck to the past (among modern essayists she referred only to Beerbohm), but in her conclusion, which referenced the current scene, she was as grim as Gerould: "The essay does not today satisfy many of the needs which literature does satisfy."[63]

Canby was less pessimistic. Drew's title was "The Lost Art of the Essay"; he called his "The Essay as Barometer." He saw the essay as a "sensitive" instrument, especially responsive to the times. There might not be as many good essays being written as there used to be, he admitted, but "it is not the fault of the essay. . . . [I]t is the time that is out of joint." An essay results from "matured and leisured thought blending with personality and [the] moulding [of] a style." Doing this requires time and tranquillity, something no one possesses in the "trepidant thirties." He added mournfully, "No one discusses immortality on a sinking ship." Times will change, and the essay with its "sensitive needle" will be our best "instrument" for indicating the "end of the world depression," but even then, the essayist will have to convert younger readers who have grown up in a nation that "live[s] on wheels between the morning and evening newspaper" and is losing its "sense of home."[64]

A month later Canby summoned that fragile sense of home when he appeared with Loveman and Morley on a radio program called *An American Fireside*. The three editors pretended to gather in the offices of the *Saturday Review* to put together the magazine's spring book issue. First names, light banter, capsule summaries of books, and anecdotes about behind-the-scenes happenings at the magazine made listeners feel like a part of the magazine's family, gathered together at the (figurative) hearth. At one point, and somewhat disconsolately, Morley asked about a piece on Thomas Wolfe, "What is it, Amy, a critical essay?" "No," she replied reassuringly. "It's a personal sketch."[65]

JOB OFFER

A year after Gerould's plebiscite, in the spring of 1936, White was offered the editorship of the *Saturday Review*. For almost four decades Henry Seidel Canby, the magazine's only editor since its inception in 1924, had been one of the most persistent and energetic advocates of Arnoldian uplift and middlebrow culture in America—first as a professor at Yale, then as a book reviewer, lecturer, editor, biographer, anthologist, grammarian, essayist, critic, and chief of the Book-of-the-Month Club's panel of judges. In 1930, distraught at what he perceived to be the direction of American politics and culture, Canby suffered a nervous breakdown, which prompted a period of reminiscence and reassessment. In the two years prior to White's job offer, Canby had published a memoir of his childhood in Wilmington, Delaware, *The Age of Confidence: Life in the Nineties* (1934), and a study of American higher education rooted in recollections of his years at Yale, *Alma Mater: The Gothic Age of the American College* (1936). Canby's magazine, with its new infusion of Luce and Lamont capital, was also undergoing changes, having recently switched from a newspaper to a quarto format. Canby would stay on as "chairman of the Board of Editors," but had decided to step down as editor.[66]

It was Christopher Morley who wrote White asking if he might be interested in succeeding Canby. White knew all the editors of the *Review* (the offices of both magazines were in the same building on West Forty-fifth Street), but Morley was probably tapped to make the inquiry because he was the magazine's practicing essayist and had published White's early light verse in "The Bowling Green." White knew that he was not, like Canby, either an editor or impresario, but his reply was courteous. He wrote Morley that he liked his magazine very much, but could not edit it because he was "no editor even with a small E" and, on top of that, a "literary defective." His reading of Morley's letter had given him "many a chuckle," he said, for he recognized right off that its "melancholy implication" was "all so plain—casting about for someone who wasn't 'literary,' you thought immediately of ME." He did admit to Morley that he was "hot for a change" and hoped soon to "rearrange my affairs so that I can devote my limited energy & curious talents to the sort of writing nearest to my heart & pen." White's rearranging would take another two years; in the meantime, Bernard DeVoto signed on to edit the *Saturday Review of Literature*.[67]

Three years later, finally feeling that the change had been made and he was going to be able to do the writing he wanted to do, White had a vision of what could have been. One day after lunch at the Seymour Hotel, he sent Katharine the following note:

> Dear Mrs. White ("Tootsie"):
> Lunching alone at the Seymour (Manhattan cocktail, cream of tomato, turkey club sandwich with fried sweets, meringue glacé, and coffee) who do I see but a party of ten, Miss Loveman in charge, arranging, introducing, making all go well, with the Editor of the Review at elbow's point with the beautiful Martha Gellhorn, so blonde, so young, selling so well, and on the other side the Booky Monthy man [Canby] with the dandruff, and other authors, critics, writers, full of anecdote and the #3 luncheon; as literary a sight as you could find all along 45th St., and sitting there alone, with last night's cigar still smouldering in my viscera and today's glace untouched in the hard light, I looked at the happy gathering and said, "There but for the grace of DeVoto, sit I."
> Mr. White[68]

EUSTACE TILLEY'S ABDICATION, 1937

In the spring of 1937 E. B. White did not yet feel so free and clear; in fact, he felt "unhappy and cooped up."[69] He had been writing his paragraphs for "Notes and Comment" for a decade and was tired of it. He had, moreover, battled depression off and on his whole life, and a recent series of personal losses had added to the despair he was feeling about his work. In the previous eighteen months, he had lost both his parents as well as his good friend Clarence Day; his wife, Katharine, had suffered a miscarriage; and James Thurber had remarried and left the *New Yorker* to freelance.

White was a notorious hypochondriac, but now his body began to revolt in serious ways. He suffered from dizzy spells and gastrointestinal problems that he alternately played up or tried to dismiss, though he seemed always to recognize that they were intimately connected to his writing problems. "A writer, detecting signs of decay in his own stuff," he quipped at the time, "secretes internal poisons which would make even a diseased tonsil sit up and take notice." Friends and relatives also took notice. His brother urged him to leave journalism and "find a more monumental medium than a newspaper column." White himself was thinking along the same lines and once again contemplating a leave of absence. He wanted to move everyone to the farm in Maine, but Katharine had been at the magazine even longer than he and was now the fiction editor. If they left New York, she would, as Brendan Gill put it later, be "giving up the best job held by any woman in America."[70] Their young son, Joel, was six and starting school.

White proposed a compromise. He would take a sabbatical, bounce between New York and Maine, and begin something more substantial, though what he did not know. At the end of May, he tried to explain himself in a long letter to Katharine but was obviously conflicted. "In the main, my plan is to have none," he confessed. ". . . I am quitting my job. In a sense, I am quitting my family—which is a much more serious matter, and which is why I am writing this letter." In a postscript, he warned, "You let yourself in for this, marrying a man who is supposed to write something, even though he never does." In a second postscript, he suggested that a reply "would be a drain on your valuable time." Finally, he expressed his willingness to "argue the whole matter out if it fails to meet with your approval or pleasure."[71]

Apparently, the nonplan met with her approval (though perhaps not her pleasure), and White left for Maine, spending much of August tooling along the coast in his thirty-foot sailboat, the *Astrid*. Before shipping out, he mailed in some last pieces to the *New Yorker*. In one he bid New York farewell and went public, after a fashion, with his plans. His valedictory took the form of a mock profile of Eustace Tilley, in which White tries on a Crayon- or Elia-like persona. The piece is sly and revealing. White had his alter ego feeling caught between the city and the country, between a genteel past and a modern present, between high literary culture and the buzzing mass media.

"We looked up Mr. Eustace Tilley this week," the piece began, "on the eve of his departure from the city—his 'maiden' departure as he pointed out." The interviewer (once again, that weaselly "we") surveyed Tilley's room at the Plaza: "Everywhere, scattered about the place, were grim reminders of his genteel background: a cold bottle of Tavel on the lowboy, a spray of pinks in a cut-glass bowl, an album held with a silver clasp, and his social-security card copied in needlepoint and framed on the wall." Like White himself (and later, White's intrepid mouse-boy, Stuart Little), Tilley escapes this safe gentility by heading north. Up there, says Tilley, he hopes to find "the time to examine" such items as "the new Knopf book about a man who had a good time" as well as "Hitler's ban on all art that he doesn't understand," and "to hear again the wildest sound in all the world." The interviewer supposes that this last comment refers to the howl of "timber wolves" but is promptly set straight: "'I mean cockcrow,' snapped Tilley, who by this time was becoming visibly agitated."[72]

Whether Tilley fared well or not we never learn, but White's own trip was a bust. He did not—not yet—confront Hitler or find the Thoreauvian wakefulness he sought. Instead, he spent twelve days on the sailboat (half of them fogbound), visited his boyhood home, wrote a painful six-part poem about a midlife crisis (which he stuck in a drawer), and finally limped home to Katharine and New York. In retrospect, he referred to the fall and winter of 1937, when he went off to Maine, as his "abdication."[73]

Having found out that White was puttering about in Maine, Thurber scolded him in a long letter from France: "You may be a writer in farmer's clothing but you are still a writer. . . . This is not a time for writers to escape to their sailboats and their farms. What we need is writers who deal with the individual plight. . . . You are not the writer who should think that he is not a writer." By the time White could muster a reply, he was back in Manhattan though still in a funk. He wrote Thurber that he *might* be a writer, but if so, he was "the second most inactive writer living, and the third most discouraged." Yes, he agreed, "the individual plight is the thing." Twice recently he had been convinced again of that—first while he sat with his mother as she died of cancer and second while watching his young son stand in front of a meeting room full of people and recite the 117th Psalm at a school pageant. He wanted to celebrate such struggles and write something that lasted, but he worried that all he had in him were the snickering bits he wrote for "Notes and Comment": "You spend your days chuckling at the obstinacies of French waiters and Italian cooks, but always knowing that much of life is insupportable and that no individual play can have a happy ending." He promised he would keep "groping toward something which will express all this in a burst of choir music," but he was not sure he could pull it off. "Today with the radio yammering at you and the movies turning all human emotions into cup custard, the going is tough. Or I find it tough."[74]

The going *had* been tough, but, as White knew, not as tough on him it had been for most Americans. In the spring of 1937, the New Deal was working and recovery had begun, but times were still bad. Unemployment was half of what it had been at the worst moment of the Depression—March 1933—but 7.7 million, or 14.3 percent of the civilian workforce, were still jobless.[75]

DWIGHT MACDONALD'S LEFTIST CRITIQUE
OF THE *NEW YORKER*

By late 1937, as White was limping home from his abdication and trying to figure out what to do next, Dwight Macdonald criticized the political quiescence of White and the *New Yorker*. The article, titled "Laugh and Lie Down," was his first for the *Partisan Review* and kicked off a decades-long war waged by the New York intellectuals against middlebrow culture. The next few years would see similar pieces in various magazines by Lionel Trilling, Stanley Edgar Hyman, and Robert Warshow.[76] In Macdonald's piece one finds, in nascent form, criticisms that will become familiar. Middlebrow culture is ultimately prudish and anti-intellectual. It is symptomatic of a mass culture that degrades us all. It simplifies and commercializes. It forsakes the modernist critique and the risky difficulty of the avant-garde and, by so doing, serves the interests of the ruling class. And for Macdonald it all started with the *New Yorker*:

> More persistently than any other American magazine the *New Yorker* has exploited a distinctive attitude towards modern life. The typical *New Yorker* writer has given up the struggle to make sense out of a world which daily grows more complicated. His stock of data is strictly limited to the inconsequential. His *Weltanschauung*—a term which would greatly irritate him—is the crudest sort of philistine "common sense." But unlike most exponents of "common sense," the *New Yorker* type is spectacularly incompetent in the practical affairs of everyday life. He is abashed by machines, easily dominated by extraverts, incapable of making out an income tax return, in constant difficulties with the gas company, his landlord, and The State. Out of these limitations the *New Yorker* extracts its peculiar kind of humor: the humor of the inadequate.

Macdonald is after the Little Man here, a type that, for him, represents a retreat from thought, competence, Europe, and political engagement. White would have agreed, at least in part. He too was frustrated with the humor of the inadequate, the claustrophobic paragraphs of "Notes and Comment," the quips about waiters and cooks, and the preciousness of Eustace Tilley, but he remained committed to the individual plight. He might joke about not being literary, but he was also tired of playing dumb and would have heard the sneer in Macdonald's use of "philistine" and *"Weltanschauung."*

According to Macdonald, American humor in the nineteenth century celebrated frontier independence and native know-how. Cornpone humorists joined prairie politicians in making fun of city slickers and challenging the moneyed interests of the East, but World War I "destroyed the populist position in humor as in politics." After the war the economy boomed, America became a player on the world stage, and New York emerged as the center of things. As a result, "Populist humor gave way to sophisticated humor; Petroleum V. Nasby yielded to Robert Benchley." In this changing climate, argued Macdonald, Americans looked toward two places for a new, more cosmopolitan humor: first, to Mencken, with his learning and his ready dismissal of "Methodists," the booboisie, and the Sahara of the Bozarts, and then, to the arch wits of the Algonquin Round Table. The *New Yorker,* Macdonald claims, "was established to exploit commercially" the "sophisticated readers" who were drawn to one or both of these kinds of humor. What he did not realize was that White found Mencken too strident and cynical, and the Algonquin Wits too arch and cute, and so was looking for new models in Thoreau and Montaigne.

Macdonald's analysis emphasized the tension between urbanism and provincialism, and because he sided with high European culture and associated it with cosmopolitan New York, he dismissed America's other traditions. Though critical of *New Yorker* humor for having lapsed into ineffectual bumbling, Macdonald preferred the snipes of the Algonquins and Mencken's scorn to the cracker-barrel irony of the West, which, for him, was not just simple and unsophisticated but also backward and reactionary. He conflated populism, for instance, with Bryan and fundamentalism: "Bryan was the personal symbol of all that was most hateful and absurd to the East."[77] Though seeming to be objective, Macdonald ignores the West's more progressive movements: the Grange, the Wobblies, Minnesota's Farmer-Labor Party, La Follette's Progressives.

He was not alone. During the thirties New York intellectuals and party functionaries consistently condescended to the writing of the fellow travelers they called "proletarian regionalists," often conflating it with the nostalgic and racist regionalism of the Agrarians. In a 1933 *New Republic* article titled "The Significance of Sections," Constance Rourke answered the New York leftists and criticized them for ignoring the rest of the country: "Even if the revolution starts in a ten-floor loft in New York, or in the textile mills of a Southern village or a plant on the River Rouge, a knowledge of these regional differences would seem essential for the enterprise of initiating class struggle on an broad scale."[78] In *American Humor: A Study in the National Character* (1931), Rourke had already gone beyond Macdonald's two types—adding the blackface minstrel to the Yankee peddler and backwoodsman as distinctly American types—and argued that these types might offer models of critique and possibility even New Yorkers could learn from.

Macdonald's own provincialism led him to valorize "the humor" generated by the "intelligentsia of the big cities" and announce it as superior to that of the provinces. He approved, for instance, of the *New Yorker*'s joining Mencken early on to expose the Scopes affair, a move that he saw as having helped the magazine survive its first years and establish itself in the city and suburbs, but then came the Crash and with it, he believed, much backsliding. At first, the *New Yorker* felt a need, whether moral or strategic, to separate itself from "Big Business," but the separation was incomplete. The "honeymoon with the oligarchy" might now be over, but "the marriage has not been disolved [*sic*]." By aiming some of its satire away from the provinces and toward Wall Street, and softening its critique of the West, the *New Yorker* increased its national readership, but the trade-off was that the "brash Menckenians and the aggressively sophisticated Algonquins have been superseded by the timorous and bewildered Thurber." Macdonald suggested that this creeping temerity made it easier for the magazine to acquire, even during the Depression, advertisements for furs, liquor, luxury cars, and lavish vacations. He was probably right. The magazine's annual advertising income did increase more than sixtyfold between 1925 and 1934, but the *New Yorker* had always been a middle-class magazine, and Macdonald's attempt to rewrite the history of its early years led him into dogmatism. Of the *New Yorker*'s recent fiction, for instance, he wrote, "Poverty is suggested rather than bluntly described, and their underdogs are drawn, not from the proletariat, whose sufferings are meaningful and hence tragic, but rather from the ranks of the declassed." These stories (edited by Katharine White) were certainly not examples of socialist realism, but the proletariat never had a monopoly on the "meaningful" or "tragic," and it is Macdonald's romanticizing of the working class that led him to say that it did.

Macdonald also linked political nerve to sexual daring. According to him, "The *New Yorker* is the last of the great family journals. Its inhibitions stretch from sex to the class struggle. It can be read aloud in mixed company without calling a blush to the cheek of the most virtuous banker." The complaint was familiar (it echoed, for instance, Sinclair Lewis's indictment of "tea-table gentility" in his 1930 Nobel Prize address) but also facile.[79] Macdonald's rhetoric smacked of Village bohemianism, and the apocalyptic certainty of a phrase like "last of the great family journals" suggested an ultraleft belief in capitalism's imminent demise.

6

Leaving the *New Yorker*

Though capitalism was more resilient than Macdonald thought, 1937 did find it in crisis. The year opened with the Flint sit-down strike, which was followed by waves of strike activity in both auto and steel. The United Auto Workers, which had recently bolted from the American Federation of Labor to join the Congress of Industrial Organizations (CIO), won a great victory at Flint on February 11. After occupying their plant for forty-four days, workers there finally signed an agreement with General Motors that recognized the UAW and won major improvements in wages, hours, and working conditions. A week later 63,000 workers struck Chrysler (two-thirds of them using the sit-down tactic) and quickly won a contract.[1] UAW membership jumped from about 60,000 to 150,000 that spring, and the Communist-led CIO doubled its membership to approximately 3 million that year.[2]

By late spring, however, labor strife grew bloody, and capital regained the offensive. Police killed ten workers and wounded one hundred in the Memorial Day Massacre outside a Republic Steel plant in Chicago, and over the next few weeks thirteen more workers were killed during strikes in six states as "Little Steel" held off the Steel Workers Organizing Committee and Ford defeated the UAW. On the cultural front Paramount suppressed newsreel footage of the Memorial Day Massacre, and the Works Progress Administration shut down a production of Marc Blitzstein's radical opera about the steel struggle, *The Cradle Will Rock*.[3] This was the background against which White abdicated and Macdonald wrote.

At the same time, Roosevelt began to miscalculate and overreach. In November 1936 he had won reelection in a landslide, beating Alf Landon in every state except Maine and Vermont and taking the Electoral College 503 to 8. He took his victory as a mandate to expand and consolidate the New Deal.

In early February he shocked Congress, the nation, and even some of his close advisers by proposing to alter permanently the federal court system, including the Supreme Court, by appointing an additional judge for every sitting judge over the age of seventy who refused to retire. Practically, this meant an immediate expansion of the Supreme Court from nine to fifteen. Opponents quickly decried his "court-packing" plan as a threat to the balance of powers.

At first Roosevelt fought back. In March he delivered a fiery "victory dinner" speech to supporters at the Mayflower Hotel, arguing that "the field will not be plowed" if he could not drive all three "horses" of the federal government. He attacked his opponents as "economic royalists," raised the specter of communism ("If we do not have the courage to lead the American people where they want to go, someone else will"), and closed by yelling "Now!" after eight bits of evidence that made this specter real (for example, "Here are strikes more far-reaching than we have ever known, costing millions of dollars—now!").[4]

Roosevelt's hubris riled White. In his next "Notes and Comment" he criticized the president's speech:

> This is balderdash. The opposition to his plan to bring the judiciary into line is from people who care not about their property, their profits, and their old Lincoln limousines, but who care about their freedom from authority—which was what started the first big doings in this country and may well start the last. We ourself applauded Mr. Roosevelt's program four years ago, but we decline to follow a leader, however high-minded, who proposes to take charge of affairs because he thinks he knows all the answers. Mr. Roosevelt is not ambitious personally, but he has turned into an Eagle Scout whose passion for doing the country a good turn every day has at last got out of hand. His "Now" remarks were a giveaway—the utterances of a petulant saviour. America doesn't need to be saved today; it can wait till tomorrow. Meanwhile, Mister, we'll sleep on it.[5]

The Left, tolerating no delay, focused on White's conclusion. Ingersoll thought the piece was "well turned," but hated its "gentle complacency." Macdonald dismissed it as "quite badly written," another example of the *New Yorker*'s refusal "to recognize the existence of wars, strikes, and revolution." The mainstream press was more sympathetic. Luce's *Time* identified White as the author of the piece and argued that this "unusually earnest thrust from the White rapier in a *New Yorker* paragraph . . . gave the President and his court plan a pinking far more effective than the bludgeonings of his customarily solemn critics."[6]

White was becoming clearer about what he would need to do to resolve the tensions he had been feeling. He preferred a lighter touch and disagreed with Roosevelt's podium banging and the serious certainty of the Left, but his *New Yorker* paragraphs still felt too light. Macdonald probably had bigger things in mind when he criticized the writing, but it was the phony editorial "we" that disturbed White: "Once in a while, we think of ourself as 'we,' but not often. The word 'ourself' is the giveaway, the plural 'our,' the singular 'self,'—united in a common cause."[7] Something had to give. He was upset that *Time* had revealed him as the writer of the court piece but ashamed of the anonymity the *New Yorker*'s "we" provided; he was not a joiner but was loyal to Ross; he was tired of easy amiability but unwilling to turn shrill.

As White mulled these contradictions during the summer of 1937, Roosevelt was forced to back away from his court plan. Chief Justice Charles Evans Hughes spoke out against it, public support evaporated, and in July the plan's main backer in the Senate, Joseph Robinson of Arkansas, died unexpectedly. Roosevelt's problems were compounded when the economic recovery screeched to a halt. Conservatives of both parties had joined to cut spending, the Federal Reserve raised the discount rate, and Roosevelt's attack on the "economic royalists" scared Wall Street. The economy fell into the "Roosevelt recession." In just a few months industrial production fell 40 percent, stock prices dropped 48 percent, and unemployment jumped from 14.3 to 19.1 percent. Hitler had recently invaded the Rhineland, the Spanish civil war was raging, and now Germany ended the Treaty of Versailles in order to back Japan's invasion of China. Roosevelt had been edging toward more international involvement, but now the recession strengthened the isolationists in Congress and he had to reverse his field, even though Eleanor, who was forsaking pacifism for antifascism, was pressuring him not to.[8]

White, however, did not feel sorry for Roosevelt. As he put it to Thurber:

> The two happiest people in America are Benchley and Franklin Roosevelt. Benchley's high spirits are those of a retired reformer, who got all his good deeds behind him safely in his twenties. . . . Roosevelt is happy because it has never occurred to him that he really doesn't understand what's wrong with things anymore than anyone else does. He is in gales of laughter most of the time. . . . Maybe I could write a piece entitled "What's So Funny?", in which I ask the President what the hell he is grinning about. But the likelihood is I won't.

The paragraph continued with his mourning the recent death of Marquis, "one of the saddest people of our generation."[9] White was unhappy and disenchanted, though not finally with New York and the *New Yorker*. As he admitted later, "I was probably disenchanted with *me*."

But with the coming of spring, having resolved again to do important work, he finally convinced Katharine to leave New York, maintain tenuous ties to the *New Yorker,* and move to Maine. That summer, two days before actually leading his "little family out of the city like a daft piper," the editor of *Harper's* invited him to lunch and offered him a signed monthly column of twenty-five hundred words. White accepted on the spot. "I was a man in search of the first person singular," he recalled, "and lo, here it was—handed to me on a platter before I even left town."[10]

ONE MAN'S MEAT:
HITLER, HOGS, AND ENCHANTMENT

Alluding to Lucretius and invoking the essay's tradition of liberal skepticism, White called his column "One Man's Meat." It debuted in October 1938 after a summer of advertising and proved immediately successful. Within three weeks *Harper's* added 11,200 new subscribers, and newsstand sales jumped 20 percent. According to Robert Root, the columns "established White's reputation as an essayist," and Roger Angell, White's stepson, thought they "were the making of him as a writer."[11]

Longer, more political, and more personal than most of his work for the *New Yorker,* these essays, when they were collected in 1942 and in an enlarged edition in 1944, changed not only the direction of White's career but that of the American essay as well. They helped extricate it from the fifty-year-long debate that, as the reaction to the Gerould plebiscite showed, had become more polarized, strident, and prescriptive than ever—one side arguing that an essay should be gentle, polite, and never polemical, the other calling for increased substance and engagement. Gerould had claimed that the "perfect essayist" might be able to write "a good essay on Hitler or on hogs, and I should be enchanted to read it—but he has not done it yet, and I am not yet enchanted." Forty years later, in the introduction to a new edition of the book, White used Gerould's term to describe that period in his life when he wrote this book that included essays about both Hitler and hogs: "Once in everyone's life there is apt to be a period when he is fully awake, instead of half asleep. I think of those five years in Maine as the time when this happened to me. Confronted by new challenges, surrounded by new acquaintances—including the characters in the barnyard, who were later to reappear in *Charlotte's Web*—I was suddenly seeing, feeling, and listening as a child sees, feels, and listens. It was one of those rare interludes that can never be repeated, a time of enchantment."[12] He is using the term *awake* in a Thoreauvian sense, and it was to Montaigne and Thoreau that he returned for models of honesty and pointedness when writing these essays.

White was distinctly American and had long made Thoreau, not Lamb, his model. Both temperamentally and philosophically, Thoreau was his kinsman. In fact, he seems occasionally to have worried that he might be too far lost in Thoreau. In "The Retort Transcendental," which appears in *The Second Tree from the Corner,* White re-created himself as a Walter Mittyesque little man so infused with Thoreau that his replies to people consist entirely of quotes from *Walden.* Of Thoreau's book White wrote, "Every man, I think, reads one book in his life, and this one is mine."[13] He first read Walden at Cornell, reread it throughout his life, and gave it as a present to at least one of his first girlfriends and later to Katharine. He refers to *Walden* often in his essays and "Notes and Comment" pieces. Early in *One Man's Meat* he wrote an essay about driving from Maine to Concord to visit the pond, casting it in the form of a letter to Thoreau.

White studied the ways in which Thoreau dealt with the problem of how to write in the first-person singular without lapsing into isolation or self-indulgence. White was moving to Maine but did not want to see it solely as a retreat, for he was about to take up battle with the isolationists. Thoreau went to Walden, but while there, he regularly walked the train tracks into town, hosted a runaway slave at his cabin, argued the abolitionist cause at the Concord Lyceum, and visited a poor Irish family at Baker farm. His sojourn at Walden took him deeper into the natural world but also out into society. He was, wrote White one year on the anniversary of Thoreau's death, "torn all his days between two awful pulls—the gnawing desire to change life, and the equally troublesome desire to live it." His genre-defying book, with its chapters at once so self-contained and interconnected, reflects this tension. The book allowed him to move through a range of voices and rhetorical acts wherein his multifaceted self and varied concerns could be revealed. Some may have regarded Thoreau as a "poseur," said White, but it was not so simple as all that: "He was a poseur all right, but the pose was struck not for other people to study but for *him* to study—a brave and ingenious device for a creative person to adopt. He posed for himself and was both artist and model, examining his own position in relation to nature and society with the most patient and appreciative care."[14] This is the model of an essayist White was looking for, the essayist as a concerned and conscientious explorer of both the world and the first-person singular.

Thoreau gave White a way to begin to tackle important and difficult political issues within the form of the personal essay, but there were also significant differences between the two men, and White was keenly aware of them.

At the end of his letter to Thoreau in *One Man's Meat*, he offers an accounting of the expenses incurred during his trip to Walden. He notes $6.20 for hotels, meals, and a pair of walking shoes, and another $1.50 for a baseball bat and glove, "gifts to take back to a boy." The total of these expenses, he tells Thoreau, was "almost what you spent for food for eight months." White admits that he cannot defend expenditures for meals, lodging, and shoes, for "they reveal a meanness and grossness in my nature that you would find contemptible," but he does defend the gifts for his son as a "kind of impediment with which you were never on even terms." He also takes a poke at Thoreau's bachelorhood: "You must remember that the house where you practiced the sort of economy that I respect was haunted only by mice and squirrels. You never had to cope with a shortstop."[15]

By poking fun at Thoreau's extreme solitude and the purity of his positions, White is also making peace with himself, his own middle-class choices, and his readers. White's family and obligations kept him from sounding a note like Thoreau's that was "so pure as to be noncorrupting." Thoreau, wrote White, could write such a "queer" book because, in some sense, "he never really grew up." White, in his adulthood, hoped only for some "rare interlude" when he was for a time "fully awake, instead of half asleep." His own time of enchantment might share some similarities with Thoreau's time at Walden, but even in Maine White lived a conventional domestic life.[16]

In *One Man's Meat*, White also held on to the lighter tones of the colyumnists who had called him to New York in the first place. They had taught him how to speak to his predominately white, middle-class American audience. If he turned to Thoreau (and Montaigne), so also did he rely on Broun, Benchley, and Morley, and in so doing he broadened the range of his voice, experimented with the form of the essay, and wrote both more personally and more polemically. He moved away from the persona of the Little Man that he, Benchley, Broun, and Thurber had developed at the *New Yorker* and that Ingersoll and Macdonald had criticized, but he retained that character's skepticism and humor.

Most important, White took up the battle against isolationism. His first columns ran during the confusing period between Munich and Pearl Harbor, when the Popular Front against fascism was rudderless and on the defensive. For nineteen months, from the signing of the Nazi-Soviet Non-Aggression Pact on August 19, 1939, until Hitler's ill-advised invasion of Russia on June 22, 1941, the Communist Party and its fellow travelers remained silent about the rise of fascism. Socialists like Norman Thomas and pacifists like the War Resisters League allied themselves with conservatives such as Charles Lindbergh, Father Coughlin, and *Chicago Tribune* publisher Col. Robert

McCormick under the umbrella of the isolationist America First Committee. Even anti-Stalinists like Dwight Macdonald and others associated with the *Partisan Review* took an isolationist position. Ostensibly against Nazism, they wrote in an open letter to the magazine, "Our entry into the war under the slogan 'Stop Hitler!' would actually result in the immediate introduction of totalitarianism over here."[17] Isolationist sentiment held sway across the political spectrum until Pearl Harbor. As late as August 1941, an extension of the Selective Service Act passed in the House by a single vote.

White's strategy in the *One Man's Meat* essays consisted of appropriating a form familiar to his readers—the fireside chat—and giving it new weight. Vincent Bertolini has argued that the voice of the genteel essayist as fireside storyteller was often that of the sentimental bachelor uncle in for the holidays, a subjectivity that brought with it a homoerotic subtext, but the voice could also be that of the father, gathering the family at the hearth. When White was writing, Americans were anxious about the Depression and the war, about their homes and homeland, and it was this second voice they wanted to hear. In his essays White drew readers into his own family, referring often to his wife, his son, and their daily lives. He was trying to figure out what was best for his own family in a troubled world, with hopes that it might offer insight to other families as well. In an installment written in June 1940, he pondered the Battle of France, argued America needed to rearm, and, in a technique borrowed from Marquis, interrupted his column with a snippet of mock dialogue: "Voice: How do you know what's good for the people? Stinging Reply: I know what's good for me."[18] The narrator in *One Man's Meat* held clear, decided positions on war and democracy, but was also accessible, funny, and down-to-earth. The balancing act was not unlike the one Roosevelt had been performing for ten years in his radio chats.

During this period White called reluctantly and carefully for intervention, yet deliberate as he was he remained in advance of Roosevelt, or at least in advance of Roosevelt's public positions. In October 1938, in the fifth installment of "One Man's Meat," White criticized Chamberlain's Munich "horse trade," but admitted he had taken to the roof of his barn during the negotiations in order to reshingle and get away from it all. The roof, he said, "seemed a queer place to be during a world crisis," but he added that he was installing a new weathervane that "would show which way the wind blew" and that the roof with its "clarity" and "altitude" might really be "the best place anybody could pick for sitting out a dance with a prime minister and a demigod." He asked rhetorically, "Who has the best view of things, anyway, a prime minister in a closet or a man on a barn roof?" Roosevelt, on the other hand, still felt compelled to send Chamberlain a congratulatory telegram that simply said, "Good man!"[19]

That winter White was trying to deny the inevitable. He wrote his book editors that the "imminence of war . . . seems as illusory and incredible as war itself," and he was "waiting for someone to take me aside and tell me that it isn't true about Austria. But nobody does." In September he expressed annoyance with a houseguest who "approached the war intellectually, through Versailles," but in the evening, "we all sat and chewed," while listening during dinner to the king of England announce Britain's entrance into the war on the radio. "War," White averred, "comes to each of us in his own fashion."[20]

During the winter of 1939 and 1940 he focused on hogs in order to ignore Hitler. "Europe in tatters," he wrote in February, "is something that ought to occupy an honest man's attention, but lately it has seemed too big for me. I prefer to curl up in a comfortable chair with *The Rural New Yorker,*" a husbandman's how-to periodical with advice about livestock and crops. At the first of the year, he wrote that he hoped one day "to have a fireside chat with my government" about the poor prose in the instructions for his tax form.[21] In June, France fell to the Germans, and for White, the war became unavoidable and jokes became harder to come by. Ross had been at him to write something, anything, for the *New Yorker,* but he had put him off even though his contract with *Harper's* allowed it. Now, as the Nazis marched into Paris, White changed his mind. Suddenly, his monthly deadline seemed too slow in coming, and he fired off a comment piece to Ross. The Nazi threat was "total," and our response must be equal to it: "One thing begins to become clear: military defence, pure defence, is no good today. Or, rather, it is not good enough." There must be "total moral resistance" to the Nazis as well. "Democracy," he wrote, "is now asked to mount its honor and decency on wheels, and to manufacture, with all the electric power at its command, a world which can make all people free and perhaps many people contented."[22] It might seem now like a fine point, but the editorial called for "military defence," not military intervention, for rearmament and putting American industry in the service of Great Britain, not deployment of troops. This position anticipated the Lend-Lease Act, which Roosevelt would not propose until the following December in his famous "Arsenal of Democracy" fireside chat. But as qualified and careful as the editorial was, it was still almost too much for the more isolationist Ross, who seems to have printed it only in order to maintain ties with White in hopes that he might one day lure him back from *Harper's.*

For White the piece was a kind of Rubicon, all the more decisive because he made himself write it at an especially difficult time in his life. Two months earlier, in April, Eugene Saxton, his editor at Harper and Brothers, had asked him to write a "primer for American youth" that would make "the case for American democracy and the American way of life." White reluctantly agreed, but after banging away at it for far too long in a New York hotel room, he wrote Saxton to say he was "ill-equipped for the job," could not continue, and was "cracking up, anyway." The problem, he wrote, had to do with himself and with the times: "These are tough days for minor poets and lackwits and we tend to get out of our field."[23] But in June, jostled by the fall of France, he not only sent off the editorial to Ross but also returned to Saxton's young people's pamphlet, salvaging it as an installment of "One Man's Meat" that would prove to be his strongest statement yet about why the battle against fascism must be joined. Because fascism was so irrational and uncompromising, he wrote, "I resent the patronizing air of persons who find in my plain belief in freedom a sign of immaturity."

This freedom in which he believed was two-sided. First, there was the "instinctive freeness" a person "experiences as an animal dweller on a planet," the feeling of freedom that arises from experiencing that "haunting intimation . . . of nature publishing herself through the 'I,'" of nature offering some sort of answer to that fundamental existential question "What is 'I'?"

The second kind of freedom was the one "more generally understood, more widely admired, more violently challenged and discussed." It included the "practical liberties [one] enjoys as a privileged member of human society."

Hitler, wrote White, knows full well that the written word helps keep these practical liberties alive: "The written word, unlike the spoken word, is something every person examines privately and judges calmly by his own intellectual standards, not by what the man standing next to him thinks." White then quoted Hitler, who wrote that "one is able to win people far more by the spoken than by the written word." Finally, Hitler added contemptuously, "Let it be said to all knights of the pen and to all the political dandies, especially of today: the greatest changes in this world have never been brought about by a goose quill! No, the pen has always been reserved to motivate these changes theoretically."[24]

White must have heard in this dismissal of the quill-wielding knights of the pen and political dandies an eerie echo of the antigenteel, anti-intellectual, snidely homophobic attacks on essayists that had recently been made by American leftist literary critics. The most notorious of these attacks was Mike Gold's tirade against Thornton Wilder in the *New Masses* and the *New Republic* during the spring and fall of 1930. Gold attacked Wilder as a "fairylike little Anglo-American curate" who represented a "small sophisticated class that has recently arisen in America—our genteel bourgeoisie." Wilder's writing, he sniffed, is nothing more than "a daydream of homosexual figures in graceful gowns moving archaically among the lilies." Braley had imagined the essay as a rebellious Little Lord Fauntleroy crawling out of the grave, dusting himself off, and chatting with the sexton. Waters had seen the essay as a lavender-scented little old lady who might or might not be passing away. Gold now associated Wilder with some kind of homosexual, vampiric necrophiliac. He is, said Gold, "a beautiful, rouged, combed, well-dressed corpse, lying among the sacred candles and lilies of the past, and sure to stink if exposed to sunlight." Then, lest we miss the connection to the essay, Gold likened Wilder's work to that of Walter Pater, whose style was "so beloved among the fairies of Oxford." This gay bashing was too much even for some of Gold's comrades and fellow travelers. *New Masses* reviewer Joshua Kunitz argued with him in subsequent issues, and Sinclair Lewis wrote in to say that he would reluctantly retain his subscription even though Gold had said, "Walter Pater wrote like a fairy for a fairy."[25]

Pater and Oxford had been under attack by Gold and the Left in 1930, but now Hitler was blitzing all of England. White recognized that an attitude like Hitler's, which led to the burning of books and the censoring of the press, was not unknown in America. Dogmatists of the Left and Right had joined not only to label the essay effete and antiquated but also to defend isolationism. It was this double squeeze that made the moment so dangerous. White's liberal belief in individuality and skeptical thought might seem like a small thing to place against such certainty, but it was what he had. "The least a man can do at such a time," he wrote, "is to declare himself and tell where he stands."[26] It was a step forward from the gentle complacency of which he had been accused by Ingersoll and Macdonald.

During the rest of 1940 and into the summer of 1941, White continued to hone his method of mixing the small with the large, rubbing skepticism against belief, and using his own experience as a way to speak out about the international situation. Even a bit about his dachshunds, Fred and Millie, became an occasion to talk about the open-mindedness of his country neighbors and the growth of tolerance in the country since the time of World War I, when "if a man owned a dachshund he was suspected of being pro-German." In an entry titled "Sanitation," an anecdote about cleaning out his barn and poisoning "mine enemies the rats" was juxtaposed with a note about the "re-Germanizing" of Alsace, where tombstones were being reinscribed in German and men named Henri were now called Heinrich. During a trip to Florida that winter he took an informal poll of his snowbird neighbors about whether "the remaining democracies of the world should unite" (the verdict was four to three in favor). Another column discussed a Florida neighbor who kept foisting isolationist "pamphlets, books, and marked-up newspapers" on the Whites. "She tracks in sand, as well as ideas," wrote White, "and I have to sweep up after her two or three times a day."[27]

During this period he also used his essays to keep in touch, at least indirectly, with the president and first lady. He borrowed the form and title for his June 1941 entry from Mrs. Roosevelt's "My Day" column, acknowledging his debt in the essay's first line. His November 1940 entry discussed a three-ton allotment of lime the government had given him to spread on his fields. He appreciated the grant and used it, but admitted that he felt looked after, a bit less self-sufficient, and even resentful, like "a person who has had a favor done him whether he liked it or not." He still supported the administration, noting that he had just voted for it again, but admitted that he had some qualms about the welfare state and wondered wickedly if the president ever got "any free lime for his Hyde Park place."[28]

One essay from this time especially reveals White's increasing commitment to the struggle against fascism. In his December 1940 essay he departed from the quips and asides of most of his columns and took on the America Firsters in a direct and sustained way. He used the entirety of that month's piece to critique Anne Morrow Lindbergh's *Wave of the Future*. Released that summer, the book had topped the best-seller lists, sold fifty thousand copies in the first two months, and quickly appeared as a *Reader's Digest* condensed book (even though it was only forty-one pages long to begin with). As an acclaimed author, wife of a national hero, and mother whose baby had been kidnapped and murdered, Lindbergh held the attention of many readers, and her humanitarian spin of the isolationist argument tapped into American uncertainty about the war. Gallup polls during the period showed that the overwhelming majority of Americans opposed U.S. entry into the war while simultaneously favoring military aid to Great Britain.[29]

White interwove his case against Lindbergh with a narrative about reading her book in his truck while waiting to see his doctor. He attacked the book's rhetorical tricks and faulty logic, carefully acknowledging where he agreed with her before exposing how she slid into an apology for fascism. He wrote that he did not, like Lindbergh, see democracy as "sick of an incurable disease" and fascism as "the wave of the future," nor did he see Germany as the world's agent of change or resistance to change as "a sin against nature." He did see the future as a complicated work in progress rather than a "unified dream" and democracy as the "most futuristic thing" he had heard of.[30] His deliberate, but impassioned, critique was widely read and quoted, and it helped shift attention away from Lindbergh's celebrity to her argument.

Thirteen years earlier White had discussed a book by Lindbergh's husband in the *New Yorker*. That book, a celebrity autobiography simply entitled *We*, came out immediately after Lucky Lindy's transatlantic flight in 1927, causing some to question its authorship. To answer the doubters his publisher produced samples from a handwritten manuscript. Appreciative of the irony that Lindbergh's title presented to one required to use the editorial "we," White frolicked among the pronouns in his short piece about the book: "In Putnam's window, in Forty-fifth Street, are displayed six pages of manuscript written in longhand by Charles A. Lindbergh, or more properly, "us"— Lindbergh and fountain pen. . . . From the many revisions and fresh starts in the manuscript, we gathered that Lindbergh does not write easily, and we felt a spirit of kinship immediately. . . . Sixty thousand words is what they say it contains. We assume he wrote it in his spare time."[31] White's sly and gentle approach to *We* is in sharp contrast to the unflinching seriousness of his critique of *The Wave of the Future,* but much had changed in the years since Lindbergh's solo flight. Twice the Lindberghs had publicly toured German aircraft production facilities—first in 1936 during the Berlin Olympics and again in 1938, when Hermann Göring, Hitler's second in command, had presented Lindbergh with the Service Cross of the German Eagle. This medal was the highest decoration Germany could bestow on a foreigner and similar to one the Nazis had given Henry Ford two months earlier, apparently in appreciation for his anti-Semitic diatribes in the *Dearborn Independent.*

Lindbergh's tours convinced him not only that the Reich was invincible but also that a German victory was for the best. Lindbergh's supposedly objective analysis of the situation was rooted in racism and anticommunism. The battle was not, as he saw it, between democracy and fascism but between European civilization and the "pressing sea of Yellow, Black, and Brown." To save themselves from "racial suicide," the Western nations must "band together to preserve that most priceless possession, our inheritance of European blood." Aviation was, for him, "almost a gift from heaven to those Western nations who were already the leaders of their era," especially Germany. Because aviation, technology, engineering, and discipline were key, the decadent so-called democracies of France and England should defer to dynamic Germany and its Luftwaffe, for only Germany "can either dam the Asiatic hordes or form the spearhead of their penetration into Europe." Lindbergh claimed, "Our civilization depends . . . on a Western wall of race and arms which can hold back either a Genghis Khan or infiltration of inferior blood." The Russian communists, he believed, were using the black and yellow races to advance their own cause. "Oriental guns are turned westward," he wrote, "Asia presses toward us on the Russian border, all foreign races stir restlessly."[32]

Anne Morrow Lindbergh generally played good cop to her husband's bad cop, but her unity with him was clear. Who, she asked rhetorically, is "the potential invader of Europe, the real threat of European civilization? Ask the Balkan and the Baltic states. Ask Finland; ask Rumania; ask Turkey." With

Europe "bled white by wars and prostrated by devastation," she continued, Russia's "advance will be slow, inevitable, and deadly—like a flow of lava." Hitler and Stalin were just individuals to her. They were secondary, interchangeable, and nothing to fear: "They have felt the wave of the future and they leapt upon it. The evils we deplore in these systems are not in themselves the future; they are scum on the wave of the future."[33]

White could not have disagreed more, but even now in the spring of 1941, at the height of his outrage, he harbored doubts about his strategy for opposing fascism and its apologists, but he used his doubt to fashion one of his most innovative essays. In a piece called simply "Spring," White moved among several sets of associations in thirteen loosely connected sections. What Carl Klaus calls the disjunctiveness of this piece suggests the distracted state of White's mind at the time. The thread that holds the essay together is his desire to reconcile his daily life on his saltwater farm with the rise of fascism. He opens with remarks about his own "doubt" as to whether his "hog has been bred, although she has been keeping company," moves next to a letter he received from a New York librarian about a representative of Superman, Incorporated, visiting the library's children's room, and then turns to how his family is currently reading *Little Women* aloud in the evenings. As Klaus and Robert Scholes have suggested, White's references later in the essay to "the Nazi idea of *Frühling*," the "German spring drive," and the warm air of April in Maine as coming in "not like an invader but like a friend" all point to a recasting of the Superman reference in terms of Hitler's celebration of the Übermensch, which in turn puts a new spin on White's quip in the essay's third section about Alcott as the "author of *Little Supermen* and *Little Superwomen*."[34]

White tried to distract himself from this disturbing conjunction of Hitler and hogs by focusing on his daily chores, especially tending his chickens, but he continued to be haunted by doubts about the value of what he was writing. In his end-of-1940 report, he convinced himself that his chickens supported the war effort and took real pride in the fact that during the previous twelve months he had been able to send 381 dozen eggs to market. It was a small contribution to the war effort, he admitted, but if only he "didn't have to earn a living by writing," he was sure he "could show a profit of a dollar a bird a year" instead of the loss he had just suffered. In darker moments, however, he lost this sense of irony and questioned whether he might be nothing more than "a middle-aged hack" whose "time isn't worth the paper he is not writing anything on." Now, as a wall of flames burned across Europe, he worried that his essays were not a backfire lit against it but instead just small coals glowing in the brooder stove of his henhouse: "In this spring of 1941 a man tends his fire in a trance that is all the deeper because of its dream-like unreality, things being as they are in the world. I sometimes think I am crazy—everyone else fighting and dying or working for some cause or writing to his senator, and me looking after some Barred Rock chickens." Finally, he rallied and claimed the worth of this fireside chat, these essays, these coals in a brooder stove, these incubating eggs: "Countries are ransacked, valleys drenched with blood. Though it seems untimely, I still publish my belief in the egg, the contents of the egg, the warm coal, and the necessity of pursuing whatever fire delights and sustains you."[35]

By June, White's commitment to intervention was so strong it prompted him to send an uncharacteristically harsh letter to Ross, criticizing the *New Yorker*'s wishy-washy style and failure "to say things that need saying." His criticism was sharp, but his use of the first-person plural shows he was not exempting himself: "The war is so damn near that it is no longer possible to use printer's ink in place of blood in a man's circulatory system, and Tilley's hat and butterfly return to plague us all. I couldn't bounce off a paragraph a week on the subject of the war, full of 'we's' and 'us's,' when I wasn't sure what key we were all trying to play in."[36]

The next day, having received a long letter from Ross that expressed genuine confusion on what road to take, White wrote back, softening his tone a bit and admitting, "I am as bewildered as anybody else." He acknowledged that his decision to take a clear and public position on the war was a move away from the Montaignean skepticism he always believed a good essayist should maintain, but given present circumstances, what else could he do? "Sometimes this 'moral' frame seems incompatible, or inconsistent, with skepticism. A skeptic doesn't like to believe anything, for fear it will ruin his intelligence (or his backhand drive), and on the other hand, a believer can't be too skeptical or it affects his faith. That is why everybody is all mixed up."[37] Though White was constitutionally a skeptic, he had never been (and certainly was not now) as apolitical as Ross, and he was becoming more politically committed by the day.

THE FOUR FREEDOMS

White's defense of democracy and his criticism of the isolationist position, especially his critique of Lindbergh's book, had not gone unnoticed in Washington.

The Roosevelt administration had wanted to take the Lindberghs on more directly for more than a year, but proisolation sentiment prevented it. On

May 16, 1940, before a joint session of Congress, Roosevelt called for the government to build fifty thousand military aircraft. Two days later, in a nationwide radio address, Charles Lindbergh countered that the country "must stop this hysterical chatter of calamity and invasion that has been running rife these last few days." He argued, "Our danger in America is an internal danger." We should not be "meddling with affairs abroad," he claimed, but a "small minority" who unfortunately "control much of the machinery of influence and propaganda" was pushing intervention. The usually unruffled Roosevelt was livid but did not want to express his anger publicly. Over lunch the day after Lindbergh's speech, he told Secretary of the Treasury Henry Morgenthau Jr., "If I should die tomorrow, I want you to know this. I am convinced Lindbergh is a Nazi." A day later, in a letter to Henry Stimson (whom he was about to appoint secretary of war), he wrote, "When I read Lindbergh's speech I felt that it could not have been better put if it had been written by Goebbels himself."[38]

During the presidential campaign that summer and fall, neither Roosevelt nor Republican nominee Wendell Willkie took a full interventionist stand, though Willkie expressed strong support for Britain. Roosevelt felt vulnerable because of anti–third term sentiment and the growing influence of America First, which claimed 450 chapters and almost eight hundred thousand members. As the campaign wound down, he was ahead, but Willkie was rising in the polls. Roosevelt's advisers worried that opposition to America's first peacetime conscription, set to begin with a Selective Service lottery on October 29, might enable Willkie to close the gap. The president was worried, too. He had been finishing his stump speech by promising American families, "Your boys are not going to be sent into any foreign wars, except in cases of attack." The next day in Boston, he grabbed the headlines by dropping the final qualifying phrase. He rationalized that it was no longer necessary but also hoped the deletion might give him a tactical advantage.[39]

It did. After beating Willkie by almost 5 million votes and 449 to 82 in the Electoral College, Roosevelt felt emboldened to go after the isolationists. In his January 6 State of the Union address, later called the "Four Freedoms" speech, he introduced an ideological justification for war: a defense of the freedoms of speech and religion and the freedoms from want and fear. After he listed each freedom he added that it should be established "everywhere in the world," which the isolationists saw as imperialistic and overreaching. Even liberal supporters of the administration complained that Roosevelt was using the war as a pretext for expanding the New Deal worldwide. Robert Maynard Hutchins, president of the University of Chicago, claimed the speech was overly ambitious and a recipe for "perpetual war." Senator

Robert La Follette Jr. said, "I urge that we make the 'four freedoms' prevail in America before we try to ram them down the throats of people everywhere in the world."[40]

Two weeks later in his third inaugural address, Roosevelt and his speech-writer, the poet, playwright, and former *Fortune* editor Archibald MacLeish, upped the ante again, taking a not-so-subtle jab at the Lindberghs and their ilk, by calling them unpatriotic defeatists: "There are men who believe democracy as a form of government and a frame of life is limited or measured by a kind of mystical and artificial fate—and that, for some unexplained reason, tyranny and slavery have become the surging wave of the future and freedom is an ebbing tide. But we Americans know this is not true."[41]

There were also disagreements among interventionists about what America's goals should be in the war. Immediately after Roosevelt's inauguration, in the February 17, 1941, issue of *Life,* Henry Luce published his famous "American Century" article. Luce argued for a different kind of alliance with Great Britain than the one proposed by Roosevelt. America should act, as he put it, like a "Good Samaritan," but it must also take advantage of the war. "We must accept whole-heartedly our duty and our opportunity," he wrote, "as the most powerful and vital nation in the world and in consequence to exert upon the world the full impact of our influence, for such purposes as we see fit and by such means as we see fit." Luce's view was in opposition to Roosevelt's idea of Lend-Lease, which would establish a much more equal relationship with Britain and the Allies than what Luce was proposing. The administration and its supporters quickly challenged Luce's notion of American superiority. In April Max Lerner called in the *New Republic* for a "people's century" and "a federation of nations" that would promote democracy both during and after the war.[42]

During the early spring of 1941, while White was tending his brooder stove and writing about his belief in the egg, the Nazis took Greece, Yugoslavia, and Crete, and Rommel swept across Libya. Roosevelt lobbied Congress (with Willkie's help) to pass the Lend-Lease Act; Lindbergh testified against it in both houses. On March 11, after two months of debate, the Senate voted 60 to 31 and the House 317 to 71 to pass an amended version of Lend-Lease. The worsening situation in Europe played a role in getting the necessary support, but so did Roosevelt's use of analogy. Former Algonquin Robert Sherwood, now a Pulitzer Prize–winning playwright and Roosevelt speechwriter, claimed Roosevelt won the Lend-Lease battle when he likened the loans of matériel to Britain and the Allies to lending your neighbor a garden hose when his house is on fire. If the fire is about to spread to your house, you don't dicker about how much the hose is worth or when you will get it back.[43]

The Lend-Lease victory enabled Roosevelt and his aides to criticize Lindbergh even more aggressively. Interior Secretary Harold Ickes led the charge. In early April he called Lindbergh "America's number one Nazi fellow traveler" and *The Wave of the Future* the "Bible of every American Nazi, Fascist, Bundist and appeaser." When those remarks received support from the public and the press, Roosevelt himself, supposedly speaking off the cuff at a news conference, explained that he could not call Lindbergh up for active duty because he was a "Vallandingham." Roosevelt explained that Ohio congressman Clement L. Vallandingham had been a leading Copperhead, or Northern supporter of the South during the Civil War. The president continued the history lesson by reminding the reporters that there had also been "appeasers at Valley Forge" who pleaded with Washington to quit. Finally, he suggested they reread Thomas Paine, who had written about "the summer soldier and sunshine patriot" who failed America during the "times that try men's souls." It was a calculated risk—to call an American hero a traitor— and the right kind of outrage on Lindbergh's part might have turned opinion his way, but Lindbergh rose to the bait instead. In a huff, he resigned from the Army Air Corps, an act most people viewed as a petulant shirking of duty.[44]

Over the summer, as Roosevelt lay low and White went fishing at a lake with his ten-year-old son, Lindbergh grew more and more obsessed with the president. At a May 23 America First rally in Madison Square Garden, he declared that Americans had as much choice in the 1940 election "as the Germans would have been given if Hitler had run against Göring." When Hitler invaded Russia in July, Roosevelt extended Lend-Lease to the Soviet Union. This decision confirmed for Lindbergh what he had thought all along—that Roosevelt meant to let the German bulwark crumble so communist and Asiatic hordes could overrun Europe. At the end of the summer, he announced that America faced three main dangers: Roosevelt, Britain, and the Jews. The Jews were the "greatest danger" because of "their large ownership and influence in our motion pictures, our press, our radio, and our government." Finally, he warned the country that "we are about to enter a dictatorship" and the "only danger to us is from within."[45]

Then came Pearl Harbor. America First disbanded four days later, and Lindbergh asked to reenlist in the Air Corps. Secretary Stimson, on orders from Roosevelt, personally refused Lindbergh, deeming him untrustworthy. The Lone Eagle spent the war years as a consultant for Ford Motor Company and test pilot for United Aircraft.

In contrast, the administration recruited White to help with the war effort immediately after Pearl Harbor. MacLeish, now director of the innocuously named Office of Facts and Figures in Washington, D.C., and acting on the advice of his assistant, John Fleming, asked White to help create a pamphlet on the Four Freedoms. The pamphlet, the president had stipulated, was to be prepared "for the widest possible distribution." When White agreed to the request, Fleming, an old friend from Cornell, followed up with a note telling White that everyone in Washington was "enormously pleased."[46] MacLeish and Fleming picked White because of his past unity with the administration, but also because he had demonstrated he could write quickly and clearly for the wide audience they sought.

White turned out to be the right man for the job, though at first when faced with the abstract and contentious conversation of his more intellectual cow-riters—Malcolm Cowley, Max Lerner, and Reinhold Niebuhr—he felt as if he were in over his head. Fleming quickly and quietly lent White his support. Sensing that the pamphlet could be undone by too much intellectualizing, he convinced MacLeish to put White in charge of rewriting the whole thing rather than just drafting the freedom-of-speech section as they had originally planned. White wrote Katharine from Washington that he would now have to boil down the "forbidding and dreary" prose of the others so that the pamphlet could do what it was supposed to do: "instruct and inspire filling station helpers and manicurists" and "explain to a great many young men why they are about to get stuck in the stomach."[47]

Weary of Washington and eager to get back to Maine, White rewrote the pamphlet in three weeks and turned in a final draft at the end of February, but he found the work hard. "It is always sobering," he wrote Katharine, "to encounter the intellectual idealists at work, for they seem to live in a realm of their own, making their plans for the world in much the same way that any common tyrant does." The finished pamphlet, of which four hundred thousand copies were issued, earned him wide respect in Washington. A month later in a New Yorker editorial he called for the federal information bureaus to be consolidated in a single agency under the leadership of radio newsman Elmer Davis.[48] On June 13 Roosevelt did exactly that, establishing the Office of War Information, with Davis as director.

The consolidation did not go smoothly. From the outset, conflicting interests pulled the OWI in different directions. The racism, anti-Semitism, and anti–New Deal sentiments that had driven the most reactionary elements of the isolationist movement did not go away. Southern Democrats criticized an OWI-produced pamphlet titled Negroes and the War, which was meant to counter Japanese propaganda that questioned whether African Americans had a real stake in the war. When the American Jewish Congress asked for help exposing Nazi atrocities, the head of the OWI's Domestic Branch, newspaper publisher and Willkie Republican Gardner Cowles, put them off, claiming that all advertising space was being devoted to issues such as war industries and rationing. Conservatives suspected that wartime agencies constituted an attempt to expand the New Deal and make it permanent.

Past experience left many Americans leery of foreign entanglements. They recalled with resentment Wilson's "war to end all wars" and the disappointing failure of the League of Nations. Polls, including an OWI poll in the summer of 1942, found that a third of Americans would accept a separate peace with Germany, about the same number were uncertain what we were fighting for, and almost half distrusted British and Soviet motives.[49] Davis and most of the writers and artists within the OWI believed Americans must be brought to a deeper understanding of what was at stake. If their countrymen were motivated only by self-defense, support for the Allies might weaken and endanger postwar efforts to build a lasting peace. These writers and artists saw their work as informational and educational. They wanted to talk directly to the people about the issues, emphasizing the horrors of fascism. Others within the OWI, including Cowles, disagreed with this strategy. Many in this second group were entertainment industry executives (some of them "dollar-a-year men"), newspaper publishers, and admen who had been brought on board because of their connections and supposed expertise. They believed in targeting audiences, staying positive, selling the war, and rallying people to buy bonds and recycle cans. At first the two groups went their own ways, but tensions soon developed. As Sydney Weinberg has put it, "Serious pamphlets like 'The Four Freedoms' . . . contrasted sharply with radio announcements dedicated to the principle of 'a truth a day keeps Hitler away.'"[50]

The midterm elections of 1942 exacerbated the situation. Democrats retained narrow margins in both houses, but Republicans picked up nine seats in the Senate and forty-seven in the House. Conservatives on both sides of the aisle were suspicious of the OWI because it was populated with Popular Front interventionists including MacLeish, Sherwood, Cowley, Waldo Salt, Howard Fast, Dorothea Lange, Muriel Rukeyser, John Houseman, Ben Shahn, Nicholas Ray, and Josephine Herbst, and radical émigrés such as Bertolt Brecht and André Breton. Right-wing columnist Westbrook Pegler called the OWI "a hideout for privileged intellectuals, New Deal cowards, and communists." Martin Dies's House Un-American Activities Committee began to investigate the OWI and soon forced out Cowley, Herbst, Rukeyser, Houseman, Ray, and others. Davis, a strong advocate of freedom of speech, acknowledged later that he was forced to fire thirty-five employees for alleged Communist Party connections.[51]

A coalition of Republicans and southern Democrats in Congress moved at the same time to cut the agency's funding and exercise more oversight.

These conservatives saw "information" as "propaganda" and tended to side with Cowles and the advertising approach. Writers and artists within the OWI had historically been given great leeway, which they defended as freedom of speech. Sometimes, however, they overstepped and openly challenged government policy. Shahn, for instance, created a poster criticizing Vichy collaboration at the same time the State Department was maintaining diplomatic relations with Marshal Pétain and his government. Often, however, the writers and artists were simply focusing on the grim realities of war, emphasizing unity with the Allies, or targeting fascism. Tensions increased within the agency when a Coca-Cola executive was brought in to oversee the graphics division. He criticized Shahn's images as too negative and said he preferred the work of Norman Rockwell. Shahn and Francis Brennan, who had worked at *Fortune* with MacLeish, responded with a parody poster in which the Statue of Liberty was lifting up not a torch but four bottles of Coke. The poster's tagline was "The War That Refreshes: Try All Four Delicious Freedoms!"[52]

Meanwhile, conservative papers, especially Robert McCormick's *Tribune* syndicate, stepped up their attack on the OWI. The *Washington Times-Herald*, a McCormick paper, targeted MacLeish in particular because he had hand-picked most of the OWI writers. They saw his internationalism—he was now advocating for One Worldism and the establishment of a United Nations–type organization—as a threat to American sovereignty. To MacLeish's dismay, Luce, his old boss at *Fortune*, even reprinted one of the *Times-Herald's* unfounded attacks in *Time*.

In his column written for *Harper's* in November 1942 White used irony to make it clear where he stood on the struggle Davis and MacLeish were waging with the advertising experts:

> There are two distinct wars being fought in the world. One is the actual war, bloody and terrible and cruel, a war of ups and downs. The other is the imaginary war that is the personal responsibility of the advertising men of America—the war you see pictures of in the full-page ads in the magazines. This second war is a lovely thing. We are always winning it, and the paint job stays bright on the bombers that gleam in the strong clear light of a copywriter's superlative adventure. . . . This vicarious ecstasy of the ad men always makes me think of the hero of James Thurber's story called "The Secret Life of Walter Mitty."[53]

Harper's followed in February with a long exposé, "Davis and Goliath: The OWI and Its Gigantic Assignment." Other middlebrow magazines, including the *Saturday Review* and the *New Republic,* also defended MacLeish, Davis, and OWI, but it was too little, too late.[54] The agency was being decimated. MacLeish had tendered his resignation earlier, but Davis talked him out of it; now, in January 1943, he resigned for good. In April there was a big dustup over the suppression of a pamphlet on potential food shortages, and thirty-eight writers resigned. In June Congress eliminated the Domestic Branch of the OWI.

Ironically, one of the OWI's greatest successes occurred simultaneously with this dismantling. In 1942 Norman Rockwell, inspired by Roosevelt's State of the Union speech, had sketched ideas for a series of posters to promote the Four Freedoms. At his own expense he had traveled to Washington to pitch his ideas to the OWI. The administrators he met with put him off, telling him they were looking for "real artists," not mere illustrators, though if he liked, perhaps he could provide some sketches for a U.S. Marine calisthenics manual they were doing. A discouraged Rockwell took his idea to the *Saturday Evening Post,* for which he had been illustrating since 1916. The *Post*'s new editor, Ben Hibbs, was trying to separate the magazine from its conservative past. Hibbs had replaced Wesley Stout, who in March 1942 had printed an inflammatory isolationist article titled "The Case against the Jew." Angry letters, canceled subscriptions, and the threat of a boycott had prompted Stout's resignation. In February and March 1943 Hibbs printed Rockwell's now iconic images in four successive issues of the *Post* along with essays on each of the freedoms. Pulitzer Prize winner Booth Tarkington wrote about freedom of speech, middlebrow popularizer Will Durant about freedom of religion, poet and former OWI writer Stephen Vincent Benét about freedom from fear, and Philippine immigrant, novelist, farmworker, and Popular Front activist Carlos Bulosan about freedom from want. The series elicited thousands of letters and requests for reprints, which the OWI helped fill. The agency eventually distributed 4 million copies worldwide. In April 1943 the OWI and Treasury Department launched a tour of Rockwell's original paintings to department stores in sixteen cities that attracted 1.2 million visitors and sold $133 million in war bonds.[55]

As Robert Westbrook has pointed out, Rockwell's Four Freedoms paintings emphasized "private interests," "political obligations," and families: a lone working-class man speaking up at a town meeting, people of all creeds worshiping together, three generations of a family enjoying Thanksgiving dinner, and a father and mother checking on their sleeping children, the parents troubled by the headlines about the London blitz in the paper the father is holding.[56] Like White's *One Man's Meat* essays, the images spoke about the personal stake Americans had in the war. Critics on the Left have dismissed

Rockwell's iconic paintings as kitsch, hopelessly middlebrow, and insidious examples of "capitalist realism," but at the time they were mainly criticized from the Right.[57] Edith Nourse Rogers, a Republican congresswoman from Massachusetts, complained that Rockwell had not recognized a fifth free-dom—"freedom of private enterprise." A conservative critic from New York asked, "Why don't you make pictures of the American Freedoms instead of the New Deal Freedoms?"[58]

White would have understood the criticisms Rockwell received for senti-mentality and New Deal boosterism. He too worried about losing himself in small-town nostalgia or political abstractions. In the spring 1941 piece that linked Hitler and hogs, and eggs and fires, White recalled that when he had first told city friends about his move to Maine, one of them, "with an ugly sneer," said, "I trust that you will spare the reading public your little adven-tures in contentment." The allusion was to a book of farming essays published by David Grayson in 1907. Grayson's book was in the genteel-essay tradition that included Ik Marvel's *Wet Days at Edgewood*, which White recalled as a favorite in his parents' parlor. What White may have known, but most read-ers did not, was the fact that just as Ik Marvel was a pseudonym for Donald Grant Mitchell, David Grayson was a pseudonym for Ray Stannard Baker. Baker published under his own name as a muckraking journalist and editor for *McClure's* and the *American Magazine,* but hid his authorship of *Adventures in Contentment* and its sequel, *Adventures in Friendship,* for nearly a decade. He was a progressive reformer and internationalist, served as Wilson's press secretary at Versailles, and wrote an eight-volume biography of Wilson that won the Pulitzer Prize in 1940. White was not as divided as either Mitchell or Baker, but he did worry about the possibility and identified himself in *One Man's Meat* as leading "a dual existence—half farmer, half literary gent."[59]

The comparison to Grayson stuck with White. He recognized the danger of his book being thought of as just another attempt to revive the gentleman-farmer essay of the Gilded Age. When his *Harper's* essays were being prepared for book publication in 1942, he wrote his editor with ideas about how the collection might be marketed: "I think it would be a mistake to put the book out as another one of those Adventures in Contentment, or as an Escape from the City, or How to Farm with a Portable Corona. This is a book of essays on a wide variety of subjects, both urban and rural; it is not a tract on subsistence farming, and it is not a handbook of retreat. It is, as you know, intensely per-sonal, but not designed to prove anything." The book may not have been out to prove anything, but it did argue for the active, critical involvement of the individual citizen in a democratic society. In the foreword White wrote, "It is a book of, for, and by an individual." In this declaration of the individual nature of reading and writing, one also hears not only an invocation of the Gettysburg Address but also White's earlier critique of Hitler's demagoguery. "Individualism and the first person singular," concluded White, "are closely related to freedom, and are what the fight is about."[60]

In the book itself White made it clear that race hatred and nationalism could limit our understanding of freedom. Shortly after Pearl Harbor, he wrote a profile of his wife's aunt Poo, a lady of old Maine stock and the "Victorian mold," who in middle age shocked everyone and married Hyozo Omori, "a young Japanese of distinguished lineage." Aunt Poo stayed on in Tokyo for thirty years after her husband's death in 1912 to run a settlement house. "Against a backdrop of war and Japanese brutality," his trumpeting of her work in the Tokyo slums may seem to some to "take on the quality of a bitter jest," but he insisted Aunt Poo's "thirty years' ministering to the poor people of an alien race" and "her insistence on their good qualities" constituted "a valuable antidote to the campaign of hate that war breeds."[61]

One Man's Meat was released on June 12, 1942, the day before the OWI was created. The reviews were excellent. Canby celebrated the book as a return to "the main line" of American writing represented by Franklin, Thoreau, Twain, and Lincoln, a line that "comes from somewhere significant, and is going somewhere for results." In the *Nation,* Diana Trilling linked White not only to Thoreau but to Montaigne as well and applauded him for holding on to "the humanistic tradition" despite the pressures of the times. In the *New Republic,* Stanley Edgar Hyman continued to link White to the *New Yorker* (even though all but three of the pieces in *One Man's Meat* had appeared first in *Harper's*), but acknowledged that the book was "*New Yorker* editorial writing at its best," adding that "the touch is always light, but the punch can be heavy and full of conviction." Irving Edman, in the *New York Herald Tribune Books,* declared White "our finest essayist, perhaps our only one."[62] The first edition sold well enough—about twelve thousand copies—to warrant a second. In 1944 his publisher released "A New and Enlarged Edition" that included ten additional columns published in *Harper's* after February 1942.

When the second edition came out, a federal election was nearing in which Roosevelt was expected to run for an unprecedented fourth term. Republicans and some conservative Democrats were concerned about the president's consolidation of power during wartime. Suspecting that the eleven million soldiers overseas overwhelmingly supported their commander in chief, they amended the Soldier's Voting Act of 1942. That legislation had required the states to provide absentee ballots to soldiers during wartime; the amended version only recommended it. Senator Robert Taft of Ohio, "Mr. Republican," pushed through another amendment that prevented the OWI and other agencies from distributing any books, pamphlets, movies, magazines, or other materials that might affect a federal election. At first, conservative elements within the army and navy interpreted this law quite broadly. Among the books they banned were Charles Beard's economic interpretation of U.S. history, a biography of Justice Holmes, and *One Man's Meat*.

The press and civil liberties organizations responded immediately, just as they had during the OWI controversy. The *Saturday Review of Literature* criticized the banning of these books in an editorial titled "Censoritis," and the Council on Books in Wartime, an organization of writers, booksellers, publishers, and librarians dedicated to the proposition that books should be seen as "weapons in the war of ideas," opposed the ban in statements picked up by the *New York Times* and other outlets.[63]

In a letter White asked his brother Stanley if he had seen the *New York Times* piece. The military's ruling, he claimed, gave him "more pleasure than anything that has happened in a long time." He was sure the book's few favorable references to the administration and its criticisms of Roosevelt's opponents were the reason it was suppressed: "At least the soldier vote is now safe, and the boys can pick up their presidential preferences from the comic strips and other reliable American sources. I am beginning to feel a little more like an author now that I have had a book banned. The literary life, in this country, begins in jail."[64]

Public criticism continued, the ban was soon lifted, and afterward *One Man's Meat* (and three other books by White) was released in an "Armed Services Edition" of 150,000 copies and two "Overseas Editions," one in French and one in German, of 50,000 copies each. These pocket-size disposable paperbacks were designed to be carried by soldiers in the field and distributed to Allied supporters. In time White received letters of appreciation from scores of servicemen. "This," he wrote later, "relived my mind, as I had been uneasy about indulging myself in pastoral pursuits when so many of my countrymen were struggling for their lives, and for mine."[65]

White had not been cultivating his own garden. Neither had he been advocating for the best of all possible worlds. Instead, he had brought a skeptical liberalism to bear on the issues of the day. He was, as he put it, a soft talker and not a joiner, and certainly not a card-carrying member of the Popular Front, but he had become involved in the struggle against fascism. That involvement had elevated his prose, released him from the *New Yorker*'s anonymous "we," and helped him create a new kind of American essay—one that was awake and engaged, that could talk about Hitler and hogs, and still be enchanting.

Epilogue:

"Once More to the Lake," History,

and Freshman Composition

T hough he had passed away fifteen years earlier, E. B. White played an important role in the 2000 New York senatorial campaign. That year Hillary Clinton, in a candidates' debate with Rick Lazio, sought to dispel accusations of carpetbagging by referring to a 1949 essay by White in which he argued that the city has always had a way of turning the newly arrived into real New Yorkers. During the spin session after the debate, as Lazio stood helpless beside him, New York's conservative governor, George Pataki, tried to defend his protégée but spun out of control. Clinton, said Pataki, had "quoted some guy, Wyatt or somebody—I don't think he was from Brooklyn—with some definition of a New Yorker that she must have read somewhere." A reporter explained that White had written for the *New Yorker* magazine for many years, but Pataki pressed on, indulging in his own brand of Know-Nothing nativism, blind to the fact that he was digging himself into a hole: "Well . . . maybe the average member of the media who lives in Manhattan, when they're quoting New York, would use E. B. White, or whatever his name is. I don't think people from Brooklyn or Peekskill would have quoted that person."

When he got home that night, Pataki was reminded by his daughter Emily, a student (like her father before her) at Yale, that "that person" was one of her childhood favorites and that the governor had read *Charlotte's Web* aloud to her and her three younger siblings when they were kids.

The next morning's mea culpa was halfhearted. The governor's spokesman admitted that Emily "gave [her father] an earful last night," but tried to keep the jabs at Manhattan's media elite in place. Then, the governor's office released a hard-hitting announcement: "The Governor values learning. He thinks everyone should be reading *Charlotte's Web* to their kids."[1]

Lazio lost the election by more than thirteen points. There were many reasons for this, of course, but Pataki's shot at Clinton and White did not help.

The governor's ill-advised and misinformed remarks are indicative of the kind of confused response White's work has received. On the one hand, book reviewers have been positive in their praise. In 1946 Warren Beck lauded him for his "rehabilitation of the informal essay, which in recent times has often ailed, either of a hectic preciosity or a boisterous madness." Writing in the *Sewanee Review* in 1978, Spencer Brown argued that White's "position in the essay" was like "that of the schooner *America* off the Isle of Wight. 'Who is second?' asks Queen Victoria. 'Madam, there is no second.'" In 1984, the year before White's death, *Harper's* editor Russell Lynes thanked him for restoring the essay "to a good name, something it had not enjoyed in journalistic circles since the Edwardians."[2]

But for most readers, just as it was for Governor Pataki, White's work as an essayist has been eclipsed by the tremendous popularity of his children's books and, to a lesser extent, his style manual. *Stuart Little,* first published in 1945, has sold four million copies. *Charlotte's Web* appeared in 1952 and has sold more than twenty million. These children's books, which have also been made into popular films, were followed in 1959 by a revised edition of *The Elements of Style,* which his former Cornell professor Will Strunk had first printed privately in 1918. That book, which is a popular gift to high school graduates and widely adopted by writing teachers, has sold more than ten million copies.[3]

Just as White as an essayist had to compete with White as children's author, grammarian, and humorist, so has the essay as a genre had to compete with misconceptions of what it is. It is seen as a kind of miscellaneous hodgepodge of a genre, neither here nor there and sometimes at odds with itself. It is lost somewhere in the larger category of "creative nonfiction," a self-contradictory term that only accentuates the essay's problems. Nonfiction, as Scott Russell Sanders has pointed out, is itself "an exceedingly vague term, taking in everything from telephone books to *Walden,* and it's negative, implying that fiction is the norm against which everything else must be measured. It's as though, instead of calling an apple a fruit, we called it a non-meat." The addition of the adjective *creative* is of little help. *Creative* as opposed to what, one wonders? *Destructive?* This fuzzy definition is but one of the reasons the personal essay slid down the hierarchy of genres during the twentieth century, a century in which the essay was increasingly dismissed as an old-fashioned and easily accessible genre written by generalists for a middlebrow audience. It has become, in the self-deprecating term used by an alternative anthology and journal devoted to it, the "fourth genre."[4] These tensions continue to haunt the essay as a genre and affect how it is taught. Indeed, how it is taught has reinforced the essay's diminished status.

In a groundbreaking 1999 article, Lynn Bloom argued that the essay canon is now fundamentally a teaching canon as opposed to a historical, critical, or national canon. The essays people know, the ones used to define the genre, are the essays that appear most frequently in freshman composition anthologies. Novels are circulated among book clubs and reviewed in magazines, plays are produced and reviewed, and poems are memorized and given to lovers as gifts, but on the whole, essays serve as models used to teach nineteen-year-olds how to write.

Such teaching is hard work. New teaching assistants facilitate multiple sections of freshman composition in which they are expected to introduce the entire writing process from brainstorming through proofreading as well as remediate and sometimes even teach writing across the curriculum. Editors select essays for first-year writing anthologies with the needs of these young teachers and their students in mind. Is the selection current and accessible? Can it be used to model this or that rhetorical mode? Is it short enough to be used in a one-hour class? Is it in the public domain, and if not, how much will the permissions cost? Will it help diversify the anthology in terms of race, ethnicity, and gender? Does it help establish a balance between classic and contemporary essays? Between emerging authors and established big names?

These concerns are real and understandable, but they push toward the inclusion of shorter, simpler, and more "teachable" essays. If the anthologies include longer, more layered, and more difficult essays, those essays are often excerpted, or flattened and simplified by the accompanying apparatuses (for example, headnotes, discussion questions, writing prompts). According to Bloom, this trend toward shorter, simpler pieces enforces the idea that the personal essay is a less literary genre. She argues that it has come to be seen as a service genre. Once belletristic, the essay is seen less as art itself and more as a means to an end, a form used to write about the inherently more artistic genres. It is the tool of teachers—specifically teachers of composition—who are themselves not seen as writers or artists but as mere facilitators or, at their worst, grammarians and fussbudgets.

The teaching tool of choice in first-year writing courses (along with a grammar handbook) is the essay anthology, and as Bloom points out, "All anthologies (not just [first-year] Readers) deracinate their material—old or new—from its original context and replant it in the anthologist's soil." Essays in particular, she adds, "acquire new, potentially very different coloration when transplanted, especially if they illustrate rhetorical modes in belletristic anthologies, which always emphasize form and subordinate history and culture."[5]

Bloom's extensive study of first-year writing anthologies published between 1946 and 1996 shows that the most widely taught American essay of the last half of the twentieth century was E. B. White's "Once More to the Lake." White wrote this essay in August 1941, and it appeared as his "One Man's Meat" column in the October 1941 issue of *Harper's*. It focuses on a fishing trip he took with his young son to a lake in Maine. According to Bloom, only Swift's "Modest Proposal," the Declaration of Independence, and Orwell's "Politics and the English Language" and "Shooting an Elephant" appeared more often in freshman composition readers during the period she studied. But despite the fact that it has been so widely reprinted and taught, White's essay has received relatively little critical attention. According to the *MLA International Bibliography*, only 5 articles on White's essay appeared between 1963 and 1998. (By way of contrast, critics produced 13 articles on "Thanatopsis" and 139 on "Death of a Salesman" during the same time period.)

Robert Root has examined how first-year writing anthologies have used White's essay and, in so doing, contributed to the deracination Bloom identified. In his 1995 study of forty-one randomly chosen recent anthologies, Root found "Once More to the Lake" reprinted in twenty-four. He investigated those anthologies to see how White's essay was classified in the tables of contents, what kinds of apparatus accompanied it, and the stated rationales for including it. Root found that the essay was used to model a wide mix of rhetorical modes and highlight an even wider variety of themes, often in the same anthology. Some anthologies provided alternate tables of contents (rhetorical and thematic). In the rhetorical tables of contents, he found White's essay categorized as narrative, descriptive, and expository, though, intriguingly, never as persuasive. It was also labeled using less classical terms, including *remembering, comparison, first-person perspective*, a *personal essay*, and a *classic essay*. The thematic tables of contents were also a jumble. By Root's count they listed the essay as "'Autobiography' (4 times), 'Nature' (5), 'Childhood' or 'Children' or 'Family' (5), 'Self-Discovery' (4), 'Mortality' (6), 'Sports and Leisure' (3), 'Places' (3), and 'Humor,' 'Relationships,' and 'Love and Brotherhood' (1 each)."[6]

These apparent contradictions could be seen as a statement about the impurity of genres and the complexity of White's essay, and occasionally anthologists have favored such an interpretation. One pair of editors concluded that "no piece of real prose is ever so pure as our systems of classification" and bemoaned the inevitable "flaws" of thematic organization before asking ironically, "Is E. B. White's theme, in 'Once More to the Lake,' Mortality? Aging? Youth and Age? or, How I Spent My Summer Vacation?" But in the end, even these editors provided a rhetorical index that placed the essay under three different modes, two patterns of development, and one genre. Rationales for including the essay at all were as various and abstract as the categories in the tables of contents, declaring that White's essay is timeless, inspiring, universal, worth imitating, and so on. Root's concern is with how such scattershot categorization confuses, narrows, and reduces the essay for young readers. "Clearly," he states, "such classifications, so demonstrably contradictory, misdirect the student's attention to the essay, by making it representative of a narrow category rather than interactive with the reader."[7]

The anthologies' apparatuses exacerbated this problem. Root found, for instance, that the headnotes usually offered skimpy, sometimes inaccurate biographical or bibliographical information, with no mention of White's column, his move to *Harper's,* or the long struggle against fascism. Editors often included the date of composition—August 1941—but they rarely pointed it out or discussed its significance. Root suggested that they probably included it only because White himself had done so in *One Man's Meat* and again in the 1977 edition of *The Essays of E. B. White.* Though the one set of editors gestured ironically toward the dangers of reducing White's piece to a "How I Spent My Summer Vacation" essay, many others offered writing prompts that demonstrated no such irony. These prompts urged students to write about their summer vacation (for example, places they have visited twice, family vacation spots, and so on) or to describe a summertime weather event like the climactic thunderstorm in White's essay.

In my own experience students tend to read "Once More to the Lake" in one of two ways. If they are undergraduates and feeling homesick, it reminds them of home and family and often touches them deeply; if they are graduate students and see themselves as sophisticated, they are more likely to dismiss it as sentimental and old-timey. To many in both groups, the ending with its the cold splash of mortality seems abrupt and unearned. Both of these readings view the essay as a nostalgia piece about fathers and sons and the cycles of time and nature—with one group embracing that nostalgia and the other rejecting it. While both readings can be supported, they follow from the context the anthologies have provided for the essay and can close off alternate readings. Often, the graduate students (or advanced undergraduates) remember their first encounter with the essay as freshmen in college and seem to want to distance themselves from that experience and see themselves as now beyond it, though at the same time they may, as teaching assistants, be teaching the essay the way it was originally taught to them.

Even in graduate or advanced undergraduate literature courses that treat White's essay as an important American essay and not just a prompt for a summer-vacation essay, the piece has not necessarily received as full a reading as it deserves. Again, this may have to do with how it has been anthologized. The two major anthologies most likely to be used in such courses are Lopate's *Art of the Personal Essay* and Atwan and Oates's *Best American Essays of the Century*. These important texts have both appeared in paperback editions, stayed in print for more than a decade, and done much to help establish an essay canon that is not just pedagogical, as Bloom pointed out, but also historical and critical. Both anthologies include "Once More to the Lake" and celebrate its importance, but their praise for White and his essay is qualified, indeed almost backhanded. In the introduction to her anthology, Oates promises, "That staple of traditional essay collections, the unhurried musing of a disembodied (Caucasian, male, privileged) consciousness, is missing here, except for its highest, most lyric expression in E. B. White's 'Once More to the Lake.'" Lopate's take is not too different. He describes White's persona as that of "a friendly, gentlemanly family man, curious about nature and city life, undidactic, modest, civic-minded, mildly nostalgic and elegiac." And again, like Oates, he apologizes as he praises, "At times White's persona threatens to become irksomely bland in its genial self-effacement, but his intelligence and humor save the day." Lopate says he is including "Once More to the Lake" because it demonstrates "how ambitious a reach White's essays had—formally, emotionally, philosophically, and politically—behind their deceptively unassuming tone."[8]

Caught between admiration for White's accomplishment and discomfort with his identity, neither Oates nor Lopate go much further with their analysis. Lopate, for instance, explains little about how White's ambition is made real or why White might have adopted such a deceptively unassuming tone. Perhaps Lopate is heeding Root's warning and trying not to narrow the categories and dictate to the reader, but given that the categories have already been narrowed and that readers, especially student readers, have already been trained to see White's essay almost exclusively as a nostalgia piece, a correction seems in order.

The late James Slevin offered a possible approach. Slevin's case study was of a different White essay, a short piece titled "Democracy," but he was concerned with the same problems I have raised here. Like Root, Slevin looked at the study questions that accompany White's essay in *The Norton Reader*, analyzed "what it means for students to become a 'Norton' reader," and concluded, "The aim of reading in the *Norton*'s textual apparatus seems to be a thoroughly ahistorical understanding of the text as an object of analysis and, a related matter, as White's property." Slevin proposed as antidote: looking at the essay "in the context of its original appearance in 'The Talk of the Town' section of the July 3, 1943, issue of the *New Yorker*, along with several of the essays, stories, and advertisements that surround it." He then examined White's text—its title, tone, persona, and so forth—in relation to this original context, a context that included "ads for Cadillacs and fur coats and nail polish" and "a story about a lady and her maid who can't speak proper English." This work enabled Slevin to see the essay in a new way, to find in it "acts of exclusion, neglect, and domination" that he had not seen before. He cautioned that his goal was not to present an "exposé" of White or "a fidgety dramatization of his failure to be politically correct," but rather "to make a larger point, not about White's failure but about the misshapen ways of reading that delimit our understanding of what texts do." It was a point, Slevin concluded, that required him to recognize what White's essay "was *doing* in 1943 in the pages of *The New Yorker*, just as it is *doing* something today in the pages of the *Norton Reader*."[9]

"Once More to the Lake" appeared originally in the October 1941 issue of *Harper's*. Looking at the essay in that context reminds one constantly of the awful situation White and his first readers faced and how their anxieties must have pushed them to look for answers, meaning, and consolation in nature and history. A cursory glance at the magazine's table of contents, illustrations, and advertisements make this clear. Pearl Harbor was two months away, but the magazine was already full of war news. It included articles with titles such as "The Great Defense Migration," "Education for Freedom," "The Farm Bloc and the War," and "Physical Fitness and the Draft." Alcoa bought a full-page ad trumpeting what the company was doing to ready the nation for war. Against this backdrop, "Once More to the Lake" comes increasingly to be seen as being not just about a week in the woods but also about the catastrophic direction the American Century was taking.

In *Harper's*, White's essay simply appeared under the name of his column. It did not receive the title "Once More to the Lake" until the next year, when it appeared in the book edition of *One Man's Meat*. The new title might allude to Milton's *Lycidas* or Shakespeare's *Henry V*, or both, but in any case it reflects an attempt by White to set the essay in a literary tradition and open it up to new interpretations. Milton's lament for his drowned friend Edward King opens:

> Yet once more, O ye laurels, and once more
> Ye myrtles brown, with ivy never-sere,
> I come to pluck your berries harsh and crude,

And with forc'd fingers rude
Shatter your leaves before the mellowing year.

Evoking this pastoral elegy to a young man "dead ere his prime" connects the essay to nature's ritual renewal, to death and mythic rebirth.[10] The Shakespearean version is more martial, alluding as it does to King Henry rallying his troops at the gap in the city wall during the siege of Harfleur: "Once more unto the breach, dear friends, once more; / Or close the wall up with our English dead." In the eighteen months prior to the essay's publication, Denmark, Norway, the Low Countries, France, Romania, and Yugoslavia had fallen to the Axis. Britain was under siege.

The essay's first sentences, however, do not look sadly toward Britain and the war but look humorously at White's personal past:

> One summer, along about 1904, my father rented a camp on a lake in Maine and took us all there for the month of August. We all got ringworm from some kittens and had to rub Pond's Extract on our arms and legs night and morning, and my father rolled over in a canoe with all his clothes on; but outside of that the vacation was a success and from then on none of us ever thought there was any place in the world like that lake in Maine. We returned summer after summer—always on August 1st for one month.[11]

Three aspects of this opening are especially striking—1904, the humorous take on the father, and the length and regularity of the family's vacation in Maine.

The year 1904 had been on White's mind and the minds of his middle-class readers that summer. In June 1941, just before White and his son Joel headed off to Belgrade Lakes and his family's traditional vacation spot, the *New Yorker* began to serialize Sally Benson's autobiographical stories about growing up in St. Louis at the turn of the century as the city prepared for the 1904 World's Fair. Later that year, the stories were released as a book titled *Meet Me in St. Louis*. Two years later, in November 1944, between Iwo Jima and the Battle of the Bulge, MGM's musical based on the stories opened with Judy Garland in the lead. The musical's famous numbers, including "The Trolley Song" and "Have Yourself a Merry Little Christmas," took America's families away from the war for a moment and back to a seemingly simpler time.

A second look at 1904 reveals that it was not quite so simple and idyllic. It was the last year of the decadelong great merger movement that led to the creation of U.S. Steel, the world's first billion-dollar corporation, a monopoly that controlled 60 percent of the industry and grossed more income than the

U.S. government, and in February of that year, the Russo-Japanese War, the century's first global war, had begun. November would bring the election of the trust-busting essayist Teddy Roosevelt as president.

White's family was probably not too different from the one portrayed in Benson's *New Yorker* stories, with its parlor piano and spacious Queen Anne house, but White would have recalled as well that the funny innocence of the annual idyll in Maine nearly came to an end in 1905. That was the year Samuel White, who had worked his way up from bundle boy to president of the Horace Waters Piano Company, was taken to court by the heirs of the man who founded the company. They accused him of stock manipulation; it would take two appeals and six years before a higher court cleared Samuel White of all wrongdoing.

A look at the ads in the October 1941 *Harper's* reveals some of the specific cultural desires of White's middle-class readers. For just five dollars Associated American Artists offered "Signed Original Etchings and Lithographs . . . identical to many owned by great museums." The Gramophone Shop offered a series of imported phonograph records, "the surfaces [of which were] superior to domestic records." A Little, Brown ad asked, "Are you 'up' on current books and authors?" and urged readers to take a "simple test." The White who composed the Sterling Finney ads and subscription invitations for the early *New Yorker* must have looked on these *Harper's* ads with an ironic understanding of himself and his readers. Halfway through "Once More to the Lake" there is a long, tone-breaking two-sentence paragraph that demonstrates the depth of White's ambivalence toward his class and the attitudes that held it together:

> Summertime, oh summertime, pattern of life indelible, the fade-proof lake, the woods unshatterable, the pasture with the sweet fern and the juniper forever and ever, summer without end; this was the background, and the life along the shore was the design, the cottages with their innocent and tranquil design, their tiny docks with the flagpole and the American flag floating against the white clouds in the blue sky, the little paths over the roots of the trees leading from camp to camp and the paths leading back to the outhouses and the can of lime for sprinkling, and at the souvenir counters at the store the miniature birch-bark canoes and the post cards that showed things looking a little better than they looked. This was the American family at play, escaping the city heat, wondering whether the newcomers at the camp at the head of the cove were "common" or "nice," wondering whether it was true that the people who drove up for Sunday dinner at the farmhouse were turned away because there wasn't enough chicken.[12]

The range of the sentence is stunning. It opens with a burst of purple prose, internal rhymes, apostrophic call to the past, and biblical echoes, and then moves through a spate of patriotic gushing, only to slam shut in a moment of uncompromising irony in which lime is sprinkled in a smelly outhouse and the store's Americana grow smaller and smaller and phonier and phonier. Then, as a first-time reader tries to absorb all that this sentence serves up, the paragraph's second sentence targets quickly, subtly, and clearly the way in which the privilege and bigotry of the middle class, White's middle class, were cloaked in snobbish euphemisms, euphemisms that crippled all the parties involved.

The good old days might not have been so good, but now—again—war was about to make things even worse. In the summer of 1941, as White and his boy retreated to Belgrade Lakes to canoe, storm clouds were gathering, and White's essay concludes with a climactic thunderstorm. When he describes the storm as "the revival of an old melodrama that I had seen a long time ago with childish awe" and sighs that in the intervening years "America had not changed in any important respect," we can hear him rejecting that false and romantic notion that World War I was "the war to end all wars." When he remarks on "a curious darkening of the sky, and a lull in everything that made life tick," and describes how the storm rolls in off the North Atlantic with a "crackling light against the dark and the gods grinning and licking their chops in the hills," we can hear him mourning the sickening return of war. Then, when the storm is over and White's little boy decides to go down to the lake for a swim, the essay's shocking denouement links the author's own sad and desperate love to the horrible war America was about to join: "When the others went swimming my son said he was going in too. He pulled his dripping trunks from the line where they had hung all through the shower, and wrung them out. Languidly, and with no thought of going in, I watched him, his hard little body, skinny and bare, saw him wince slightly as he pulled up around his vitals the small, soggy, icy garment. As he buckled the swollen belt suddenly my groin felt the chill of death."[13]

Returned to 1941, "Once More to the Lake" opens up in new ways. It becomes larger and, as Lopate said, more ambitious. Might not the same be true of other American essays if they too were released from the first-year writing anthologies and read against history?

NOTES

PREFACE

1. Theodor Adorno, "The Essay as Form," 158.
2. Lillian Smith to Frank Taylor, May 2, 1944, *How Am I to Be Heard? Letters of Lillian Smith*, 83.

INTRODUCTION: DEFENDING THE ESSAY

1. The term *custodians of culture* was coined by Henry May. See his book *The End of American Innocence: A Study of the First Years of Our Own Time, 1912–1917*, esp. chap. 4.
2. E. B. White to Gus Lobrano [October? 1934], *Letters of E. B. White*, 121.
3. E. B. White, foreword to *Selected Essays of E. B. White*, vii.
4. Graham Good, *The Observing Self: Rediscovering the Essay*, vii.
5. Suzanne Ferguson, "The Rise of the Short Story in the Hierarchy of Genres," 176.
6. Pierre Bourdieu, *The Field of Cultural Production*, 46ff, 75–76.
7. Ibid., 48.
8. Ehrenreich and Ehrenreich formulated this position in a much-debated 1977 article. See John Ehrenreich and Barbara Ehrenreich, "The Professional-Managerial Class."
9. Pierre Bourdieu, *Distinction: A Social Critique of the Judgment of Taste*, 48, 323, 325–26.
10. See, for instance, Gerald Early, ed., *Speech and Power: The African-American Essay and Its Cultural Content from Polemics to Pulpit*, vols. 1–2; Phillip Lopate, ed., *The Art of the Personal Essay: An Anthology from the Classical Era to the Present*; Robert Atwan and Joyce Carol Oates, eds., *The Best American Essays of the Century*; John D'Agata, ed., *The Next American Essay* and *The Lost Origins of the Essay*.
11. Lee Gutkind launched *Creative Nonfiction* in 1993, Dinty Moore founded *Brevity: A Journal of Concise Literary Nonfiction* in 1997, Michael Steinberg and David Cooper followed with *Fourth Genre: Explorations in Nonfiction* in 1999, and Joe Mackall and Dan Lehman published the first issue of *River Teeth: A Journal of Nonfiction Narrative* in 1999.
12. Creative nonfiction is, as Wendy Bishop put it in a special issue of *College English* devoted to creative nonfiction in 2003 (65, no. 3), "suddenly sexy"; *Pedagogy* published

an issue on creative nonfiction in the spring of 2004. The Bedell NonfictioNOW Conference is a biennial feature at the University of Iowa.

13. "The AWP Official Guide to Writing Programs," *http://guide.awpwriter.org/*.

14. Raymond Williams, *Keywords: A Vocabulary of Culture and Society*, 310; Michel Foucault, "Afterword: The Subject and Power," 212.

15. See Henry Luce, "The American Century"; and Max Lerner, "The People's Century." Wallace delivered his speech on May 8, 1942, and reprinted it in *The Century of the Common Man* the following year.

16. Warren Susman, "Culture and Commitment," 192.

17. Almost all of the contributors to *The Ambiguous Legacy*, for instance, refer to the twentieth century as the "American Century." See Michael J. Hogan, ed., *The Ambiguous Legacy: U.S. Foreign Relations in the "American Century"*; Harold Evans, *The American Century*; David Levering Lewis, *W. E. B. Du Bois: The Fight for Equality and the American Century, 1919–1963*; Ronald Steel, *Walter Lippman and the American Century*; Joshua Freeman et al., eds., *Who Built America? Working People and the Nation's Economy, Politics, Culture, and Society*; and David S. Mason, *The End of the American Century*. Information about the Project for the New American Century is available at http://www.newamericancentury.org/.

18. My thinking follows that of Michael Denning, who argues that the American Century ended almost as soon as Henry Luce named it. For Denning, the period between 1945 and 1989 is the age of three worlds—"the capitalist First, the communist Second, and the decolonizing Third." If we in the United States have too often preferred to see that time as a continuation of the American Century, says Denning, there is a reason: "A distinctive American ideology emerged in the age of three worlds: 'democracy' came to be seen as a peculiarly 'American' product, and was wrenched apart from socialism and Marxism, both now counterposed to Americanism. Inside the United States, notions of Americanism, the 'American way of life,' and American exceptionalism flourished, and 'un-American activities' were the subject of Congressional investigations" (*Culture in the Age of the Three Worlds*, 26, 13).

19. The terms *cultural politics* and *aesthetic ideologies* belong to Michael Denning, who is building on Alan Trachtenberg's work. Denning, *The Cultural Front: The Laboring of American Culture in the Twentieth Century*, xix, 202; Trachtenberg, introduction to *Paul Strand: Essays on His Life and Work*, ed. Maren Strange (New York: Aperture Foundation, 1990), 4, quoted in Denning, *Cultural Front*, 473–74n9.

20. See Richard Ohmann, *Selling Culture: Magazines, Markets, and Class at the Turn of the Century*, 297–339; David Savran, *A Queer Sort of Materialism: Recontextualizing American Theater*; John Louis Howland, "Between the Muses and the Masses: Symphonic Jazz, 'Glorified' Entertainment, and the Rise of the American Musical Middlebrow, 1920–1944"; Jaime Harker, *American the Middlebrow: Women's Novels, Progressivism, and Middlebrow Authorship between the Wars*; Nicola Humble, *The Feminine Middlebrow Novel, 1920s to 1950s: Class, Domesticity, and Bohemianism*; and Teresa Mangum, *Married, Middle-brow, and Militant: Sarah Grand and the New Woman Novel*.

21. Hilaire Belloc, "By Way of Preface: An Essay upon Essays upon Essays (1929)." Carl Klaus and I are presently editing a collection, *Essayists on the Essay: Four Centuries of Commentary (forthcoming, 2011)*, which will help bring these pieces to light.

22. Lynn Z. Bloom, "The Essay Canon."

23. Janice Radway, *A Feeling for Books: The Book-of-the-Month Club, Literary Taste, and Middle-Class Desire*, 258; Anthony Giddens, *The Class Structure of the Advanced Societies*, 111 (emphasis in the original). Radway ascribes the idea to Stuart Blumin but offers no

citation. Neither does she mention Giddens, whose distinction seems to be the source of view of middle-class ideology. Indeed, his remark has become a touchstone among scholars of the middle class. It is employed by Ohmann, *Selling Culture*, 171–72; Cindy Sondik Aron, *Ladies and Gentlemen of the Civil Service: Middle-Class Workers in Victorian America*, 16; Robert Lanning, *The National Album: Collective Biography and the Formation of the Canadian Middle Class*, 186; Andrew Carl Holman, *A Sense of Their Duty: Middle-Class Formation in Victorian Ontario Towns*, 15; Thomas Winter, *Making Men, Making Class: The YMCA and Workingmen, 1877–1920*, 8n17; Debby Applegate, "Henry Ward Beecher and the 'Great Middle Class': Mass-Marketed Intimacy and Middle-Class Identity," 109; Amy Schrager Lang, *The Syntax of Class: Writing Inequality in Nineteenth-Century America*, 17; and Sarah C. Maza, *The Myth of the French Bourgeoisie: An Essay on the Social Imaginary, 1750–1850*, 118.

24. Stuart Blumin, *The Emergence of the Middle Class: Social Experience in the American City, 1760–1900*, 9–10.

25. Michel de Montaigne, *The Complete Essays of Montaigne*, 139; Ralph Waldo Emerson, "Friendship," in *The Collected Works of Ralph Waldo Emerson*, 2:119; E. B. White, *Charlotte's Web*, 184.

26. See Walter Pater, "Dialectic." A recent study of this phenomenon is Kuisma Korhonen's *Textual Friendship: The Essay as Impossible Encounter from Plato and Montaigne to Levinas and Derrida*.

27. Warren Susman, "'Personality' and the Making of Twentieth-Century Culture"; F. Scott Fitzgerald, *The Great Gatsby: The Authorized Text*, 6.

28. It is a goal that has remained central to the essayist's project, as the opening of Edward Hoagland's 1976 essay on the essay, "What I Think, What I Am," testifies: "Our loneliness makes us avid column readers these days. The personalities in the San Francisco *Chronicle*, Chicago *Daily News*, New York *Post* constitute our neighbors now."

29. Roosevelt did use "Ladies and gentleman" to open three of his fireside chats, and, during the war years, he appealed to national loyalty by using "My fellow Americans" to open nine others, but "My friends" was his standard opening and the one most associated with the chats. See Franklin Roosevelt, *Ah That Voice: The Fireside Chats of Franklin Delano Roosevelt* and *FDR's Fireside Chats*.

30. Richard Wrightman Fox argues, for instance, that the culture of personality began to vie with that of character as early as 1875. See his article "The Culture of Liberal Protestant Progressivism, 1875–1925."

31. E. B. White, "Intimations," in *One Man's Meat*, 222 (hereafter cited as *OMM*).

32. E. B. White, *The Wild Flag: Editorials from the "New Yorker" on Federal World Government and Other Matters*, 21.

33. See White, "Compost" [June 1940], in *OMM*, 129: "Today joined a society called Friends of the Land, as at my time of life a man should belong to a club so that he will have somewhere to sit in the afternoon." In her review of *One Man's Meat*, Diana Trilling wrote, "Well, Mr. White has joined no club except a society called Friends of the Land, but he believes in many good things. Being a humanist himself, he is a firm believer, for one thing, in man's humanity" ("Humanity and Humor," 118).

1. THE GENTEEL ESSAY AND THE GENTLEMAN AT THE FIRESIDE

1. Joan Shelley Rubin, *The Making of Middlebrow Culture*, xvii; Nathaniel Peffer, "Editors and Essays: A Note on Magazines Like *Harper's*," 83.

2. The quotation is from Susman, "'Personality,'" 273, who cites Philip Rieff, *The Triumph of the Therapeutic Uses of Faith after Freud* (New York: Harper and Row, 1966), 2.

3. See May, *End of American Innocence*, esp. chap. 4.

4. See, for instance, Rubin, *Making of Middlebrow Culture*, 10–12; May, *End of American Innocence*, 30–79; and Arthur Frank Wertheim, *The New York Little Renaissance: Iconoclasm, Modernism, and Nationalism in American Culture, 1908–1919*, 3–4.

5. Matthew Arnold, *Culture and Anarchy: An Essay in Political and Social Criticism*, 49, 176, viii, 23ff. His American lectures were collected as *Discourses in America* (London: Macmillan, 1885). The standard work on Arnold's influence in America is John Henry Raleigh's *Matthew Arnold and American Culture*. See also Rubin, *Making of Middlebrow Culture*, 14–15; Alan Trachtenberg, *The Incorporation of America: Culture and Society in the Gilded Age*, 155–56; and Lawrence Levine, *Highbrow/Lowbrow: The Emergence of Cultural Hierarchy in America*, 223–24.

6. Leslie Stephen, "The Essayists," 64.

7. Owen Wister, preface to *An Apology for Old Maids, and Other Essays*, by Henry Dwight Sedgwick, xiii.

8. Virginia Woolf, "Melodious Meditations," in *The Essays of Virginia Woolf*, 2:80–81.

9. Montaigne, *Complete Essays*, 504, 611, 595.

10. Nathaniel Hawthorne, "Fire Worship (1843)," 156, 150, 151, 158.

11. Henry David Thoreau, *Walden and Resistance to Civil Government*, 161, 169–70.

12. Herman Melville, "I and My Chimney," 154, 109–10, 132, 148, 155. The story appeared first in *Putnam's Magazine* (March 1856). My reading is indebted to those of R. Bruce Bickley, *The Method of Melville's Short Fiction*, 49–54; Ann Douglas, in *The Feminization of American Culture*, 317–18; and Vincent Bertolini, "Fireside Chastity: The Erotics of Sentimental Bachelorhood in the 1850s," 723–25.

13. On the autobiographical context, see Bickley, *Method of Melville's Short Fiction*, 49. For Curtis's comments on the story, see Herschel Parker, *Herman Melville: A Biography*, 259.

14. James Russell Lowell, "Rousseau and the Sentimentalists," 205.

15. Frank Norris quoted in Malcolm Cowley in his foreword to *After the Genteel Tradition: American Writers, 1910–1930*, 10.

16. Walter Blair, "The Essay: A Standard Form Takes on New Qualities," 97.

17. Lawrence Buell, *Literary Transcendentalism: Style and Vision in the American Renaissance*, 79; Ralph Waldo Emerson, "Address at the Woman's Rights Convention, September 20, 1855," 20.

18. Ralph Waldo Emerson, March 1842, *Selections from Ralph Waldo Emerson: An Organic Anthology*, 126.

19. Ibid., March 13, 1839, 124–25.

20. Ralph Waldo Emerson, *Journals and Miscellaneous Notebooks, 1838–1842*, 224, 265; Emerson, October 18, 1839, *Emerson in His Journals*, 227; Emerson, February 19, 1840, *Journals and Miscellaneous Notebooks*, Journal E, 338; Ralph Waldo Emerson to William Emerson, February 25, 1840, quoted in James Elliot Cabot, *A Memoir of Ralph Waldo Emerson*, 399.

21. Robert Atwan, "'Ecstasy & Eloquence': The Method of Emerson's Essays," 110–12; Emerson, "Montaigne; or, The Skeptic," from *Representative Men*, in *Selections from Emerson*, 293; Emerson, June 24, 1840, *Emerson in His Journals*, 240–41.

22. Emerson, "Montaigne; or, The Skeptic," 293; Emerson, June 24, 1840, *Emerson in His Journals*, 240–41; Emerson, March 29–31, 1837, *Emerson in His Journals*, 160.

23. Henry David Thoreau to Ralph Waldo Emerson, July 8, 1843, *The Writings of*

Henry David Thoreau: Journal, 6:94.

24. Emerson, October 7, 1840, in *Selections from Emerson*, 144–45.

25. Lopate, introduction to *Art of the Personal Essay*, li.

26. Thomas Carlyle to Emerson, November 3, 1844, *The Correspondence of Thomas Carlyle and Ralph Waldo Emerson, 1834–1872*, 80–82.

27. Henry James, review of *A Memoir of Ralph Waldo Emerson*, by James Elliot Cabot (1887), in *Literary Criticism*, 250, published originally in *Macmillan's Magazine* (December 1887); Bronson Alcott, *Concord Days* (Boston: Roberts Brothers, 1872), 36, quoted in Ronald A. Bosco and Joel Myerson, *Emerson in His Own Time: A Biographical Chronicle of His Life, Drawn from Recollections, Interviews, and Memoirs by Family, Friends, and Associates*, 58.

28. Joel Porte, "The Problem of Emerson," 85 (quoting Stephen Whicher, "Emerson's Tragic Sense," in *Emerson: A Collection of Critical Essays*, ed. Milton Konvitz and Stephen Whicher [Englewood Cliffs, N.J.: Prentice-Hall, 1962], 39), 93, 94.

29. Atwan, "'Ecstasy & Eloquence,'" 114.

30. Porte, "The Problem of Emerson," 108, 114.

31. Charles Brockden Brown, "The Man at Home," 27.

32. Ironically, Irving borrowed these two characters from German folktales. See Perry Miller, afterword to *The Sketch Book of Geoffrey Crayon, Gent.*, by Washington Irving, 377.

33. Irving quoted in William L. Hedges, *Washington Irving: An American Study, 1802–1832*, 14; Irving, "The Author's Account of Himself," in *Sketch Book*, 14; Irving, "English Writers on America," in *Sketch Book*, 64–64.

34. Bickley, *Method of Melville's Short Fiction*, 29.

35. Irving, "The Author's Account of Himself," 15. Bruce Bickley brought to my attention Charles Dickens's debt to Irving. For Dickens's correspondence with Irving, see Norman Page, *Charles Dickens: Family History*, 146.

36. Walter Benjamin, *Charles Baudelaire: A Lyric Poet in the Age of High Capitalism*, 61, 34. David Seed applies Benjamin to Dickens in his "Touring the Metropolis: The Shifting Subjects of Dickens's London Sketches."

37. Joseph Dennie, "On the Pleasures of Study," 100–101.

38. Douglas, *Feminization of American Culture*, 237.

39. Thoreau, October 28, 1853, *Writings of Thoreau*, 5:459.

40. Nathaniel P. Willis, "Letters from under a Bridge," 244; Curtis quoted in Robert E. Spiller et al., eds., *Literary History of the United States*, 833.

41. David Hall, "The Victorian Connection," 562, 574.

42. Roscoe Conkling, *Life and Letters of Roscoe Conkling: Orator, Statesman, Advocate* (New York: Charles Webster, 1889), 540–41, quoted in Richard Hofstadter, *Anti-Intellectualism in American Life*, 188–89.

43. Douglas, *Feminization of American Culture*, 236–37.

44. George Washington Plunkitt quoted in Hofstadter, *Anti-Intellectualism in American Life*, 187–88.

45. Ethel Parton, "A New York Childhood: The Seventies in Stuyvesant Square," 32, 44. See also Joyce W. Warren, *Fanny Fern: An Independent Woman*, 279.

46. Ethel Parton, "Fanny Fern: An Informal Biography," unpublished manuscript in the Sophia Smith Collection, Smith College, quoted in Joyce W. Warren, introduction to *Ruth Hall, and Other Writings*, by Fanny Fern, xiii.

47. Willis, letter to Sarah Eldredge Farrington, n.d., Sophia Smith Collection, Smith College, quoted in Warren, *Fanny Fern*, 93.

48. James Parton, review of *Fern Leaves, Home Journal,* June 4, 1853, quoted in Warren, *Fanny Fern,* 109, 194.

49. Fern, *Ruth Hall,* 207.

50. Melissa J. Homestead, "'Every Body Sees the Theft': Fanny Fern and Literary Proprietorship in Antebellum America," 235.

51. Sales figures from James D. Hart, *The Popular Book: A History of America's Literary Taste,* 98.

52. Donald Grant Mitchell, "Original Preface," in *Reveries of a Bachelor; or, A Book of the Heart by Ik Marvell,* viii, ix, vii.

53. Mitchell, *Reveries of a Bachelor,* 17, 37.

54. Bertolini, "Fireside Chastity"; Mitchell, *Reveries of a Bachelor,* 60.

55. Mitchell, *Reveries of a Bachelor,* xix.

56. Douglas, *Feminization of American Culture,* 239; Mitchell, *Reveries of a Bachelor,* 3, 67.

57. M. E. W., "With an Old Magazine," 249.

58. Benjamin Ellis Martin, "In the Footprints of Charles Lamb, Part I," 280.

59. M. E. W., "With an Old Magazine," 249; "Minor Notices," 179.

60. Charles Lamb, preface to *Essays of Elia,* 347; William Hazlitt, "Washington Irving," in *The Spirit of the Age; or, Contemporary Portraits,* 379.

61. William Hazlitt, "On Depth and Superficiality," in *Selected Essays of William Hazlitt, 1778–1830,* 272, originally published in *The Plain Speaker* (1826).

62. Hamilton Mabie, "The Essay and Some Essayists, Part II," 50.

63. Tudor Jenks, "The Essay," 212, 213; "Essays," 879; "Contemporary Essays," 269.

64. Florence Converse, "Among Literary Shallows," 711.

65. Carl Klaus, "Essayists on the Essay," 170; Hamilton Mabie, "The Essay and Some Essayists, Part I," 506; Jennette Barbour Perry, "The Romantic Essay," 358–59; Louise Collier Willcox, "Some Recent Essays," 780.

66. Richard Burton, "The Essay as Mood and Form," 87, 89–91.

67. Malcolm Cowley, foreword to *After the Genteel Tradition,* 9.

68. F. M. Colby, "Recent American Essays, in Two Parts: Part I," 319; Brander Matthews, "Concerning Certain Contemporary Essayists."

2. THE "DEATH" OF THE ESSAY

1. Ehrenreich and Ehrenreich, "The Professional-Managerial Class," 18.

2. W. Alfred Jones, "Essay Writing: The Champion," 13; Stephen, "The Essayists," 64; Jenks, "The Essay," 213; Richard Burton, "The Predominance of the Novel," 354–55; Stephen, "The Essayists," 64.

3. Agnes Repplier, "The Passing of the Essay," 231, 235, 232, 228–29, 232.

4. T. J. Jackson Lears, *No Place of Grace: Antimodernism and the Transformation of Culture, 1880–1920,* 60–96.

5. The definitive biography is George Stewart Stokes, *Agnes Repplier: Lady of Letters.*

6. Clara Laughlin, "Concerning Essays," 349.

7. Benjamin Wells, "Contemporary American Essays," 487, 495–96, 487.

8. H. A. Clarke, "The Survival of the Essay," 431–32; Matthews, "Concerning Certain Contemporary Essayists."

9. See Thomas Schlereth, *Victorian America: Transformations in Everyday Life, 1876–1915,* esp. chap. 1, "Moving," 7–32.

10. Henry Ford and Samuel Crowther, *My Life and Work*, 72. Douglas Brinkley notes that the date when Henry Ford first made this famous statement is not known. In *My Life and Work*, Ford implies that it was 1908 or 1909, when he was launching the Model T, but Brinkley cites the June 1913 (tenth anniversary issue) of *Ford Times* (6, no. 9), 366, which reprints the quotation and says it was first made around 1903, when the Ford Motor Company was founded (*Wheels for the World: Henry Ford, His Company, and a Century of Progress, 1903–2003*, 783n1). To further complicate matters, Warren Susman offers a 1907 date ("'Personality,'" 276).

11. Booth Tarkington, *The Magnificent Ambersons* (Garden City, N.Y.: Doubleday, 1918), 274, quoted in Brinkley, *Wheels for the World*, 114.

12. Harry Braverman, *Labor and Monopoly Capital: The Degradation of Work in the Twentieth Century*, 147.

13. Brinkley, *Wheels for the World*, 181, 155.

14. Antonio Gramsci, *Selections from the Prison Notebooks of Antonio Gramsci*, 277–318.

15. [Hamilton Mabie?], "Recent Examples of the Essay," 765, 768; "The Contemplative Essayist."

16. On literacy and the rise of the reading public, see Christopher P. Wilson, *The Labor of Words: Literary Professionalism in the Progressive Era*, 1–16; Sammye Johnson and Patricia Prijatel, *The Magazine from Cover to Cover: Inside a Dynamic Industry*, 56–87; and Schlereth, *Victorian America*, 244–57.

17. Carl F. Kaestle, "Literacy and Diversity: Themes from a Social History of the American Reading Public," 525.

18. Schlereth, *Victorian America*, 253.

19. Several histories discuss the technological changes in American publishing during the nineteenth century. See, for instance, John Tebbel, *A History of Book Publishing in the United States* and *The Media in America*, esp. chap. 7; and Cathy Davidson, *Revolution and the Word: The Rise of the Novel in America*, esp. chap. 2.

20. Rubin, *Making of Middlebrow Culture*, 18; Ohmann, *Selling Culture*, 29.

21. Don Seitz, *Training for the Newspaper Trade* (Philadelphia: Lippincott, 1916), 25, quoted in Wilson, *Labor of Words*, 27.

22. Edward Bok, *The Americanization of Edward Bok: The Autobiography of a Dutch Boy Fifty Years After*, 296.

23. Jennifer Scanlon notes how in this column "his words sound like the opinion of the magazine rather than of an individual" (*Inarticulate Longings: The "Ladies' Home Journal," Gender, and the Promise of Consumer Culture*, 117).

24. Bok, *Americanization of Bok*, 162–63. The book was awarded the Pulitzer Prize in Autobiography in 1921.

25. Oliver Wendell Holmes Sr., "The Autocrat's Autobiography" (1858), in *The Autocrat of the Breakfast Table: Everyman His Own Boswell*, xxiii.

26. Holmes, "To the Readers of the Autocrat" (1882), in ibid., xviii–xix.

27. Holmes, "Preface to the Riverside Edition" (1891), in ibid., xx–xxi.

28. Samuel McChord Crothers, *The Gentle Reader*, 1, 2, 321.

29. Helen Marshall North, "What Americans Read," 533.

30. Christopher P. Wilson, "The Rhetoric of Consumption: Mass-Market Magazines and the Demise of the Gentle Reader, 1880–1920," 42.

31. Frank Luther Mott, "The Magazine Revolution and Popular Ideas in the Nineties," 195. Matthew Schneirov suggests that the revolution began earlier (*The Dream of a New Social Order: Popular Magazines in America, 1893–1914*, 73–102).

32. Ohmann, *Selling Culture*, 8–9, 25.

33. Kaestle, "Literacy and Diversity," 528.

34. Ohmann, *Selling Culture*, 29.

35. Kaestle, "Literacy and Diversity," 535.

36. See Wilson, *Labor of Words*, 57; and Helen Damon-Moore, *Magazines for the Millions: Gender and Commerce in the "Ladies' Home Journal" and the "Saturday Evening Post," 1880–1910*, 99.

37. Walter Hines Page, "The Uplift of a Whole Nation," *World's Work*, July 1904, 4944, quoted in Wilson, *Labor of Words*, 56.

38. Ohmann, *Selling Culture*, 217. For a fully imagined description of a family's experience reading these magazines, see the opening chapter of Ohmann's book.

39. Judith Williamson, *Decoding Advertisements: Ideology and Meaning in Advertising* (London: Marion Boyars, 1978), 51, quoted in ibid., 191.

40. Tom Reynolds, "Selling College Literacy: The Mass-Market Magazine as Early 20th Century Literacy Sponsor," 169.

41. William Dean Howells, "The Man of Literature as a Man of Business," 429, 431, 433–34, 438, 440–42. Howells later included this essay as the opening selection in his *Literature and Life*, 1–35.

42. William Dean Howells, "Editor's Easy Chair," 802–3.

3. THE ESSAY IN THE PROGRESSIVE ERA

1. Phillip Lopate, "Introduction: William Dean Howells and the Discovery of New York," xvi.

2. William Dean Howells, *A Hazard of New Fortunes*, 173–74, 396–97.

3. Clifford Edward Clark Jr., *The American Family Home, 1800–1960*, xiii.

4. Thomas Reeves, *Twentieth Century America: A Brief History*, 6.

5. Benjamin I. Page and James Roy Simmons, *What Government Can Do: Dealing with Poverty and Inequality*, 12.

6. Ohmann, *Selling Culture*, 138.

7. Schlereth, *Victorian America*, 101.

8. Henry Ward Beecher, "The Advance of a Century," *New York Tribune*, extra no. 33, July 4, 1876, quoted in Trachtenberg, *Incorporation of America*, 149.

9. Schlereth, *Victorian America*, 114.

10. See Ohmann, *Selling Culture*, 128; Schlereth, *Victorian America*, 100; and Clark, *American Family Home*, 97–98.

11. Schlereth, *Victorian America*, 119.

12. Ibid., 122.

13. Trachtenberg, *Incorporation of America*, 149. See also Lyn Lofland, *A World of Strangers: Order and Action in Urban Public Space*; and Karen Halttunen, *Confidence Men and Painted Ladies: A Study of Middle-Class Culture in America, 1830–1870*, esp. chap. 2, "Hypocrisy and Sincerity in the World of Strangers."

14. Katherine Grier, *Culture and Comfort: People, Parlors, and Upholstery, 1850–1930*; Ohmann, *Selling Culture*, 143.

15. See David A. Badillo, "Mexicanos and Suburban Parish Communities: Religion, Space, and Identity in Contemporary Chicago," 25; Irving Cutler, *Jewish Chicago: A Pictorial History*, 7.

16. Clarence Cook's articles were collected in the popular stylebook *The House Beautiful: Essays on Beds and Tables, Stools, and Candlesticks*.

17. Karen Halttunen, "From Parlor to Living Room: Domestic Space, Interior Decoration, and the Culture of Personality," 169; Lillian Hart Tryon, "Abolishing the Parlor," in *Speaking of Home: Being Essays of a Contented Woman* (Boston: Houghton Mifflin, 1916), 44–45, quoted in Russell Lynes, *The Domesticated Americans*, 154.

18. Henry Seidel Canby, *The Age of Confidence: Life in the Nineties*, 57.

19. See Clay Lancaster, *The American Bungalow, 1880–1930*, 19.

20. Sears alone sold one hundred thousand houses and the plans to many more in the thirty-one years they focused on bungalows. See Katherine Cole Stevenson and H. Ward Jandl, *Houses by Mail: A Guide to Houses from Sears, Roebuck, and Company*, 19.

21. Gwendolyn Wright, *Building the Dream: A Social History of Housing in America*, 171.

22. Virginia Woolf, "Mr. Bennett and Mrs. Brown," 212–13, 226, 229–30.

23. Virginia Woolf, "The Decay of Essay-Writing," in *Essays of Virginia Woolf*, 125–26, originally published in *Academy and Literature* (February 25, 1905). McNellie's editor's note reveals that it was an editor's title and Woolf preferred "A Plague of Essays."

24. Virginia Woolf, "The Modern Essay," 223, 217, 221, 225.

25. Virginia Woolf, "A Sketch of the Past" (1939–1940), in *Moments of Being*, 126.

26. On "homosexual panic," see Eve Kosofsky Sedgwick, *Between Men: English Literature and Male Homosocial Desire*, esp. 88–90. Woolf's use of *buggers* and her reference to James's remarks come from "A Sketch of the Past," 169ff.

27. Virginia Woolf, "Old Bloomsbury," in *Moments of Being*, 172, 168.

28. Ibid., 173.

29. The biblical claim for the *Journal* is made in *A Short History of the "Ladies' Home Journal"* (Philadelphia: Curtis Publishing, 1953), 15–17, from Curtis Publishing Company Papers, Department of Special Collections, Van Pelt–Dietrich Library, University of Pennsylvania, quoted in Scanlon, *Inarticulate Longings*, 44.

30. George Horace Lorimer, "Business Policies of the *Saturday Evening Post*," contained in "Dope Book," ca. 1920–1923, Curtis Publishing Company Papers, Special Collections, Van Pelt–Dietrich Library, University of Pennsylvania, Box 130, as quoted in Douglas B. Ward, "The Reader as Consumer: Curtis Publishing Company and Its Audience, 1910–1930," 47.

31. Bok, *Americanization of Bok*, 274–75; Edward Bok, *Successward: A Young Man's Book for Young Men*, 169. Bok's view of the mediating role of the middle class is quoted in Salme Harju Steinberg, *Reformer in the Marketplace: Edward W. Bok and the "Ladies' Home Journal*," 44.

32. The best survey of Bok's influence on middle-class housing reform is Leland M. Roth's "Getting Houses to the People: Edward Bok, *The Ladies' Home Journal*, and the Ideal House."

33. Bok, *Americanization of Bok*, 240, 241; Edward Bok, "They Live in *Ladies' Home Journal* Houses: Here Are Five Successfully Erected in Foreign Countries"; Bok, *Americanization of Bok*, 242.

34. Edward Bok, "The Magazine with a Million."

35. Edward Bok, *Twice Thirty: Some Short and Simple Annals of the Road* (New York: Charles Scribner's and Sons, 1925), 373, quoted in Damon-Moore, *Magazines for the Millions*, 64.

36. *Five Thousand Books: An Easy Guide to the Best Books in Every Department of Reading*, selected, classified, and briefly described by a corps of experienced editors under the direction of the literary bureau of the *Ladies' Home Journal*, 139–44; George S. Hellman, "Hamilton Wright Mabie," in *The Cambridge History of English and American Literature*, ed. A. W. Ward et al., 125.

37. Hamilton Mabie, "Why the Essay Is Valuable as Reading."

38. Hamilton Mabie, "The Girl and Her Graduation Essay."

39. See Schlereth, *Victorian America*, 93–94. On Chicago's "Bungalow Belt," see Maria Kefalas, *Working-Class Heroes: Protecting Home, Community, and Nation in a Chicago Neighborhood*.

40. Denning, *Cultural Front*, 187.

41. Halttunen, "From Parlor to Living Room," 160.

42. Jenks, "The Essay," 213.

43. Edith Wharton and Ogden Codman Jr., *The Decoration of Houses*, 25.

44. Henry James, *Collected Travel Writings: Great Britain and America*, 493, published originally in *North American Review* (January–February 1906), collected in *The American Scene* (1907).

45. *Historical Statistics of the United States, Colonial Times to 1957: A Statistical Abstract Supplement*, Series H321, 316, p. 211, quoted in Burton Bledstein, *The Culture of Professionalism: The Middle Class and the Development of Higher Education in America*, 297.

46. See Trachtenberg, *Incorporation of America*, 145.

47. Ehrenreich and Ehrenreich, "The Professional-Managerial Class," 15.

48. John Corbin, *Which College for the Boy? Leading Types in American Education*, originally published as a series of articles in the *Saturday Evening Post*, the one on Michigan appearing in the October 19, 1907, issue; Daniel Coit Gilman, "The Dawn of a University," in *The Launching of a University, and Other Papers: A Sheaf of Remembrances* (New York: Dodd, Mead, 1906), 262, quoted in Bledstein, *Culture of Professionalism*, 293.

49. Alexandra Oleson and John Voss, introduction to *The Organization of Knowledge in Modern America, 1860–1920*, ed. Alexandra Oleson and John Voss (Baltimore: Johns Hopkins University Press, 1979), xi, quoted in Janice Radway, "Research Universities, Periodical Publication, and the Circulation of Professional Expertise: On the Significance of Middlebrow Authority," 213. Figures (for all but 1930) are from Oleson and Voss, introduction, xi, quoted in Radway, "Middlebrow Authority," 213. The figure for 1930 comes from Bledstein, *Culture of Professionalism*, 297. His figures for the earlier years differ slightly from those of Oleson and Voss.

50. Robert Wiebe, *The Search for Order, 1877–1920*, 118; [James McCosh], *Addresses Delivered in Reference to Free High Schools before the Legislature of New Jersey, 1971* (Trenton, N.J.: Murphy and Bechtel, 1871), 8, quoted in Bledstein, *Culture of Professionalism*, 279.

51. Wiebe, *Search for Order*, 119.

52. *Historical Statistics of the United States*, Series 598–601, pt. 1, 379, quoted in Schlereth, *Victorian America*, 247.

53. Merle Curti, *The Growth of American Thought*, 682. Fritz Machlup says 83.9 percent (*The Production and Distribution of Knowledge in the United States*, table IV-3, 71).

54. Curti, *Growth of American Thought*, 682.

55. David E. Kyvig, *Daily Life in the United States, 1920–1940*, 143.

56. Wiebe, *Search for Order*, 118–19.

57. Edward A. Krug, *The Shaping of the American High School* (New York: Harper and Row, 1964), 391–93, 443–44, as cited in Schlereth, *Victorian America*, 248–49.

58. Patricia Bizzell and Bruce Herzberg, eds., *The Rhetorical Tradition: Readings from Classical Times to the Present* (Boston: Bedford, 1990), 639, quoted in Lynn Z. Bloom, "Once More to the Essay: The Essay Canon and Textbook Anthologies," 26 (emphasis in the original).

59. Bloom, "Once More to the Essay," 25.

60. Richard Connors, *Composition-Rhetoric: Backgrounds, Theory, and Pedagogy*.

61. John Trimbur, "Essayist Literacy and the Rhetoric of Deproduction," 75, 83; Roland Barthes, *The Pleasure of the Text*, 14.

62. Cameron S. Moseley, "U.S. School Publishing: From Webster and McGuffey to the Internet," 25.

63. Maurice Garland Fulton, *Expository Writing: Materials for a College Course in Exposition by Analysis and Imitation*, v.

64. Justin Smith Morrill, quoted in Frederick Rudolph, *The American College and University*, 249.

65. William James, *The Letters of William James*, ed. Henry James (Boston: Atlantic Monthly Press, 1920), 1:100–101, quoted in Bledstein, *Culture of Professionalism*, 320.

66. Bledstein, *Culture of Professionalism*, 338.

67. Henry Seidel Canby, *Alma Mater: The Gothic Age of the American College*, 196–98.

68. Gerard Stanley Lee, *The Lost Art of Reading*, 20, 22, 379, 51, 393, 297–98. Lee's celebration of Lamb and his view of the essayist as one whose personality and ability to generalize enable him to see the universal in the particular have much in common, as one might expect they would, with the position argued by his wife, Jeannette Barbour Perry, in "The Romantic Essay," her important contribution to the essay debate that appeared in the *Critic* a year earlier.

69. Reynolds, "Selling College Literacy," 176, 173.

70. William James, "The Social Value of the College-Bred," address to the meeting of the Association of American Alumnae at Radcliffe College, November 7, 1907, *Essays for College Men*, ed. Norman Foerster, Frederick A. Manchester, and Karl Young (New York: Henry Holt, 1913), 174–75, quoted in Reynolds, "Selling College Literacy," 166.

71. Henry Seidel Canby, "Literature in Contemporary America," 207.

72. Hamlin Garland, *Roadside Meetings*, 342–43.

73. Frank Doubleday, "The Young Publisher's Chances."

74. Arnold Rampersad, *The Art and Imagination of W. E. B. Du Bois*, 72, 70; Robert Stepto, *From Behind the Veil*; Elaine Wright Newsome, "W. E. B. Dubois' 'Figure in the Carpet': A Cyclical Pattern in the Belletristic Prose"; and Paul Gilroy, *The Black Atlantic: Modernity and Double-Consciousness*, 122–23.

75. W. E. B. Du Bois, *The Souls of Black Folk*, 74, 76.

76. Walter Ong, "The Writer's Audience Is Always a Fiction," 12; Du Bois, *Souls of Black Folk*, 5.

77. Du Bois, *Souls of Black Folk*, 5, 11, 6; Henry Louis Gates Jr. and Terri Hume Oliver, preface to ibid., xxvi.

78. Du Bois, *Souls of Black Folk*, 164.

79. W. E. B. Du Bois, "Constitution and By-laws of the Niagara Movement as Adopted July 12 and 13, 1905," 59; "The Niagara Movement: Address to the Nation," 63.

80. W. E. B. Du Bois, "Criteria of Negro Art," 328, published originally in the *Crisis*, October 1926.

81. Randolph Bourne, "The Handicapped—by One of Them," 61.

82. John Jay Chapman, "Coatesville," 71, 73.

83. John Muir, "Stickeen," 42.

84. Mary Winsor, "John Jay Chapman, Essayist," 454–55.

85. [Hamilton Mabie?], "Essays."

86. [Hamilton Mabie?], "The Prosperity of the Essay."

87. [Mabie?], "Recent Examples of the Essay," 767.

88. For an excellent discussion of Brander Matthews's contradictions, see Susanna

Ashton, "Authorial Affiliations; or, The Clubbing and Collaborating of Brander Matthews." On the unionization controversy, see "By the Way," 966. For a description of Matthews's Manhattan home, see Charles Hernstreet, *Literary New York: Its Landmarks and Associations:* "Crossing Central Park to the far west side, the journeyer comes to a wide, tree-lined West End Avenue, and there at Ninety-third Street, almost on the shores of the Hudson River, in a locality of beautiful homes, Brander Matthews, author of *Vignettes of Manhattan* and *A Confident To-morrow,* lives and works" (251).

89. Brander Matthews, "Literature as a Profession," 196, 195, 211.

90. See, for instance, Brander Matthews, *Cheap Books and Good Books.* The first meeting of the American Copyright League was held in Matthews's house on April 16, 1883.

91. Lawrence J. Oliver, "Theodore Roosevelt, Brander Matthews, and the Campaign for Literary Americanism"; Brander Matthews, *American Character,* 6, originally delivered as the Phi Beta Kappa lecture, Columbia University, June 1905.

92. Brander Matthews, "Three American Essayists," 139, 141–42, 145, 148; Roosevelt to Matthews, January 2, 1891, Brander Matthews Papers, Columbia University, New York, quoted in Oliver, "Campaign for Literary Americanism," 100; Roosevelt, "A Colonial Survival," *Cosmopolitan,* December 1892, 232–33, quoted in Oliver, "Campaign for Literary Americanism," 100–101.

93. Brander Matthews, "Modern Essays," 268–69.

94. "The Contemplative Essayist."

95. Richard Burton, "The Essay: A Famous Literary Form and Its Conquests," *New York Times,* April 5, 1914, BR166.

96. Claude M. Fuess, introduction to *Selected Essays,* vii–xiv.

4. NEW YORK, NEW YORK: THE ARRIVAL OF THE COLYUMNISTS

1. Stuart P. Sherman, "Graduate Schools and Literature," in *Shaping Men and Women: Essays on Literature and Life,* ed. Jacob Zeitlin (New York: Doubleday and Doran, 1928), 39, 43–44, quoted in Rubin, *Making of Middlebrow Culture,* 48; John Erskine, *My Life as a Teacher* (Philadelphia: J. B. Lippincott, 1948), 170, quoted in Rubin, *Making of Middlebrow Culture,* 166.

2. Canby, *Alma Mater,* x, quoted in Radway, "Middlebrow Authority," 204; Gerald Graff, *Professing Literature: An Institutional History,* 91ff.

3. Canby, "Literature in Contemporary America," 211; Henry Seidel Canby, *Everyday Americans,* 178, 163–64, 175–76.

4. See Claudia Goldin and Lawrence F. Katz, "Decreasing (and Then Increasing) Inequality in America: A Tale of Two Half-Centuries"; and Claudia Goldin and Robert A. Margo, "The Great Compression: The Wage Structure in the United States at Mid-Century."

5. Gordon Hutner, "The 'Good Reader' and the Bourgeois Critic," 18.

6. Agnes Repplier, "The American Essay in Wartime," 253.

7. Randolph Bourne, "Trans-national America," 86; Randolph Bourne, "A Vanishing World of Gentility," 234.

8. Randolph Bourne, "The Light Essay," 419.

9. Christopher Morley, "In Memoriam: E. V., Bill Footner, Tom Daly, Bob Holliday," 178; Robert Cortes Holliday, "Caun't Speak the Language," 210–11.

10. Robert Cortes Holliday, "An Article without an Idea," 80–84; Morley, "In Memoriam," 177.

11. Holliday, "Article without an Idea," 84.

12. H. L. Mencken, "Civilized Chicago," *Chicago Sunday Tribune* (1917), pt. 8, p. 5; he reiterated the claim in "The Literary Capital of the United States," *Nation* (London), April 17, 1920, 92, reprinted in *Chicago Daily News,* May 12, 1920. See also Greg Holden, *A Booklover's Tour of the Windy City,* 6.

13. Sherwood Anderson, *Sherwood Anderson's Memoirs,* 317.

14. Alexander Stoddart, "Journalism's Radium, the Colyumn," 274.

15. George Ade quoted in Fred Charters Kelly, *George Ade: Warmhearted Satirist,* 100; Lazar Ziff, *The American 1890s: Life and Times of a Lost Generation* (New York: Viking, 1966), 165, quoted in A. L. Lorenz, "The Whitechapel Club: Defining Chicago's Newspapermen in the 1890s," 83.

16. Quoted in Lorenz, "Whitechapel Club," 99.

17. Theodore Dreiser, *Newspaper Days,* ed. T. D. Nostwich (Philadelphia: University of Pennsylvania Press, 1991) 3, quoted in Donald L. Miller, *City of the Century: The Epic of Chicago and the Making of America,* 522.

18. The best analysis of the Dunne-Roosevelt relationship can be found in Aviva Taubenfeld, *Rough Writing: Ethnic Authorship in Theodore Roosevelt's America,* 121–57.

19. William Allen White in a letter to Ade, quoted in Kelly, *George Ade: Warmhearted Satirist,* 144.

20. George Ade, "They Simply Wouldn't Let Me Be a High-Brow."

21. Anna Morgan, *My Chicago,* 149.

22. Mary Terrill, "About Essays, and Three," 192; Charles Brooks, "The Writing of Essays," 219–20, 222; F. E. Schelling, "The Familiar Essay."

23. Berton Braley, "On Being an Essayist," 646–47; F. M. Colby, *"The Gentleman's Review."*

24. Burton Rascoe, "What of Our Essayists?" 74.

25. Malcolm Cowley, *Exile's Return: A Literary Odyssey of the 1920s,* 227; Henry Seidel Canby, "Out with the Dilettante."

26. Mary Ellis Opdycke, "Colyumism," 16.

27. Stuart P. Sherman, *Life and Letters of Stuart P. Sherman,* ed. Jacob Zeitlin and Homer Woodbridge (New York: Farrar and Rinehart, 1929), 2:683, quoted in Rubin, *Making of Middlebrow Culture,* 66.

28. Royal Cortissoz to Geoffrey Pasons, January 6, 1923, Reid Family Papers, quoted in Rubin, *The Making of Middlebrow Culture,* 63.

29. See Rubin, *Making of Middlebrow Culture,* 47–49, 63–65.

30. Ann Douglas, *Terrible Honesty: Mongrel Manhattan in the 1920s;* Carl Van Doren, "Day In and Day Out: Manhattan Wits," 182, 183, 198; Opdycke, "Colyumnism," 16.

31. Van Doren, "Day In and Day Out," 198, 182.

32. Stuart P. Sherman, "An Apology for the Essayists of the Press," 184, 177–78.

33. See C. L. Edson, *The Gentle Art of Columning: A Treatise on Comic Journalism,* which included essays by Marquis, Morley, Adams, and *Saturday Evening Post* editor George Horace Lorimer. It was followed by Hallam Walker Davis's book *The Column.*

34. Sherman, "Apology for Essayists," 173–77, 182–84.

35. Don Marquis, "The Almost Perfect State."

36. Sherman, "Apology for Essayists," 177–78.

37. White, "Farm Paper," in *OMM,* 113; White, "Don Marquis," in *Essays of E. B. White,* 255.

38. Don Marquis, *Hermione and Her Little Group of Serious Thinkers,* 59.

39. Braley, "On Being an Essayist," 646.

40. The term is Thomas Edison's, but Radway adapts it to the Book-of-the-Month Club (*Feeling for Books*, 155ff).

41. Rubin, *Making of Middlebrow Culture*, 137, 141; Radway, *Feeling for Books*, 371n66, 180–81, 183.

42. Radway, *Feeling for Books*, 179–80.

43. Woolf, "The Modern Essay," 222.

44. Radway, *Feeling for Books*, 180; Rubin, *Making of Middlebrow Culture*, 138–39, 135; Radway, *Feeling for Books*, 182.

45. White, "Marquis," 250.

46. Billy Altman, *Laughter's Gentle Soul: The Life of Robert Benchley*, 130–34, 148–58; Norris Yates, *Robert Benchley*, 36. Marion Meade, who quotes Parker, also suggests that Gruening's pacifism and German surname did not help (*Dorothy Parker: What Fresh Hell Is This?* 68).

47. Norris Yates, *The American Humorist: Conscience of the Twentieth Century*, 320; C. Wright Mills, *Letters and Autobiographical Writings*, 100, quoted in Russell Jacoby, afterword to *White Collar: The American Middle Classes*, 367; C. Wright Mills, "From the Author," *Book Find News* (1951): 5, quoted in Richard Gillam, "'White Collar' from Start to Finish: C. Wright Mills in Transition," 27; Mills, *White Collar*, xii, 328; Dwight Macdonald, "Laugh and Lie Down," 47.

48. Jonathan Freedman, *The Temple of Culture: Assimilation and Anti-Semitism in Literary Anglo-America*, 10; Mills, *White Collar*, xiii.

49. Robert Benchley, "The Brow-Elevation in Humor," 304–6.

50. Nina Miller, *Making Love Modern: The Intimate Public Worlds of New York's Literary Women*, 97.

51. Robert Benchley, "Mr. Bok's Americanization," 217.

52. See Radway, *Feeling for Books*, 199–200.

53. See Rubin, *Making of Middlebrow Culture*, 80ff.

54. Cowley, *Exile's Return*, 53, 58.

55. Andreas Huyssen, *After the Great Divide: Modernism, Mass Culture, Postmodernism*.

56. See Timothy Materer, "Make It Sell! Ezra Pound Advertises Modernism."

57. Ezra Pound, "How to Read"; Ezra Pound to Louis Zukofsky, November 2, 1928, *Pound/Zukofsky: Selected Letters of Ezra Pound and Louis Zukofsky (Correspondence of Ezra Pound)*, 18.

58. Pound to Zukofsky, July 7, 1932, *Pound/Zukofsky*, 130; Pound to Irita Van Doren, December 14, 1931[?], quoted in Rubin, *Making of Middlebrow Culture*, 90–91; Ezra Pound to William Carlos Williams, March 10, 1932, *Pound/Williams: Selected Letters of Ezra Pound and William Carlos Williams*, 132.

59. James Laughlin, speech in acceptance of the 1992 National Book Foundation's Medal for Distinguished Contribution to American Letters at the National Book Awards Ceremony, 1992, *http://www.nationalbook.org/nbaacceptspeech_jlaughlin.html*.

60. Catherine Turner, *Marketing Modernism between the Two World Wars*, 137, 209, 117; Henry Seidel Canby, *American Memoir*, 287–88.

61. Kathleen Morgan Drowne and Patrick Huber, *The 1920s*, 66–67.

62. Theodore Peterson, *Magazines in the Twentieth Century*, 78.

63. Henry Ford, as told to William A. McGarry, "Prosperity—What Is It?" *Saturday Evening Post*, April 10, 1926, quoted in Jan Cohn, *Creating America: George Horace Lorimer and the "Saturday Evening Post*," 187.

64. Cowley, *Exile's Return*, 4–5.

65. Canby, "Literature in America," 6–7.

66. Henry Seidel Canby, "Adventures in Starting a Literary Magazine," 302–3; Canby, *American Memoir*, 277–78.

67. Henry Seidel Canby, "Timely and Timeless," *Saturday Review of Literature*, August 2, 1924, 2, quoted in Christina Klein, *Cold War Orientalism: Asia in the Middlebrow Imagination, 1945–1961*, 73; Canby quoted in Joseph Wood Krutch, introduction to *Saturday Review Treasury*, ed. John *Haverstick*, xx.

68. Studies from 1963 and 1966, cited by Klein, *Cold War Orientalism*, 73.

69. Katharine White quoted in Burton Bernstein, *Thurber* (New York: Ballantine Books, 1972), 637, quoted in Scott Elledge, *E. B. White: A Biography*, 117.

70. Paula Fass, *The Damned and the Beautiful: American Youth Culture in the 1920s*. For the more on the influence of the humor magazines, see Judith Yaross Lee, *Defining "New Yorker" Humor*, esp. chap. 1, where she cites Fass's work.

71. On the 1923 issue of *Vanity Fair*, see Ben Yagoda, *About Town: The "New Yorker" and the World It Made*, 37.

72. Ross's prospectus is widely available. See, for instance, appendix 1 in Thomas Kunkel, *Genius in Disguise: Harold Ross of the "New Yorker*," 440.

73. E. B. White, "H. W. Ross" (December 15, 1951), in *Writings from the "New Yorker," 1927–1976*, 232.

74. Ohmann, *Selling Culture*, 251–52.

75. See Trysh Travis, "What We Talk about When We Talk about the *New Yorker*," 254n6.

76. Henry Ford, interview with Charles N. Wheeler, *Chicago Tribune*, March 25, 1916.

77. Carl Van Doren, "Short for Buncombe."

78. Kenneth Burke, "The Virtues and Limitations of Debunking," 171, 174, 169, 184.

79. Bourdieu, "Field of Power, Literary Field, and Habitus," in *Field of Cultural Production*, 163–64.

80. Braley, "On Being an Essayist," 647.

81. John Waters, "A Little Old Lady Passes Away," 27–29; Howard Mumford Jones, "The Demise of a Little Old Lady."

82. Yagoda, *About Town*, 58–59. By 1945 the figure was 73 percent. By 2003 the magazine had more subscribers in California (167,000) than in New York (166,000). See the Pew Research Center's Project for Excellence in Journalism, "Annual Report: Magazine Audience" (2005), *http://www.journalism.org/node/482*.

83. Denning, *Cultural Front*, 15.

84. Heywood Broun, "The Magical City," in *It Seems to Me: 1925–1935*, 112–15, originally published in the *New York Telegram*, October 31, 1930.

85. Ross quoted in Yagoda, *About Town*, 197; William Shawn, *Encyclopedia Britannica*, 1964 ed., s.v. "Harold Ross," quoted in Elledge, *E. B. White*, 119n14.

5. STARTING OUT AT THE *NEW YORKER*

1. Kenneth T. Jackson, *Crabgrass Frontier: The Suburbanization of the United States*, 84–85; Clark, *American Family Home*, 92.

2. White, introduction to *Letters of E. B. White*, 1–2.

3. Ibid., 4.

4. Jacket copy of E. B. White, *Quo Vadimus? or, The Case for the Bicycle*, quoted in Elledge, *E. B. White*, 1–2.

5. Arthur Loesser, *Men, Women, and Pianos* (New York: Simon and Schuster, 1954),

549, 552–53, cited in Ohmann, *Selling Culture*, 90.

6. Ohmann, *Selling Culture*, 90. It is a position with which Thomas Schlereth seems to agree: "Common in rural and workers' homes by the 1890s, parlor organs seemed especially suitable for the hymns and sentimental ballads so loved by the Victorians. By the turn of the century, however, anyone with serious social and musical pretensions had a piano" (*Victorian America*, 211). Stuart Blumin demonstrates that for at least a part of the urban middle class, a piano and a parlor had served as important markers much earlier. He quotes Issac Ferris from 1857: "Time was when it was sufficient for a comfortable liver to have half a house, or to have one spare front-room for company: now, the same man must have a whole house, and the first story must be thrown into parlors. . . . It is not many years since the class spoken of were only occasionally favored with a piano; now, that instrument must be set down as requisite to parlor equipment" ("Men of Business: Their Home Responsibilities," in *The Man of Business, Considered in His Various Relations* [New York, 1857], 24–25, quoted in Blumin, *Emergence of the Middle Class*, 138).

7. White, introduction to *Letters of E. B. White*, 3. Later, after his father's death, when White was helping his mother shut down the house in Mt. Vernon, the many pianos became a bit of a burden. He and Katharine had a piano in Manhattan and the house in Maine—"all we have room for." To his brother Stanley he wrote, "I don't know what your Piano Situation is, but if you should want this grand [in Mt. Vernon] in preference to whatever piano you already own, I would be glad to give it to you for the sake of keeping it in the family" (*Letters of E. B. White*, 130).

8. White to Stanley Hart White, March 11, 1954, *Letters of E. B. White*, 389. The attendance figure of twenty-five hundred is from several sources, including Elledge, *E. B. White*, 10. The sixty thousand–dollar figure is from Robert Shaplen, *Free Love and Heavenly Sinners: The Story of the Great Henry Ward Beecher Scandal* (New York: Alfred A. Knopf, 1954), 99, cited in Douglas, *Feminization of American Culture*, 242.

9. White, "Farm Paper," in *OMM*, 113. For more on the children's magazines, see "The St. Nicholas League" in *Essays of E. B. White*, 225–33.

10. White to Luella Adams, November 24, 1957, *Letters of E. B. White*, 445. In the letter White is quoting his own journal from February 24, 1920.

11. E. B. White, "The Years of Wonder," in *Essays of E. B. White*, 170–71.

12. E. B. White, "Noontime of an Advertising Man," *New Yorker*, June 25, 1949, quoted in Elledge, *E. B. White*, 99.

13. E. B. White, "Notes and Comment," *New Yorker*, April 2, 1960, quoted in Elledge, *E. B. White*, 100; E. B. White, "Here Is New York," in *Essays of E. B. White*, 125–26.

14. E. B. White, "A Step Forward," 21.

15. Yagoda, *About Town*, 40, 96.

16. *New Yorker*, April 23, 1927, 8.

17. First advertisement for the Book-of-the-Month Club (1926), reprinted in Maxwell Sackheim, *My First Sixty Years in Advertising*, 118. See also Rubin, *Making of Middlebrow Culture*, 99; and Radway, *Feeling for Books*, 193.

18. *New Yorker*, April 23, 1927, 23.

19. Yagoda, *About Town*, 96.

20. Radway, *Feeling for Books*, 29.

21. *New Yorker*, April 9, 1927, 61.

22. Roland Marchand, *Advertising the American Dream: Making Way for Modernity, 1920–1940*, 32, 13.

23. E. B. White, "Notes and Comment," *New Yorker*, May 28, 1927, 11.

24. Katharine Sergeant White to E. B. White, June 21, 1929, quoted in Elledge, *E. B. White*, 164.

25. The recountings of this story are several; see especially David McCullough, *Mornings on Horseback: The Story of an Extraordinary Family, a Vanished Way of Life, and the Unique Child Who Became Theodore Roosevelt*, 256.

26. Sherman, "Apology for Essayists," 185.

27. Samuel McChord Crothers, "Making Friends with the Essay."

28. Franklin Delano Roosevelt, *F.D.R., Columnist: The Uncollected Columns of Franklin D. Roosevelt*, 103.

29. James R. McGovern, *And a Time for Hope: Americans in the Great Depression*, 288n86.

30. Bruce Barton to George Barr Baker, July 7, 1924, Barton Papers, Box 13, file: "Coolidge, Calvin," quoted in Douglas B. Craig, *Fireside Politics: Radio and Political Culture in the United States, 1920–1940*, 145.

31. Kenneth D. Yeilding and Paul H. Carlson, introduction to Roosevelt, *Ah That Voice*, xii.

32. Paul F. Lazerfield, *Radio and the Printed Page* (New York: Duell, Sloan, and Pearce, 1940), 31–44, quoted in Rubin, *Making of Middlebrow Culture*, 274.

33. Franklin Roosevelt, *New York Times*, January 28, 1929, quoted in Frank Friedel, *Franklin D. Roosevelt: The Triumph*, 31. See also Davis W. Houck and Amos Kiewe, *FDR's Body Politics: The Rhetoric of Disability*, 53.

34. See Roosevelt, *Ah That Voice*, xiii, and *FDR's Fireside Chats*, xv. There is some speculation that the term was inspired by Roosevelt's press secretary, Steve Early, who had remarked to reporters that the president liked to think of his audience as being "a few people around his fireside" (Betty Houchin Winfield, *FDR and the News Media*, 104).

35. Yeilding and Carlson say there were only twenty-six. Roosevelt's head speechwriter, Samuel I. Rosenman, added another when he compiled the official edition of Roosevelt's papers. Other authorities upped the number to twenty-eight, claiming that the November 14, 1937, speech was mislabled due to an editorial oversight. Finally, when Mass Communications, Inc. (MCI), issued tape recordings of the fireside chats in 1973, they added the speech of May 27, 1941, and the 1944 and 1945 State of the Union addresses, which were presented over the radio in a style informal enough to include them with the others. Buhite and Levy follow MCI's lead (Roosevelt, *FDR's Fireside Chats*, xv).

36. Roosevelt to R. Leffingwell, March 16, 1942, *FDR: His Personal Letters*, vol. 1, *The Early Years*, ed. Elliott Roosevelt (New York: Duell, Sloan, and Pearce), 1298–99, quoted in Doris Kearns Goodwin, *No Ordinary Time: Franklin and Eleanor Roosevelt; The Home Front in World War II*, 320.

37. See introduction, n. 25.

38. Samuel Rosenman, *Working with Roosevelt* (New York: Harper and Brothers, 1952), 5–6, quoted in Roosevelt, *FDR's Fireside Chats*, xvii–xviii; Frances Perkins, *The Roosevelt I Knew* (New York: Viking, 1946), 72, quoted in Roosevelt, *FDR's Fireside Chats*, xix, and Goodwin, *No Ordinary Time*, 58; Henry Fairlie, "The Voice of Hope," *New Republic*, January 27, 1982, 16, quoted in Paul Fussell, *Wartime: Understanding and Behavior in the Second World War*, 181; Richard Strout, "The President and the Press," in *The Making of the New Deal: The Insiders Speak*, ed. Katie Louchheim (Cambridge: Harvard University Press, 1983), 13, quoted in Winfield, *FDR and the News Media*, 104.

39. Franklin D. Roosevelt, "The Method for Reopening Banks," in *The Public Papers and Addresses of Franklin D. Roosevelt*, 2:60.

40. July 24, 1933, Roosevelt, *Ah That Voice*, 22, and *FDR's Fireside Chats*, 36.

41. July 28, 1943, Roosevelt, *Ah That Voice*, 217, and *FDR's Fireside Chats*, 266.

42. White to Gus Lobrano, [March 1933], *Letters of E. B. White*, 112–13.

43. On the magazine's success during this period, see Yagoda, *About Town*, 96–97; Elledge, *E. B. White*, 183; and Dale Kramer and George R. Clark, "Harold Ross and the *New Yorker*," 519.

44. [Ralph Ingersoll], "The New Yorker," 88; Elledge, *E. B. White*, 182–83. Katharine White's biographer estimates that together the Whites earned between twenty-three and thirty thousand dollars in 1935 (Linda Davis, *Onward and Upward: A Biography of Katharine S. White*, 114).

45. L. Davis, *Onward and Upward*, 118; [Ingersoll], "The New Yorker," 88; Elledge, *E. B. White*, 182.

46. White to Charles Morton, May 6, 1963, *Letters of E. B. White*, 501.

47. Cited in Yagoda, *About Town*, 111.

48. White, "Swing Low, Sweet Upswing," *New Yorker*, January 7, 1933, reprinted in *Quo Vadimus?* 118, quoted in Elledge, *E. B. White*, 185.

49. White, "Notes and Comment," *New Yorker*, November 25, 1933, reprinted in *Every Day Is Saturday*, 197–98, quoted in Elledge, *E. B. White*, 184.

50. Ross to White, May 7, 1935, quoted in Elledge, *E. B. White*, 192–93. See Robert K. Root Jr., *E. B. White: The Emergence of an Essayist*, esp. chaps. 2 and 3, where he carefully traces White's struggle to create essays using the format of "Notes and Comment."

51. White to Lobrano, [October? 1934], *Letters of E. B. White*, 121.

52. Rea Irvin, the magazine's famous art director, created Eustace Tilley, but *New Yorker* writer Corey Ford named him a few months later in an ironic series called "The Making of a Magazine" that filled the back of the front cover until advertisers could be convinced to buy the page. See Yagoda, *About Town*, 47–48.

53. White, *New Yorker*, February 17, 1934, quoted in Elledge, *E. B. White*, 188.

54. See, for instance, Michael Shudson, *Advertising, the Uneasy Persuasion: Its Dubious Impact on American Society*, 209–33; and Elspeth H. Brown, *The Corporate Eye: Photography and the Rationalization of American Commercial Culture, 1884–1929*, 114. Michael Augspurger, in *An Economy of Abundant Beauty: "Fortune" Magazine and Depression America*, following *Fortune* illustrator Laurence Sisson, prefers the term *designed realism* as opposed to Macdonald's designation, *sophisticated kitsch* (76).

55. Macdonald quoted in Vicki Goldberg, *Margaret Bourke-White: A Biography*, 104; Dwight Macdonald, *Politics Past* (New York: Viking, 1970), 8–9, quoted in Denning, *Cultural Front*, 84.

56. [Ingersoll], "The New Yorker," 97, 85.

57. White chose to see himself and the *New Yorker* editors as predominantly middle class. As he later put it, "Only two staff people in the early days of *The New Yorker* had a background of Society: Ralph Ingersoll and Fillmore Hyde. The rest of us just popped out of the subway somewhere" (White to Walter Blair, February 1, 1964, *Letters of E. B. White*, 514–15). For more on Ingersoll, see Roy Hoppes, *Ralph Ingersoll: A Biography*.

58. Wolcott Gibbs, "Time . . . Fortune . . . Life . . . Luce," 21, 25; E. B. White, interview by George A. Plimpton and Frank H. Crowther, *Paris Review* 48 (Fall 1969), reprinted in *The "Paris Review": Interviews*, ed. Philip Gourevitch (New York: Picador, 2009), 4:142, quoted in Yagoda, *About Town*, 207.

59. Quoted in Elledge, *E. B. White*, 377n34.

60. Katharine Fullerton Gerould, "The Extirpation of Culture," 68; Gerould, "The Plight of the Genteel."

61. Amy Loveman, "Arm Chair Philosophy," quoted in Katharine Fullerton Gerould, "Information, Please! A Call for a Plebiscite of Magazine Readers," 393. Incendiary as these comments were, they were not as provocative as remarks Gerould made a year later in the *North American Review* in which she argued that "we need to get away from polemics; we even need to get away from statistics," and that the essay can help us do it. She admitted the nation was "in a state of war," a war over whether "to guarantee bread to everyone," and even allowed that feeding the hungry "is perhaps our major duty," but she could not resist adding, "The preoccupation with bread alone is a savage's preoccupation. . . . The preoccupation with facts to the exclusion of what can be done with them, and the incapacity for logical thinking, are both savage" ("An Essay on Essays," 417). Again, she had slipped. Many of her readers might agree that we do not live by bread alone, and that "the incapacity for logical thinking" is not good, but they resented her attempt to bank on their racism by tossing around the term *savage* so loosely.

62. Letters in response to Gerould, "Information, Please!" appeared in the January 26, 1935, and February 2, 1935, issues of the *Saturday Review of Literature*. Canby apparently tried to solicit responses from editors other than Dashiell, but not always with success. Mixed feelings within their staff, uncertainty about their readers, and Gerould's formidable presence apparently scared *Harper's*. See this response to Canby's query from Lee Foster Hartman:

> January 17, 1935
>
> Dear Henry,
>
> I hate like the devil to wash out on you, but I cannot see my way clear to making a rejoinder to Mrs. Gerould without telling her in substance that she is a first-class intellectual snob. I have long thought so, but at the same time I like her very much, so that I do not want to cross swords with her.
>
> I have asked George Leighton of our staff to try his hand at an answer and I enclose the result, which you are welcome to cut and publish as a communication to The Saturday Review, if you like. But I cannot permit this to appear as coming from Harper's Magazine. If you wish to print any part of it, I should like to have you attach some blind pen name to it. Leighton makes certain points which I do not agree with at all—in fact, I am on Mrs. Gerould's side of the fence—but I think Leighton represents a certain vigorous point of view common to a good many readers who are on the other side of thirty-five.
>
> Sincerely yours,
>
> LFH

(Henry Seidel Canby Papers, Beinecke Library, Yale University, YCAL MSS 64, Box 3, Folder 95)

63. Elizabeth Drew, "The Lost Art of the Essay," 38, 36, 49.

64. Henry Seidel Canby, "The Essay as Barometer."

65. This was apparently a onetime promotion and not an ongoing show. *An American Fireside*, March 24, 1935, Motion Picture, Broadcasting, and Recorded Sound Division, Library of Congress, Washington, D.C., quoted in Rubin, *Making of Middlebrow Culture*, 266–67.

66. On Canby's breakdown, see Rubin, *Making of Middlebrow Culture*, 123. On his new title after 1936, see his Yale papers, http://webtext.library.yale.edu/xml2html/beinecke.CANBY.con.html.

67. White to Morley, April 27, 1936, *Letters of E. B. White*, 131–32.

68. White to K. White, [March? 1939], ibid., 193–94.

69. White, introduction to *OMM*, xii.

70. White, "Notes and Comment," *New Yorker*, April 24, 1937, quoted in Elledge, *E. B. White*, 197; Stanley White to White, March 15, 1937, quoted in Elledge, *E. B. White*, 197; Brendan Gill, *Here at the "New Yorker,"* 119, quoted in ibid., 212.

71. White to Katharine White, May 31, 1937, ibid., 154–56. Linda Davis points out that departures, such as this one to Maine, formed a consistent pattern in White's life and in the couple's long marriage. Unsure what to do with his life, White took off on an eighteen-month cross-country jaunt upon graduating from Cornell. Later, when he and Katharine got together as a couple, they interrupted their courtship at the final moment—she spent the summer of 1929 in Reno obtaining a divorce, while he canoed in Ontario. During September 1935, when she suffered a miscarriage in Maine, he was in New York. They occasionally vacationed separately. The arrangement may have seemed odd, even unfair, to some, but Davis argues otherwise. "That the White marriage was close and deeply satisfying for both Katharine and Andy," she says, "is indisputable, but they, or Andy, required spaces in their togetherness. For private, forever hidden emotional reasons, they tended to separate at times when one would expect a happily married couple to draw closer" (*Onward and Upward*, 118).

72. White, "Notes and Comment," *New Yorker*, August 7, 1937, 9.

73. White, *Harper's*, October 1938, 555, quoted in Elledge, *E. B. White*, 209.

74. James Thurber, *Letters of Thurber*, 11–14, quoted in Elledge, *E. B. White*, 205; White to Thurber, [October? 1937], ibid., 166–67.

75. *Historical Statistics of the United States*, pt. 1, 126, 135, quoted in McGovern, *And a Time for Hope*, 42; Robert R. Nathan, "Estimates of Unemployment in the United States, 1929–1935," *International Labor Review* 63 (January 1936): 49–73, quoted in McGovern, *And a Time for Hope*, 4.

76. Critiques of White or the *New Yorker* or both include Lionel Trilling, "*New Yorker* Fiction"; Stanley Edgar Hyman, "The Urban *New Yorker*"; Robert Warshow, "The Working Day at the Splendide," *Nation* (November 9, 1946), and "Melancholy to the End," review of *Wild Flag*, *Partisan Review* 14 (January–February 1947): 86–88; these last two are reprinted in Robert Warshow, *The Immediate Experience: Movies, Comics, Theatre, and Other Aspects of Popular Culture*, the latter as "E. B. White and the *New Yorker*." The broader critiques of middlebrow are legion; among the most notable are Clement Greenberg's "Avant Garde and Kitsch" and Dwight Macdonald's "Masscult and Midcult I," *Partisan Review* (Spring 1960): 203–33, and "Masscult and Midcult II," *Partisan Review* (Fall 1960): 589–631, reprinted in Macdonald, *Against the American Grain: Essays on the Effects of Mass Culture*, 3–77.

77. Macdonald, "Laugh and Lie Down," 44–46.

78. Constance Rourke, "The Significance of Sections," *New Republic*, September 20, 1933, 149, quoted in Denning, *Cultural Front*, 133. Rourke's comments here are hauntingly prescient. The CIO victory at Ford's River Rouge plant did not come until 1941, but September 1934 saw the largest strike of a single industry in American history, when four hundred thousand textile workers went out from Maine to Alabama. Then, two years later, the great wave of sit-down strikes began in Akron and Flint. Macdonald was writing in the winter of 1937, on the heels of all of this activity.

79. Macdonald, "Laugh and Lie Down," 45–48; Sinclair Lewis, "The American Fear of Literature: The Nobel Prize Address (1930)," 16.

6. LEAVING THE *NEW YORKER*

1. William Z. Foster, *History of the Communist Party of the United States*, 341.

2. Robert H. Zieger, *The CIO: 1935–1955*, 53, 395n8.

3. Denning, *Cultural Front*, 286–87.

4. Franklin Delano Roosevelt, "Victory Dinner Address," in *Representative American Speeches, 1937–38*, ed. A. Craig Beard, 105, 109, 110. Five nights later he took a more measured approach in a fireside chat. See "Defending the Plan to 'Pack' the Supreme Court," in *FDR's Fireside Chats*, 83–95.

5. White, "Notes and Comment," *New Yorker*, March 13, 1937, 15.

6. Ingersoll to White, March 17, 1937, quoted in Elledge, *E. B. White*, 199; Macdonald, "Laugh and Lie Down," 50; *Time*, March 22, 1937, quoted in Elledge, *E. B. White*, 198.

7. White, "Notes and Comment," *New Yorker*, March 4, 1944, 15.

8. See Joseph P. Lash, *Eleanor and Franklin: The Story of Their Relationship Based on Eleanor Roosevelt's Private Papers*, 567.

9. White to James Thurber, January 8, 1938, *Letters of E. B. White*, 171.

10. White, introduction to *OMM*, xii–xiii.

11. Elledge, *E. B. White*, 217; Root, *Emergence of an Essayist*, 16; Roger Angell, foreword to *OMM*, viii.

12. Gerould, "Information, Please!" 395; White, introduction to *OMM*, xiii.

13. E. B. White, "Visitors to the Pond," 28.

14. White, "Notes and Comment," *New Yorker*, May 7, 1949, 23.

15. White, "Walden," in *OMM*, 70. This was one of several expense accounts in the manner of Franklin and Thoreau that White included in *One Man's Meat*; see *OMM*, 13, 53, 102ff, 107–8, 265.

16. White, "A Slight Sound at Evening," in *Selected Essays*, 235–36; White, introduction to *OMM*, xiii.

17. Quoted in Norman Moss, *Nineteen Weeks: America, Britain, and the Fateful Summer of 1940*, 163.

18. Bertolini, "Fireside Chastity"; White, "Compost," in *OMM*, 132.

19. White, "Clear Days," in *OMM*, 17; Roosevelt quoted in Nicholas John Cull, *Selling War: The British Propaganda Campaign against American "Neutrality" in World War II*, 21.

20. White to Cass Canfield and Eugene Saxton, January 18, 1939, *Letters of E. B. White*, 191; White, "Second World War," in *OMM*, 84.

21. White, "Farm Paper," in *OMM*, 113; "Fro-Joy," in *OMM*, 107.

22. White, "Notes and Comment," *New Yorker*, June 22, 1940, 11.

23. Saxton to White, April 5, 1940, quoted in Elledge, *E. B. White*, 223; White to Saxton, July 5, 1940, quoted in Elledge, *E. B. White*, 223.

24. White, "Freedom," in *OMM*, 135–39.

25. Mike Gold, "Notes of the Month" (April 1930), 4; Gold, "Notes of the Month" (May 1930), 3; Gold, "Wilder: Prophet of the Genteel Christ," 266–67; Sinclair Lewis, "A New Subscriber Disagrees (Letter)," 22.

26. White, "Freedom," in *OMM*, 135–39.

27. White, "Sanitation," in *OMM*, 148; "The Trailer Park," in *OMM*, 180–85; "On a Florida Key," in *OMM*, 178.

28. White, "Lime," in *OMM*, 158.

29. The figures for an April 1941 poll showed 19 percent in favor of America entering the war and 70 percent in favor of military support of Great Britain. See Max Wallace,

The American Axis: Henry Ford, Charles Lindbergh, and the Rise of the Third Reich, 276. On Lindbergh's book and its reception, see Justus D. Doenecke, *Storm on the Horizon: The Challenge to American Intervention, 1939–1941*, 53–55.

30. White, "The Wave of the Future," in *OMM*, 165, 167.

31. E. B. White, "We," 12.

32. Charles Lindbergh, "Aviation, Geography, and Race," 64, 67; Charles Lindbergh, "What Substitute for War?" *Atlantic Monthly*, March 1940, 307, quoted in Doenecke, *Storm on the Horizon*, 214; Lindbergh, "Aviation, Geography, and Race," 67.

33. Anne Morrow Lindbergh, "A Prayer for Peace," *Reader's Digest*, January 1940, 5, quoted in Doenecke, *Storm on the Horizon*, 19; Anne Morrow Lindbergh, "The Wave of the Future: A Confession of Faith," 281.

34. White, "Spring," in *OMM*, 186–90; Carl Klaus, "Excursion of the Mind: Toward a Poetics of Uncertainty in the Disjunctive Essay"; Robert Scholes and Carl Klaus, *Elements of the Essay*, 59. On the history of the piece, see Root, *Emergence of an Essayist*, 98–104.

35. White, "Report," in *OMM*, 102; "Camp Meeting," in *OMM*, 78; "Security," in *OMM*, 13; "Spring," in *OMM*, 190–91.

36. White to Harold Ross, June 25, [1941?], *Letters of E. B. White*, 212.

37. White to Ross, [June 26, 1941?], ibid.

38. "Lindbergh Decries Fears of Invasion," *New York Times*, May 20, 1940, 1; Charles Lindbergh, "The Air Defense of America," radio address of May 19, 1940, entered in the *Congressional Record*, May 20, 1940, 3034–35; Roosevelt quoted in Goodwin, *No Ordinary Time*, 48; Roosevelt's letter to Stimson letter quoted in Wallace, *American Axis*, 241.

39. Albert Fried, *FDR and His Enemies*, 192; Goodwin, *No Ordinary Time*, 187–88.

40. Hutchins and La Follette quoted in Doenecke, *Storm on the Horizon*, 43.

41. Quoted in Goodwin, *No Ordinary Time*, 210. On *MacLeish*'s role, see James MacGregor Burns and Susan Burns, *The Three Roosevelts: Patrician Leaders Who Transformed America*, 438.

42. Luce, "The American Century," 63; Lerner, "The People's Century."

43. Robert Sherwood, *Roosevelt and Hopkins: An Intimate History*, 221.

44. Fried, *FDR and His Enemies*, 197–98.

45. Lindbergh, speeches in Des Moines, Iowa, September 11, 1941; Fort Wayne, Indiana, October 3, 1941; and Madison Square Garden, October 30, 1941, quoted in ibid., 203–5.

46. John Fleming to White, January 10, 5, 1942, quoted in Elledge, *E. B. White*, 232.

47. White to K. White, [February 4, 1942], *Letters of E. B. White*, 225, 224.

48. Ibid., [January 31? 1942], *Letters of E. B. White*, 223; White, "Notes and Comment," *New Yorker*, March 12, 1942. See Elledge, *E. B. White*, 234; and Scott Donaldson, *Archibald MacLeish: An American Life*, 362. It should be noted that there was already strong support for this position within the administration. MacLeish, Rosenman, and Harry Hopkins had already been lobbying Roosevelt to take this step. See Sydney Weinberg, "What to Tell Americans: The Writers' Quarrel in the Office of War Information," 77.

49. Weinberg, "What to Tell Americans," 78; David A. Horowitz, *Beyond Both Left and Right: Insurgency and the Establishment*, 189–90.

50. Weinberg, "What to Tell Americans," 81.

51. Westbrook Pegler quoted in John W. Henderson, *United States Information Agency*, 34; Denning, *Cultural Front*, 81–83; Howard Blue, *Words at War: World War II Era Radio Drama and the Postwar Broadcasting Industry Blacklist*.

52. Weinberg, "What to Tell Americans," 86. See also Daniel Belgrad, *The Culture of Spontaneity: Improvisation and the Arts in Postwar America*, 24. Belgrad points out that there are several versions of this story. There may, in fact, have been more than one poster.

53. White, "A Week in November," in *OMM*, 265–66.

54. See Michael Darrock and Joseph P. Dorn, "Davis and Goliath: The OWI and Its Gigantic Assignment"; and Malcolm Cowley, "The Sorrows of Elmer Davis." William Rose Benét emphasized the class and regional bias behind the Cowles and ad-executive approach ("They're not the Hicks that you take them for. / They know what is needed to win this war.") and finished with this couplet: "In closing, I'll only say, 'God save us! / It isn't your fault at all, Elmer Davis.'" See Benét, "Oh boy, but there's an ocean / Of joy in promotion" (poem), *Saturday Review of Literature*, May 8, 1943, 22, quoted in Weinberg, "What to Tell Americans," 85–86. On the OWI controversy, see Allan Winkler, *The Politics of Propaganda: The Office of War Information, 1942–1945*; Arthur Schlesinger Jr., *A Life in the Twentieth Century: Innocent Beginnings, 1917–1950*, 277–94; and Winfield, *FDR and the News Media*, 157–70.

55. Stuart Murray and James McCabe, *Norman Rockwell's Four Freedoms*, 25–28, 72–73, 91.

56. Robert Westbrook, "Fighting for the American Family: Private Interests and Political Obligation in World War II," 203ff.

57. See, for example, Marshall Singer, "Capitalist Realism by Norman Rockwell," 45; and Tomas Posiszyl, "Socialist Evening Realistic Post." Much of this work builds on the dismissal of Rockwell as kitsch, which has been a staple of Frankfurt School–inspired criticism since Greenberg's "Avant-Garde and Kitsch," *Partisan Review* (1939).

58. Quoted in Murray and McCabe, *Norman Rockwell's Four Freedoms*, 65, 67.

59. White, "Spring," in *OMM*, 189; "Questionnaire," in *OMM*, 234.

60. White to Eugene Saxton, January 28, 1942, *Letters of E. B. White*, 220; White, foreword to *OMM*, vii–viii.

61. White, "Aunt Poo," in *OMM*, 239, 240, 243–44.

62. Henry Seidel Canby, ". . . But No Man's Poison"; Diana Trilling, "Humanity and Humor," 118; Hyman, "The Urban *New Yorker*," 91; Irving Edman, "Earthy, Humorous, Accessible," *New York Herald Tribune Books*, June 14, 1942, 2, quoted in Root, *Emergence of an Essayist*, 5.

63. Norman Cousins, "Censoritis"; "Ban on Books by Army and Navy Is Opposed by Literary Council," *New York Times*, June 18, 1944, 29.

64. White to Stanley White, June [1944], *Letters of E. B. White*, 254–55.

65. White, introduction to *OMM*, xi.

EPILOGUE: "ONCE MORE TO THE LAKE," HISTORY, AND
FRESHMAN COMPOSITION

1. The Pataki story was national news. See, for instance, Clyde Haberman, "NYC: Highfalutin' but Hardly Proud of It," *New York Times*, October 9, 2000, B1; and Gail Collins, "Public Interests: Inside George's Web," *New York Times*, October 10, 2000, A27.

2. Warren Beck, "E. B. White," 115; Spencer Brown, "The Odor of Durability," 146; Russell Lynes, "The Divided Life of Stuart Little's Father," 10.

3. For sales figures, see Jill Lepore, "The Lion and the Mouse"; Deb Aronson, *E. B. White*, 60; Catherine Kim, "*Elements of Style* Celebrates 50 Years: Cornell Alumni

Created Preeminent Style Guide," *Cornell Daily Sun,* March 27, 2009. *Publisher's Weekly* (December 17, 2001) lists *Charlotte's Web* as the best-selling children's paperback of all time.

4. Scott Russell Sanders, interview with Scott Russell Sanders, 123; Robert L. Root Jr. and Michael Steinberg, eds., *The Fourth Genre: Contemporary Writers of/on Creative Nonfiction* and *Fourth Genre: Explorations in Nonfiction.*

5. Bloom, "The Essay Canon," 418.

6. Robert L. Root Jr., "Once More to the Essay: Prose Models, Textbooks, and Teaching," 91–92.

7. Donald Hall and D. L. Emblem, eds., *A Writer's Reader,* 2nd ed. (Boston: Little, Brown, 1979), vi–vii, as cited in Root, "Once More to the Essay," 91; Root, "Once More to the Essay," 93.

8. Joyce Carol Oates, "Introduction: The Art of the (American) Essay," xx; Lopate, "E. B. White," headnote to *Art of the Personal Essay,* 532.

9. James Slevin, "Reading/Writing in the Classroom and the Profession," 125, 127, 138.

10. See, for instance, Roger S. Platizky, "'Once More to the Lake': A Mythic Interpretation." I would like to thank an anonymous outside reader for the University of Missouri Press for pointing me toward *Lycidas* as a possible source for White's title.

11. White, "Once More," in *OMM,* 198.

12. Ibid., 200–201.

13. Ibid., 203.

Bibliography

Ade, George. "They Simply Wouldn't Let Me Be a High-Brow." *American Magazine,* December 1920, 50–51, 197–99.

Adorno, Theodor. "The Essay as Form." Trans. Bob Hullot-Kentor. *New German Critique* (Spring–Summer 1984): 151–71.

Altman, Billy. *Laughter's Gentle Soul: The Life of Robert Benchley.* New York: W. W. Norton, 1997.

Anderson, Sherwood. *Sherwood Anderson's Memoirs.* Ed. Ray Lewis White. Chapel Hill: University of North Carolina Press, 1969.

Angell, Roger. Foreword to *One Man's Meat,* vii–x. 1942. Reprint, Gardiner, Maine: Tilbury House, 1997.

Applegate, Debby. "Henry Ward Beecher and the 'Great Middle Class': Mass-Marketed Intimacy and Middle-Class Identity." In *The Middling Sorts: Explorations in the History of the American Middle Class,* ed. Burton J. Bledstein and Robert D. Johnston, 107–24. New York and London: Routledge, 2001.

Arnold, Matthew. *Culture and Anarchy: An Essay in Political and Social Criticism.* London: Smith, Elder, 1869.

Aron, Cindy Sondik. *Ladies and Gentlemen of the Civil Service: Middle-Class Workers in Victorian America.* New York: Oxford University Press, 1987.

Aronson, Deb. *E. B. White.* New York: Rosen Publishing Group, 2005.

Ashton, Susanna. "Authorial Affiliations; or, The Clubbing and Collaborating of Brander Matthews." *Symploke* 7, nos. 1–2 (1999): 165–87.

Atwan, Robert. "'Ecstasy & Eloquence': The Method of Emerson's Essays." In *Essays on the Essay: Redefining the Genre,* ed. Alexander J. Butrym, 106–15. Athens: University of Georgia Press, 1989.

Atwan, Robert, and Joyce Carol Oates, eds. *The Best American Essays of the Century.* Boston: Houghton Mifflin, 2000.

Augspurger, Michael. *An Economy of Abundant Beauty: "Fortune" Magazine and Depression America.* Ithaca: Cornell University Press, 2004.

Badillo, David A. "Mexicanos and Suburban Parish Communities: Religion, Space, and Identity in Contemporary Chicago." *Journal of Urban History* 31, no. 1 (2004): 23–46.

Barthes, Roland. *The Pleasure of the Text.* Trans. Richard Miller. New York: Hill and Wang, 1975.

Beard, A. Craig, ed. *Representative American Speeches, 1937–38.* Vol. 2. New York: H. W. Wilson, 1938.

Beck, Warren. "E. B. White." In *Critical Essays on E. B. White,* ed. Robert L. Root Jr., 114–21. New York: G. K. Hall, 1994. Originally published in *College English* 35 (April 1946): 175–81.

Belgrad, Daniel. *The Culture of Spontaneity: Improvisation and the Arts in Postwar America.* Chicago: University of Chicago Press, 1998.

Belloc, Hilaire. "By Way of Preface: An Essay upon Essays upon Essays (1929)." Preface to *One Thing and Another: A Miscellany from His Uncollected Essays,* selected by Patrick Cahill, 11–14. London: Hollis and Carter, 1955.

Benchley, Robert. "The Brow-Elevation in Humor." In *Love Conquers All,* 303–6. New York: Henry Holt, 1922.

———. "Mr. Bok's Americanization." In *Love Conquers All,* 216–20. New York: Henry Holt, 1922.

Benjamin, Walter. *Charles Baudelaire: A Lyric Poet in the Age of High Capitalism.* Trans. Harry Zohn. London: Verso, 1973.

Bertolini, Vincent. "Fireside Chastity: The Erotics of Sentimental Bachelorhood in the 1850s." *American Literature* 68, no. 4 (1996): 707–37.

Bickley, R. Bruce. *The Method of Melville's Short Fiction.* Durham: Duke University Press, 1975.

Blair, Walter. "The Essay: A Standard Form Takes on New Qualities." In *American Literature: A Brief History,* ed. Walter Blair, Theodore Hornberger, and Randal Stewart, 95–101. Chicago: Scott, Foresman, 1964.

Bledstein, Burton J. *The Culture of Professionalism: The Middle Class and the Development of Higher Education in America.* New York: W. W. Norton, 1976.

Bloom, Lynn Z. "The Essay Canon." *College English* 61, no. 4 (1999): 401–30.

———. "Once More to the Essay: The Essay Canon and Textbook Anthologies." *Symploke* 8, nos. 1–2 (2000): 20–35.

Blue, Howard. *Words at War: World War II Era Radio Drama and the Postwar Broadcasting Industry Blacklist.* Lanham, Md.: Scarecrow Press, 2002

Blumin, Stuart. *The Emergence of the Middle Class: Social Experience in the American City, 1760–1900.* New York: Cambridge University Press, 1989.

Bok, Edward. *The Americanization of Edward Bok: The Autobiography of a Dutch*

Boy Fifty Years After. New York: Charles Scribner's Sons, 1920.

——. "The Magazine with a Million." *Ladies' Home Journal,* February 1903, 16.

——. *Successward: A Young Man's Book for Young Men.* Philadelphia: Curtis Publishing, 1899.

——. "They Live in *Ladies' Home Journal* Houses: Here Are Five Successfully Erected in Foreign Countries." *Ladies' Home Journal,* March 1916, 1.

Bosco, Ronald A., and Joel Myerson. *Emerson in His Own Time: A Biographical Chronicle of His Life, Drawn from Recollections, Interviews, and Memoirs by Family, Friends, and Associates.* Iowa City: University of Iowa Press, 2003.

Bourdieu, Pierre. *Distinction: A Social Critique of the Judgment of Taste.* Trans. Richard Nice. Cambridge: Harvard University Press, 1984.

——. *The Field of Cultural Production.* Various translators. Ed. Randal Johnson. European Perspectives, a Series in Social Thought and Cultural Criticism, ed. Lawrence D. Kristzman. New York: Columbia University Press, 1993.

Bourne, Randolph. "The Handicapped—by One of Them." In *The Best American Essays of the Century,* ed. Robert Atwan and Joyce Carol Oates, 57–70. Boston: Houghton Mifflin, 2000.

——. "The Light Essay." *Dial* 65 (November 16, 1918): 419–20.

——. "Trans-national America." *Atlantic Monthly,* July 1916, 86–97.

——. "A Vanishing World of Gentility." *Dial* 64, no. 76 (1918): 234–35.

Braley, Berton. "On Being an Essayist." *Bookman,* August 1920, 646–48.

Braverman, Harry. *Labor and Monopoly Capital: The Degradation of Work in the Twentieth Century.* New York: Monthly Review Press, 1974.

Brinkley, Douglas. *Wheels for the World: Henry Ford, His Company, and a Century of Progress, 1903–2003.* New York: Viking, 2003.

Brooks, Charles S. "The Writing of Essays." In *Modern Essays and Stories,* ed. F. H. Law, 219–222. New York: Century, 1922. Excerpted from "The Posture of Authors." *Century,* August 1920, 466–71.

Broun, Heywood. *It Seems to Me: 1925–1935.* New York: Harcourt, Brace, 1935.

Brown, Charles Brockden. "The Man at Home." In *The Rhapsodist, and Other Uncollected Writings,* ed. Harry R. Warfel, 27–98. New York: Scholars' Facsimiles and Reprints, 1943. Originally published in the *Weekly Magazine* (Philadelphia), February 3, 1798.

Brown, Elspeth H. *The Corporate Eye: Photography and the Rationalization of American Commercial Culture, 1884–1929.* Baltimore: Johns Hopkins University Press, 2005.

Brown, Spencer. "The Odor of Durability." Review of *Essays of E. B. White* [and *The John McPhee Reader*]. *Sewanee Review,* Winter 1978, 146–52.

Buell, Lawrence. *Literary Transcendentalism: Style and Vision in the American Renaissance.* Ithaca: Cornell University Press, 1973.

Burke, Kenneth. "The Virtues and Limitations of Debunking." In *The*

Philosophy of Literary Form: Studies in Symbolic Action, 168–90. 1941. Reprint, Berkeley and Los Angeles: University of California Press, 1974.

Burns, James MacGregor, and Susan Burns. *The Three Roosevelts: Patrician Leaders Who Transformed America*. New York: Grove, 2002.

Burton, Richard. "The Essay as Mood and Form." In *Forces in Fiction*, 85–99. Indianapolis: Bowen-Merrill, 1902.

———. "The Predominance of the Novel." *Dial* 16 (1894): 354–56.

"By the Way." *Outlook*, September 6, 1916.

Cabot, James Elliot. *A Memoir of Ralph Waldo Emerson*. Vol. 2. Boston: Houghton Mifflin, 1890.

Canby, Henry Seidel. "Adventures in Starting a Literary Magazine." In *Saturday Review Treasury*, ed. John Haverstick, 297–305. New York: Simon and Schuster, 1957.

———. *The Age of Confidence: Life in the Nineties*. Illustrated by Albert Kruse. New York: Farrar and Rinehart, 1934.

———. *Alma Mater: The Gothic Age of the American College*. New York: Farrar and Rinehart, 1936.

———. *American Memoir*. Boston: Houghton Mifflin, 1947.

———. ". . . But No Man's Poison." Review of *One Man's Meat*, by E. B. White. *Saturday Review of Literature*, June 13, 1942, 7.

———. "The Essay as Barometer." *Saturday Review of Literature*, February 16, 1935, 488.

———. *Everyday Americans*. New York: Century, 1920.

———. "Literature in Contemporary America." In *The America of Today: Being Lectures Delivered at the Local Lectures Summer Meeting of the University of Cambridge*, ed. Gaillard Lapsley, 199–212. Cambridge: Cambridge University Press, 1919.

———. "Out with the Dilettante." In *Definitions: Essays in Contemporary Criticism*, 246–48. New York: Harcourt, 1922.

Carlyle, Thomas. *The Correspondence of Thomas Carlyle and Ralph Waldo Emerson, 1834–1872*. Vol. 2. Boston: Houghton Mifflin, Riverside Press, 1896.

Chapman, John Jay. "Coatesville." In *The Best American Essays of the Century*, ed. Robert Atwan and Joyce Carol Oates, 71–74. Boston: Houghton Mifflin, 2000.

Clark, Clifford Edward, Jr. *The American Family Home, 1800–1960*. Chapel Hill: University of North Carolina Press, 1986.

Clarke, H. A. "The Survival of the Essay." *Poet-lore* 9 (1897): 431–36.

Cohn, Jan. *Creating America: George Horace Lorimer and the "Saturday Evening Post."* Pittsburgh: University of Pittsburgh Press, 1990.

Colby, F. M. *"The Gentleman's Review."* In *Harper Essays*, ed. Henry Seidel Canby, 246–50. New York: Harper and Brothers. 1927. Originally published in *Harper's,* January 1920, 275–77.

——. "Recent American Essays, in Two Parts: Part I." *Bookman,* December 1904, 316–19.

——. "Recent American Essays, in Two Parts: Part II." *Bookman,* January 1905, 473–75.

Connors, Richard. *Composition-Rhetoric: Backgrounds, Theory, and Pedagogy.* Pittsburgh: University of Pittsburgh Press, 1997.

"The Contemplative Essayist." *Harper's Weekly,* May 17, 1913, 6.

"Contemporary Essays." *Atlantic Monthly,* February 1894, 262–69.

Converse, Florence. "Among Literary Shallows." *Atlantic Monthly,* May 1908, 711–12.

Cook, Clarence. *The House Beautiful: Essays on Beds and Tables, Stools and Candlesticks.* New York: Scribner, Armstrong, 1878.

Corbin, John. *Which College for the Boy? Leading Types in American Education.* New York: Houghton Mifflin, 1908.

Cousins, Norman. "Censoritis." *Saturday Review of Literature,* July 1, 1944, 12.

Cowley, Malcolm, ed. *After the Genteel Tradition: American Writers, 1910–1930.* 1937. Reprint, Carbondale: Southern Illinois University Press, 1964.

——. *Exile's Return: A Literary Odyssey of the 1920s.* 1934. Reprint, New York: Penguin, 1994.

——. "The Sorrows of Elmer Davis." *New Republic,* May 3, 1943, 591–93.

Craig, Douglas B. *Fireside Politics: Radio and Political Culture in the United States, 1920–1940.* Baltimore: Johns Hopkins University Press, 2000.

Crothers, Samuel McChord. *The Gentle Reader.* Boston: Houghton Mifflin, 1903.

——. "Making Friends with the Essay." *World Review* 4 (1927): 190.

Cull, Nicholas John. *Selling War: The British Propaganda Campaign against American "Neutrality" in World War II.* New York: Oxford University Press.

Curti, Merle. *The Growth of American Thought.* 3rd ed. 1944. Reprint, New Brunswick, N.J.: Transaction Publishers, 1982.

Cutler, Irving. *Jewish Chicago: A Pictorial History.* Charleston, S.C.: Arcadia Publishing, 2000.

D'Agata, John, ed. *The Lost Origins of the Essay.* St. Paul, Minn.: Graywolf, 2009.

——, ed. *The Next American Essay.* St. Paul, Minn.: Graywolf, 2002.

Damon-Moore, Helen. *Magazines for the Millions: Gender and Commerce in the "Ladies' Home Journal" and the "Saturday Evening Post," 1880–1910.* Albany: State University of New York Press, 1994.

Darrock, Michael, and Joseph P. Dorn. "Davis and Goliath: The OWI and Its Gigantic Assignment." *Harper's,* February 1943, 225–37.

Davidson, Cathy. *Revolution and the Word: The Rise of the Novel in America.*

Expanded ed. 1986. Reprint, New York: Oxford University Press, 2004.

Davis, Hallam Walker. *The Column.* New York: Alfred A. Knopf, 1926.

Davis, Linda. *Onward and Upward: A Biography of Katharine S. White.* New York: Harper and Row, 1987.

Dennie, Joseph. "On the Pleasures of Study." In *The Lay Preacher,* ed. Milton Ellis, 100–102. New York: Scholars' Facsimiles and Reprints, 1943. Originally published in *Port Folio,* no. 113 (January 23, 1808).

Denning, Michael. *The Cultural Front: The Laboring of American Culture in the Twentieth Century.* New York: Verso, 1997.

———. *Culture in the Age of the Three Worlds.* New York: Verso, 2004.

Doenecke, Justus D. *Storm on the Horizon: The Challenge to American Intervention, 1939–1941.* New York: Rowman and Littlefield, 2000.

Donaldson, Scott. *Archibald MacLeish: An American Life.* New York: Houghton Mifflin, 1992.

Doubleday, Frank. "The Young Publisher's Chances." *Publisher's Weekly,* September 19, 1903, 452–53.

Douglas, Ann. *The Feminization of American Culture.* 1977. Reprint, New York: Doubleday Anchor, 1988.

———. *Terrible Honesty: Mongrel Manhattan in the 1920s.* New York: Farrar, Straus, and Giroux, 1995.

Drew, Elizabeth. "The Lost Art of the Essay." In *How Writers Write: Essays by Contemporary Authors,* 35–49. New York: Cromwell, 1937. Originally published in *Saturday Review of Literature,* February 16, 1935.

Drowne, Kathleen Morgan, and Patrick Huber. *The 1920s.* American Popular Culture through History Series, ed. Ray B. Browne. Westport, Conn.: Greenwood, 2004.

Du Bois, W. E. B. "Constitution and By-laws of the Niagara Movement as Adopted July 12 and 13, 1905." In *Pamphlets and Leaflets by W. E. B. Du Bois,* ed. Herbert Aptheker, 59–62. White Plains, N.Y.: Kraus-Thomason Organization, 1986.

———. "Criteria of Negro Art." In *The Oxford W. E. B. Du Bois Reader,* ed. Eric J. Sundquist, 324–28. New York: Oxford University Press, 1996.

———. "The Niagara Movement: Address to the Nation." In *Pamphlets and Leaflets by W. E. B. Du Bois,* ed. Herbert Aptheker, 63–65. White Plains, N.Y.: Kraus-Thomason Organization, 1986.

———. *The Souls of Black Folk.* Ed. Henry Louis Gates Jr. and Terri Hume Oliver. 1903. Reprint, New York: W. W. Norton, 1999.

Early, Gerald, ed. *Speech and Power: The African-American Essay and Its Cultural Content from Polemics to Pulpit.* Vols. 1–2. New York: Ecco, 1992–1993.

Edson, C. L. *The Gentle Art of Columning: A Treatise on Comic Journalism.* New York: Brentano's, 1920.

Ehrenreich, John, and Barbara Ehrenreich. "The Professional-Managerial

Class." In *Between Labor and Capital,* ed. Pat Walker, 5–45. South End Press Political Controversies Series, no. 1. Boston: South End Press, 1979. Originally published in two parts in *Radical America* 11 (March–April 1977): 7–31; (May–June 1977): 7–22.

Elledge, Scott. *E. B. White: A Biography.* New York: W. W. Norton, 1986.

Emerson, Ralph Waldo. "Address at the Woman's Rights Convention, September 20, 1855." In *The Later Lectures of Ralph Waldo Emerson: 1843–1871.* Vol. 2, *1855–1871, 15–29.* Athens: University of Georgia Press, 2001.

——. *The Collected Works of Ralph Waldo Emerson.* Vol. 2, *Essays: First Series.* Introduction and notes by Joseph Slater. Text established by Alfred R. Ferguson and Jean Ferguson Carr. 1841. Reprint, Cambridge: Harvard University Press, Belknap Press, 1979.

——. *Emerson in His Journals.* Ed. Joel Porte. Cambridge: Harvard University Press, 1984.

——. *Journals and Miscellaneous Notebooks, 1838–1842.* Ed. William H. Gilman, A. W. Plumstead, and Harrison Hayford. Cambridge: Harvard University Press, 1960–1982.

——. *Selections from Ralph Waldo Emerson: An Organic Anthology.* Ed. Stephen E. Whicher. 1957. Reprint, Boston: Houghton Mifflin, 1960.

"Essays." *Outlook,* December 3, 1904.

Evans, Harold. *The American Century.* New York: Alfred A. Knopf, 1998.

Fass, Paula. *The Damned and the Beautiful: American Youth Culture in the 1920s.* New York: Oxford University Press, 1977.

Ferguson, Suzanne. "The Rise of the Short Story in the Hierarchy of Genres." In *Short Story Theory at a Crossroads,* ed. Susan Lohafer and Jo Ellyn Clarey, 176–92. Baton Rouge: Louisiana State University Press, 1998.

Fern, Fanny. *Ruth Hall, and Other Writings.* Ed. Joyce W. Warren. New Brunswick: Rutgers University Press, 1986.

Fitzgerald, F. Scott. *The Great Gatsby: The Authorized Text.* Ed. Matthew Bruccoli. 1925. Reprint, New York: Scribner Paperback, Simon and Schuster, 1995.

Five Thousand Books: An Easy Guide to the Best Books in Every Department of Reading. Rev. ed. Philadelphia: Curtis Publishing, 1895.

Ford, Henry, and Samuel Crowther. *My Life and Work.* 1922. Reprint, Whitefish, Mont.: Kessinger Publishing, 2003.

Foster, William Z. *History of the Communist Party of the United States.* New York: International Publishers, 1952.

Foucault, Michel. "Afterword: The Subject and Power." Trans. Leslie Sawyer. Ed. Hubert L. Dreyfus and Paul Rabinow. In *Michel Foucault: Beyond Structuralism and Hermeneutics,* 208–26. 2nd ed. Chicago: University of Chicago Press, 1983.

Fox, Richard Wrightman. "The Culture of Liberal Protestant Progressivism, 1875–1925." *Journal of Interdisciplinary History* 23, no. 3 (1993): 639–60.

Freedman, Jonathan. *The Temple of Culture: Assimilation and Anti-Semitism in Literary Anglo-America.* New York: Oxford University Press, 2000.

Freeman, Joshua, et al., eds. *Who Built America? Working People and the Nation's Economy, Politics, Culture, and Society.* Vol. 2, *From the Gilded Age to the Present.* New York: Pantheon, 1992.

Fried, Albert. *FDR and His Enemies.* New York: Palgrave, 1999.

Friedel, Frank. *Franklin D. Roosevelt: The Triumph.* Boston: Little, Brown, 1956.

Fuess, Claude M. Introduction to *Selected Essays,* vi–xiv. Riverside Literature Series. Boston: Houghton Mifflin, 1914.

Fulton, Maurice Garland, ed. *Expository Writing: Materials for a College Course in Exposition by Analysis and Imitation.* New York: Macmillan, 1912.

Fussell, Paul. *Wartime: Understanding and Behavior in the Second World War.* New York: Oxford University Press, 1989.

Garland, Hamlin. *Roadside Meetings.* New York: Macmillan, 1930.

Gates, Henry Louis, Jr., and Terri Hume Oliver. Preface to *The Souls of Black Folk,* by W. E. B. Du Bois, ed. Henry Louis Gates Jr. and Terri Hume Oliver, ix–xxxv. 1903. Reprint, New York: W. W. Norton, 1999.

Gerould, Katharine Fullerton. "An Essay on Essays." *North American Review* 240, no. 3 (1935): 409–18.

——. "The Extirpation of Culture." In *Modes and Morals,* 66–94. New York: Scribner's, 1920.

——. "Information, Please! A Call for a Plebiscite of Magazine Readers." *Saturday Review of Literature,* December 29, 1934, 393, 395.

——. "The Plight of the Genteel." *Harper's,* February 1926, 310–19.

Gibbs, Wolcott. "Time . . . Fortune . . . Life . . . Luce." *New Yorker,* November 28, 1936, 20–25.

Giddens, Anthony. *The Class Structure of the Advanced Societies.* London: Hutchinson University Library, 1973.

Gill, Brendan. *Here at the "New Yorker."* New York: Random House, 1975.

Gillam, Richard. "'White Collar' from Start to Finish: C. Wright Mills in Transition." *Theory and Society* 10, no. 1 (1981): 1–30.

Gilroy, Paul. *The Black Atlantic: Modernity and Double-Consciousness.* Cambridge: Harvard University Press, 1993.

Gold, Mike. "Notes of the Month." *New Masses* 6 (April 1930): 4.

——. "Notes of the Month." *New Masses* 6 (May 1930): 3.

——. "Wilder: Prophet of the Genteel Christ." *New Republic,* October 22, 1930, 166–67.

Goldberg, Vicki. *Margaret Bourke-White: A Biography.* New York: HarperCollins, 1986.

Goldin, Claudia, and Lawrence F. Katz. "Decreasing (and Then Increasing) Inequality in America: A Tale of Two Half-Centuries." In *The Causes and Consequences of Increasing Inequality,* ed. Finis Welch, 37–82. Chicago:

University of Chicago Press, 2002.

Goldin, Claudia, and Robert A. Margo. "The Great Compression: The Wage Structure in the United States at Mid-Century." *Quarterly Journal of Economics* 107 (February 1992): 1–34.

Good, Graham. *The Observing Self: Rediscovering the Essay.* London: Routledge, 1988.

Goodwin, Doris Kearns. *No Ordinary Time: Franklin and Eleanor Roosevelt; The Home Front in World War II.* New York: Simon and Schuster, 1994.

Graff, Gerald. *Professing Literature: An Institutional History.* Twentieth Anniversary Edition. Chicago: University of Chicago Press, 2007.

Gramsci, Antonio. *Selections from the Prison Notebooks of Antonio Gramsci.* Ed. and trans. Quinton Hoare and Geoffrey Nowell Smith. New York: International Publishers, 1971.

Greenberg, Clement. "Avant Garde and Kitsch." *Partisan Review* 6, no. 5 (1939): 34–49.

Grier, Katherine. *Culture and Comfort: People, Parlors, and Upholstery, 1850–1930.* Rochester, N.Y.: Strong Museum, 1988.

Hall, David. "The Victorian Connection." *American Quarterly* 27 (December 1975): 561–74.

Halttunen, Karen. *Confidence Men and Painted Ladies: A Study of Middle-Class Culture in America, 1830–1870.* New Haven: Yale University Press, 1982.

——. "From Parlor to Living Room: Domestic Space, Interior Decoration, and the Culture of Personality." In *Consuming Visions: Accumulation and Display of Goods in America, 1880–1920,* ed. Simon J. Bonner, 157–89. New York: W. W. Norton, 1989.

Harker, Jaime. *American the Middlebrow: Women's Novels, Progressivism, and Middlebrow Authorship between the Wars.* Amherst: University of Massachusetts Press, 2007.

Hart, James D. *The Popular Book: A History of America's Literary Taste.* Berkeley and Los Angeles: University of California Press, 1963.

Haverstick, John, ed. Saturday Review Treasury. New York: Simon and Schuster, 1957.

Hawthorne, Nathaniel. "Fire Worship (1843)." In *Mosses from an Old Manse,* 150–59. Salem Edition. 1854. Reprint, Boston: Houghton Mifflin, 1893.

Hazlitt, William. *Selected Essays of William Hazlitt, 1778–1830.* Ed. Geoffrey Keynes. New York: Random House, 1930.

——. *The Spirit of the Age; or, Contemporary Portraits.* Ed. William Hazlitt [son of the author]. 3rd ed. 1825. Reprint, London: C. Templeman, 1858.

Hedges, William L. *Washington Irving: An American Study, 1802–1832.* Baltimore: Johns Hopkins University Press, 1965.

Henderson, John W. *United States Information Agency.* New York: Praeger, 1969.

Hernstreet, Charles. *Literary New York: Its Landmarks and Associations.* New York: G. P. Putnam's Sons, 1903.

Hesse, Douglas, ed. "Creative Nonfiction." Special issue, *College English* 65, no. 3 (2003).

Hoagland, Edward. "What I Think, What I Am." In *The Tugman's Passage,* 24–27. New York: Random House, 1982. Originally published in *New York Times Book Review,* June 27, 1976.

Hofstader, Richard. *Anti-Intellectualism in American Life.* 1963. Reprint, New York: Vintage, 1966.

Hogan, Michael J., ed. *The Ambiguous Legacy: U.S. Foreign Relations in the "American Century."* New York: Cambridge University Press, 1999.

Holden, Ray. *A Booklover's Tour of the Windy City.* Chicago: Lake Claremont Press, 2001.

Holliday, Robert Cortes. "An Article without an Idea." In *Broome Street Straws,* 80–87. New York: George H. Doran, 1919. Originally published as "With Malice toward None," under the pseudonym "Murray Hill." *Bookman,* August 1919, 677–79.

———. "Caun't Speak the Language." In *Walking-Stick Papers,* 201–13. New York: George H. Doran, 1918.

Holman, Andrew Carl. *A Sense of Their Duty: Middle-Class Formation in Victorian Ontario Towns.* Montreal: McGill-Queens University Press, 2000.

Holmes, Oliver Wendell, Sr. *The Autocrat of the Breakfast Table: Everyman His Own Boswell.* Riverside Literature Series. 1858. Reprint, Boston: Houghton Mifflin, 1891.

Homestead, Melissa J. "'Every Body Sees the Theft': Fanny Fern and Literary Proprietorship in Antebellum America." *New England Quarterly* 74, no. 2 (2001): 210–37.

Hoppes, Roy. *Ralph Ingersoll: A Biography.* New York: Atheneum, 1985.

Horowitz, David A. *Beyond Both Left and Right: Insurgency and the Establishment.* Urbana: University of Illinois Press, 1996.

Houck, Davis W., and Amos Kiewe. *FDR's Body Politics: The Rhetoric of Disability.* College Station: Texas A&M University Press, 2003.

Howells, William Dean. "Editor's Easy Chair." *Harper's,* October 1902, 802–5.

———. *A Hazard of New Fortunes.* 1890. Reprint, New York: Penguin, 2001.

———. *Literature and Life.* New York: Harper's, 1902.

———. "The Man of Literature as a Man of Business." *Scribner's Magazine,* October 1893, 429–46.

Howland, John Louis. "Between the Muses and the Masses: Symphonic Jazz, 'Glorified' Entertainment, and the Rise of the American Musical Middlebrow, 1920–1944." Ph.D. diss., Stanford University, 2002.

Humble, Nicola. *The Feminine Middlebrow Novel, 1920s to 1950s: Class, Domesticity, and Bohemianism.* Oxford: Oxford University Press, 2001.

Hutner, Gordon. "The 'Good Reader' and the Bourgeois Critic." *Kenyon Review*, n.s., 20, no. 1 (1998): 17–32.

Huyssen, Andreas. *After the Great Divide: Modernism, Mass Culture, Postmodernism.* Bloomington: Indiana University Press, 1986.

Hyman, Stanley Edgar. "The Urban *New Yorker*." *New Republic*, July 20, 1942, 90–92.

[Ingersoll, Ralph]. *"The New Yorker." Fortune*, August 1934.

Irving, Washington. *The Sketch Book of Geoffrey Crayon, Gent.* 1820. Reprint, New York: Signet Classics, 1961.

Jackson, Kenneth T. *Crabgrass Frontier: The Suburbanization of the United States.* New York: Oxford University Press, 1985.

Jacoby, Russell. Afterword to *White Collar: The American Middle Classes,* by C. Wright Mills, 365–80. 50th Anniversary Edition. 1951. Reprint, New York: Oxford University Press, 2002.

James, Henry. *Collected Travel Writings: Great Britain and America.* Vol. 1. Ed. Richard Howard. Library of America Edition. New York: Literary Classics of America, 1993.

———. *Literary Criticism.* Vol. 1, *Essays on Literary, American Writers, English Writers.* Ed. Leon Edel and Mark Wilson. Library of America Edition. New York: Literary Classics of the United States, 1984.

Jenks, Tudor. "The Essay." *Outlook*, July 29, 1893, 212–13.

Johnson, Sammye, and Patricia Prijatel. *The Magazine from Cover to Cover: Inside a Dynamic Industry.* 2nd ed. New York: Oxford University Press, 2007.

Jones, Howard Mumford. "The Demise of a Little Old Lady." Review of *1934 Essay Annual*, ed. Erich A. Walter. *Saturday Review of Literature*, July 28, 1934, 19.

Jones, W. Alfred. "Essay Writing: The Champion." *Essays upon Authors and Books,* 13–21. New York: Standford and Swords, 1849.

Kaestle, Carl F. "Literacy and Diversity: Themes from a Social History of the American Reading Public." *History of Education Quarterly* 28, no. 4 (1988): 523–49.

Kefalas, Maria. *Working-Class Heroes: Protecting Home, Community, and Nation in a Chicago Neighborhood.* Berkeley and Los Angeles: University of California Press, 2003.

Kelly, Fred Charters. *George Ade: Warmhearted Satirist.* Indianapolis: Bobbs-Merrill, 1947.

Klaus, Carl. "Essayists on the Essay." In *Literary Nonfiction: Theory, Practice, Pedagogy,* ed. Chris Anderson, 155–75. Carbondale: Southern Illinois University Press, 1989.

———. "Excursion of the Mind: Toward a Poetics of Uncertainty in the Disjunctive Essay." In *What Do I Know? Reading, Writing, and Teaching the Essay*, ed. Janis Forman, 39–53. Portsmouth, N.H.: Heinemann-Boynton/Cook, 1995.

Klein, Christina. *Cold War Orientalism: Asia in the Middlebrow Imagination, 1945–1961*. Berkeley and Los Angeles: University of California Press, 2003.

Korhonen, Kuisma. *Textual Friendship: The Essay as Impossible Encounter from Plato and Montaigne to Levinas and Derrida*. Philosophy and Literary Series, ed. Hugh J. Silverman. New York: Humanity Books, 2006.

Kramer, Dale, and George R. Clark, "Harold Ross and the *New Yorker*." *Harper's*, April 1943, 510–21.

Kunkel, Thomas. *Genius in Disguise: Harold Ross of the "New Yorker."* New York: Random House, 1995.

Kyvig, David E. *Daily Life in the United States, 1920–1940*. Chicago: Ivan R. Dee, 2004.

Lamb, Charles. *Essays of Elia*. Sightline Books: The Iowa Series in Literary Nonfiction, ed. Carl Klaus and Patricia Hampl. 1823. Reprint, Iowa City: University of Iowa Press, 2003.

Lancaster, Clay. *The American Bungalow, 1880–1930*. 1985. Reprint, Mineola, N.Y.: Dover, 1995.

Lang, Amy Schrager. *The Syntax of Class: Writing Inequality in Nineteenth-Century America*. Princeton: Princeton University Press, 2003.

Lanning, Robert. *The National Album: Collective Biography and the Formation of the Canadian Middle Class*. Montreal: McGill-Queens University Press, 1996.

Lash, Joseph P. *Eleanor and Franklin: The Story of Their Relationship Based on Eleanor Roosevelt's Private Papers*. New York: W. W. Norton, 1971.

Laughlin, Clara E. "Concerning Essays." *Book Buyer* 14 (May 1897): 349–52.

Lears, T. J. Jackson. *No Place of Grace: Antimodernism and the Transformation of Culture, 1880–1920*. New York: Pantheon Books, 1981.

Lee, Gerard Stanley. *The Lost Art of Reading*. New York: G. Putnam's Sons, 1903.

Lee, Judith Yaross. *Defining "New Yorker" Humor*. Jackson: University Press of Mississippi, 2000.

Lepore, Jill. "The Lion and the Mouse." *New Yorker*, July 21, 2008. *http://www.newyorker.com/reporting/2008/07/21/080721fa_fact_lepore*.

Lerner, Max. "The People's Century." *New Republic*, April 7, 1941, 465–66.

Levine, Lawrence. *Highbrow/Lowbrow: The Emergence of Cultural Hierarchy in America*. Cambridge: Harvard University Press, 1988.

Lewis, David Levering. *W. E. B. Du Bois: Biography of a Race, 1868–1919*. New York: Henry Holt, 1993.

——. *W. E. B. Du Bois: The Fight for Equality and the American Century, 1919–1963*. New York: Henry Holt, 2000.

Lewis, Sinclair. "The American Fear of Literature: The Nobel Prize Address (1930)." In *The Man from Main Street: A Sinclair Lewis Reader; Selected Essays and Other Writings, 1904–1950,* ed. Harry Edward Maule and Melville Cane, 3–17. New York: Random House, 1953.

———. "A New Subscriber Disagrees (Letter)." *New Masses* 6 (July 1930): 22.

Lindbergh, Anne Morrow. *The Wave of the Future: A Confession of Faith.* New York: Harcourt Brace, 1940.

———. "The Wave of the Future: A Confession of Faith." In *We Testify,* ed. Doris Fielding Reid and Nancy Schoonmaker, 275–92. New York: Smith and Durrell, 1941.

Lindbergh, Charles. "Aviation, Geography, and Race." *Reader's Digest,* November 1939, 64–67.

Lofland, Lyn. *A World of Strangers: Order and Action in Urban Public Space.* New York: Basic Books, 1973.

Lopate, Phillip, ed. *The Art of the Personal Essay: An Anthology from the Classical Era to the Present.* New York: Doubleday, 1994.

———. "Introduction: William Dean Howells and the Discovery of New York." In *A Hazard of New Fortunes,* by William Dean Howells, v–xxix. 1890. Reprint, New York: Penguin, 2001.

Lorenz, A. L. "The Whitechapel Club: Defining Chicago's Newspapermen in the 1890s." *American Journalism* 15, no. 1 (1998): 83–102.

Loveman, Amy. "Arm Chair Philosophy." *Saturday Review of Literature,* August 23, 1930, 65.

Lowell, James Russell. "Rousseau and the Sentimentalists" (1867). In *Among My Books,* First and Second Series (vol. 2 of 3) in *The Complete Writings of James Russell Lowell.* Vol. 4, *1870 and 1876,* 171–217. Elmwood Edition. Reprint, New York: AMS Press, 1966.

Luce, Henry. "The American Century." *Life,* February 17, 1941, 61–65.

Lynes, Russell. "The Divided Life of Stuart Little's Father." *New York Times Book Review,* October 14, 1985, 9–10.

———. *The Domesticated Americans.* New York: Harper and Row, 1963.

M. E. W. "With an Old Magazine." *Temple Bar.* Pts. 1 and 2. Reprinted in *Critic* 9, no. 228 (1888): 235–36; no. 229 (1888): 248–49.

Mabie, Hamilton. "The Essay and Some Essayists, Part I." *Bookman,* August 1899, 504–11.

———. "The Essay and Some Essayists, Part II." *Bookman,* September 1899, 49–54.

[———?]. "Essays." *Outlook,* December 3, 1904, 879–82.

———. "The Girl and Her Graduation Essay." *Ladies' Home Journal,* May 1908, 24.

[———?]. "The Prosperity of the Essay." *Outlook,* November 25, 1905, 697–99.

[———?]. "Recent Examples of the Essay." *Outlook,* December 7, 1907, 765–68.

——. "Why the Essay Is Valuable as Reading." *Ladies' Home Journal*, April 1908, 36.

Macdonald, Dwight. *Against the American Grain: Essays on the Effects of Mass Culture*. New York: Random House, 1962.

——. "Laugh and Lie Down." *Partisan Review* 4, no. 1 (1937): 44–53.

Machlup, Fritz. *The Production and Distribution of Knowledge in the United States*. Princeton: Princeton University Press, 1962.

Mangum, Teresa. *Married, Middle-brow, and Militant: Sarah Grand and the New Woman Novel*. Ann Arbor: University of Michigan Press, 1998.

Marchand, Roland. *Advertising the American Dream: Making Way for Modernity, 1920–1940*. Berkeley and Los Angeles: University of California Press, 1986.

Marquis, Don. "The Almost Perfect State." In *Modern Essays*, ed. Christopher Morley, 39–40. New York: Harcourt, Brace, 1921.

——. *Hermione and Her Little Group of Serious Thinkers*. New York: D. Appleton, 1918.

Martin, Benjamin Ellis. "In the Footprints of Charles Lamb, Part I." *Scribner's Magazine*, March 1890, 266–82.

——. "In the Footprints of Charles Lamb, Part II." *Scribner's Magazine*, April 1890, 471–86.

Mason, David S. *The End of the American Century*. Lanham, Md.: Rowman and Littlefield, 2008.

Materer, Timothy. "Make It Sell! Ezra Pound Advertises Modernism." In *Marketing Modernisms: Self-Promotion, Canonization, Rereading*, ed. Kevin J. H. Dettmar and Stephen Watt, 17–36. Ann Arbor: University of Michigan Press, 1996.

Matthews, Brander. *American Character*. New York: Thomas L. Crowell, 1906.

——. *Cheap Books and Good Books*. New York: American Copyright League, 1888.

——. "Concerning Certain Contemporary Essayists." *Harper's Weekly*, November 6, 1897, 1106.

——. "Literature as a Profession." In *The Historical Novel and Other Essays*, 193–213. New York: Charles Scribner's Sons, 1901.

——. "Modern Essays." *Munsey's Magazine* 49 (1913): 268–72.

——. "Three American Essayists." In *Americanisms and Briticisms with Essays on Other Isms*, 135–50. New York: Harper and Brothers, 1892.

May, Henry. *The End of American Innocence: A Study of the First Years of Our Own Time, 1912–1917*. New York: Alfred A. Knopf, 1959.

Maza, Sarah C. *The Myth of the French Bourgeoisie: An Essay on the Social Imaginary, 1750–1850*. Cambridge: Harvard University Press, 2003.

McCullough, David. *Mornings on Horseback: The Story of an Extraordinary Family, a Vanished Way of Life, and the Unique Child Who Became Theodore*

Roosevelt. New York: Simon and Schuster, 1982.

McGovern, James R. *And a Time for Hope: Americans in the Great Depression.* Westport, Conn.: Praeger, 2000.

Meade, Marion. *Dorothy Parker: What Fresh Hell Is This?* New York: Villard, 1988.

Melville, Herman. "I and My Chimney." In *The Apple-Tree Table and Other Sketches,* 109–66. Princeton: Princeton University Press, 1922.

Miller, Donald L. *City of the Century: The Epic of Chicago and the Making of America.* New York: Simon and Schuster, 1997.

Miller, Nina. *Making Love Modern: The Intimate Public Worlds of New York's Literary Women.* New York: Oxford University Press, 1999.

Mills, C. Wright. *Letters and Autobiographical Writings.* Ed. K. Mills with P. Mills. Berkeley and Los Angeles: University of California Press, 2000.

———. *White Collar: The American Middle Classes.* 50th Anniversary Edition. 1951. Reprint, New York: Oxford University Press, 2002.

"Minor Notices." *Critic,* October 11, 1890.

Mitchell, Donald Grant. *Reveries of a Bachelor; or, A Book of the Heart by Ik Marvell.* Rev. ed. 1850. Reprint, New York: Charles Scribner's Sons, 1891.

Montaigne, Michel de. *The Complete Essays of Montaigne.* Trans. Donald M. Frame. 1580. Reprint, Stanford: Stanford University Press, 1958.

Morgan, Anna. *My Chicago.* Chicago: Ralph Fletcher Seymour, 1918.

Morley, Christopher. "In Memoriam: E. V., Bill Footner, Tom Daly, Bob Holliday." In *Ironing Board,* 166–78. Essay Reprint Series. 1949. Reprint, Freeport, N.Y.: Books for Libraries Press, 1968.

Moseley, Cameron S. "U.S. School Publishing: From Webster and McGuffey to the Internet." In *The Book in the United States Today,* ed. William Gordon Graham and Richard Abel, 23–36. Edison, N.J.: Transaction, 1997.

Moss, Norman. *Nineteen Weeks: America, Britain, and the Fateful Summer of 1940.* New York: Houghton Mifflin, 2003.

Mott, Frank Luther. "The Magazine Revolution and Popular Ideas in the Nineties." *Proceedings of the American Antiquarian Society,* n.s., 64, no. 1 (1954): 195–214.

Muir, John. "Stickeen." In *The Best American Essays of the Century,* ed. Robert Atwan and Joyce Carol Oates, 28–44. Boston: Houghton Mifflin, 2000.

Murray, Stuart, and James McCabe. *Norman Rockwell's Four Freedoms.* New York: Gramercy, 1998.

Newsome, Elaine Wright. "W. E. B. Du Bois' 'Figure in the Carpet': A Cyclical Pattern in the Belletristic Prose." Ph.D. diss., University of North Carolina at Chapel Hill, 1981.

North, Helen Marshall. "What Americans Read." *North American Review* 150 (1890): 533–35.

Oates, Joyce Carol. "Introduction: The Art of the (American) Essay." In

The Best American Essays of the Century, xvii–xxviii. Boston: Houghton Mifflin, 2000.

Ohmann, Richard. *Selling Culture: Magazines, Markets, and Class at the Turn of the Century.* London and New York: Verso, 1996.

Oliver, Lawrence J. "Theodore Roosevelt, Brander Matthews, and the Campaign for Literary Americanism." *American Quarterly* 41, no. 1 (1989): 93–111.

Ong, Walter. "The Writer's Audience Is Always a Fiction." *PMLA* 90, no. 1 (1975): 9–21.

Opdycke, Mary Ellis. "Colyumism." *New Republic,* August 29, 1923, 15–17.

Page, Benjamin I., and James Roy Simmons. *What Government Can Do: Dealing with Poverty and Inequality.* Chicago: University of Chicago Press, 2002.

Page, Norman. *Charles Dickens: Family History.* London: Routledge, 1999.

Parker, Herschel. *Herman Melville: A Biography.* Vol. 2, *1851–1891.* Baltimore: Johns Hopkins University Press, 2002.

Parton, Ethel. "A New York Childhood: The Seventies in Stuyvesant Square." *New Yorker,* June 13, 1936, 32, 34, 36, 41–42, 44–46.

Pater, Walter. "Dialectic." In *Plato and Platonism: A Series of Lectures,* 156–76. London and New York: Macmillan, 1893.

Peffer, Nathaniel. "Editors and Essays: A Note on Magazines Like *Harper's.*" *Harper's,* December 1935, 78–84.

Perry, Jennette Barbour. "The Romantic Essay." *Critic,* April 1902, 358–60.

Peterson, Theodore. *Magazines in the Twentieth Century.* Urbana: University of Illinois Press, 1956.

Platizky, Roger S. "'Once More to the Lake': A Mythic Interpretation." *College Literature* 15, no. 2 (1988): 171–79.

Porte, Joel. "The Problem of Emerson." In *Uses of Literature,* ed. Monroe Engel, 85–114. Harvard English Studies. Cambridge: Harvard University Press, 1973.

Posiszyl, Tomas. "Socialist Evening Realistic Post." *ARTmargins,* November 12, 2003. *http://www.artmargins.com/index.php?option=com_content&vi ew=article&id=242:socialist-evening-realistic-post&catid=111:articles&Ite mid=68.*

Pound, Ezra. "How to Read." Pts. 1–3. *New York Herald Tribune Books,* January 13, 1929, 1, 6; January 20, 1929, 5–6; January 27, 1929, 5–6.

Pound, Ezra, and William Carlos Williams. *Pound/Williams: Selected Letters of Ezra Pound and William Carlos Williams.* Ed. Hugh Witemeyer. New York: New Directions, 1996.

Pound, Ezra, and Louis Zukofsky. *Pound/Zukofsky: Selected Letters of Ezra Pound and Louis Zukofsky (Correspondence of Ezra Pound).* Ed. Barry Ahearn. New York: New Directions 1987.

Radway, Janice. *A Feeling for Books: The Book-of-the-Month Club, Literary Taste, and Middle-Class Desire*. Chapel Hill: University of North Carolina Press, 1997.

——. "Research Universities, Periodical Publication, and the Circulation of Professional Expertise: On the Significance of Middlebrow Authority." *Critical Inquiry* 31 (Autumn 2004): 203–28.

Raleigh, John Henry. *Matthew Arnold and American Culture*. Berkeley and Los Angeles: University of California Press, 1957.

Rampersad, Arnold. *The Art and Imagination of W. E. B. Du Bois*. Cambridge: Harvard University Press, 1976.

Rascoe, Burton. "What of Our Essayists?" *Bookman* 55 (1922): 74–75.

Reeves, Thomas. *Twentieth Century America: A Brief History*. New York: Oxford University Press, 2000.

Repplier, Agnes. "The American Essay in Wartime." *Yale Review* 7, no. 2 (1918): 249–59.

——. "The Passing of the Essay." In *In the Dozy Hours*, 226–35. Boston: Houghton Mifflin, 1894.

Reynolds, Tom. "Selling College Literacy: The Mass-Market Magazine as Early 20th Century Literacy Sponsor." *American Periodicals* 15, no. 2 (2005): 163–77.

Roosevelt, Franklin Delano. *Ah That Voice: The Fireside Chats of Franklin Delano Roosevelt*. Comp. Kenneth D. Yeilding and Paul H. Carlson. Odessa, Tex.: Presidential Museum, 1974.

——. *F.D.R., Columnist: The Uncollected Columns of Franklin D. Roosevelt*. Ed. Donald Scott Carmichael. Chicago: Pellegini and Cudahy, 1947.

——. *FDR's Fireside Chats*. Ed. Russell D. Buhite and David W. Levy. Norman: University of Oklahoma Press, 1992.

——. *The Public Papers and Addresses of Franklin D. Roosevelt*. Vol. 2, *The Year of Crisis, 1933*. New York: Random House, 1938.

Root, Robert L., Jr., ed. *Critical Essays on E. B. White*. New York: G. K. Hall, 1994.

——. *E. B. White: The Emergence of an Essayist*. Iowa City: University of Iowa Press, 1999.

——. "Once More to the Essay: Prose Models, Textbooks, and Teaching." *Journal of Teaching Writing* 14, nos. 1–2 (1995): 87–110.

Root, Robert L., Jr., and Michael Steinberg, eds. *The Fourth Genre: Contemporary Writers of/on Creative Nonfiction*. 5th ed. 1998. Reprint, New York: Longman, 2010.

Roth, Leland M. "Getting Houses to the People: Edward Bok, the *Ladies' Home Journal*, and the Ideal House." *Perspectives in Vernacular Architecture* 4 (1991): 187–96.

Rourke, Constance. *American Humor: A Study of the National Character*. New York: Harcourt, Brace, 1931.

Rubin, Joan Shelley. *The Making of Middlebrow Culture*. Chapel Hill: University of North Carolina Press, 1992.

Rudolph, Frederick. *The American College and University*. 1962. Reprint, Athens: University of Georgia Press, 1990.

Sackheim, Maxwell. *My First Sixty Years in Advertising*. Englewood Cliffs, N.J.: Prentice-Hall, 1970.

Sanders, Scott Russell. "Interview with Scott Russell Sanders." By Robert Root. *Fourth Genre: Explorations in Nonfiction* 1, no. 1 (1999): 119–32.

Savran, David. *A Queer Sort of Materialism: Recontextualizing American Theater*. Ann Arbor: University of Michigan Press, 2003.

Scanlon, Jennifer. *Inarticulate Longings: The "Ladies' Home Journal," Gender, and the Promise of Consumer Culture*. New York: Routledge, 1995.

Schelling, F. E. "The Familiar Essay." In *Appraisements and Asperities*, 9–14. Philadelphia: Lippincott, 1922.

Schlereth, Thomas J. *Victorian America: Transformations in Everyday Life, 1876–1915*. Everyday Life in America Series, ed. Richard Balkin. 1991. Reprint, New York: HarperPerennial, 1992.

Schlesinger, Arthur, Jr. *A Life in the Twentieth Century: Innocent Beginnings, 1917–1950*. New York: Houghton Mifflin Harcourt, 2000.

Schneirov, Matthew. *The Dream of a New Social Order: Popular Magazines in America, 1893–1914*. New York: Columbia University Press, 1994.

Scholes, Robert, and Carl Klaus. *Elements of the Essay*. New York: Oxford University Press, 1969.

Sedgwick, Eve Kosofsky. *Between Men: English Literature and Male Homosocial Desire*. New York: Columbia University Press, 1985.

Seed, David. "Touring the Metropolis: The Shifting Subjects of Dickens's London Sketches." *Yearbook of English Studies* 34 (2004): 155–70.

Sherman, Stuart P. "An Apology for Essayists of the Press." In *Points of View*, 173–85. New York: Scribner's, 1924. Originally published as "The Charge of the Literary Light Brigade." *New York Times Book Review*, January 29, 1922, 12, 21.

Sherwood, Robert. *Roosevelt and Hopkins: An Intimate History*. New York: Harper and Brothers, 1948.

Shudson, Michael. *Advertising, the Uneasy Persuasion: Its Dubious Impact on American Society*. New York: Basic Books, 1984.

Singer, Marshall. "Capitalist Realism by Norman Rockwell." *Ramparts* 11 (November 1972): 45–47.

Slevin, James. "Reading/Writing in the Classroom and the Profession." In *Introducing English: Essays in the Intellectual Work of Composition*, 123–41. Pittsburgh: University of Pittsburgh Press, 2001.

Smith, Lillian. *How Am I to Be Heard? Letters of Lillian Smith*. Ed. Margaret Rose Gladney. Chapel Hill: University of North Carolina Press, 1993.

Spiller, Robert E., Willard Thorp, Thomas H. Johnson, Henry Seidel Canby, and Richard M. Ludwig, eds. *Literary History of the United States*. 3rd ed. London: Macmillan, 1963.

Steel, Ronald. *Walter Lippman and the American Century*. Boston: Little, Brown, 1980.

Steinberg, Salme Harju. *Reformer in the Marketplace: Edward W. Bok and the "Ladies' Home Journal."* Baton Rouge: Louisiana State University Press, 1979.

Stephen, Leslie. "The Essayists." In *Men, Books, and Mountains*, ed. S. O. A. Ullman, 45–73. Minneapolis: University of Minnesota Press, 1956. Originally published in *Cornhill Magazine* (1881).

Stepto, Robert. *From Behind the Veil*. Urbana: University of Illinois Press, 1979.

Stevenson, Katherine Cole, and H. Ward Jandl. *Houses by Mail: A Guide to Houses from Sears, Roebuck, and Company*. Washington, D.C.: Preservation Press, 1986.

Stoddart, Alexander. "Journalism's Radium, the Colyumn." *Independent* 93, no. 3611 (1918): 274, 289–93.

Stokes, George Stewart. *Agnes Repplier: Lady of Letters*. Philadelphia: University of Pennsylvania Press, 1949.

Susman, Warren. "Culture and Commitment." In *Culture as History: The Transformation of American Society in the Twentieth Century*, 184–210. New York: Pantheon Books, 1985.

——. "'Personality' and the Making of Twentieth-Century Culture." In *Culture as History: The Transformation of American Society in the Twentieth Century*, 271–85. New York: Pantheon Books, 1985.

Taubenfeld, Aviva. *Rough Writing: Ethnic Authorship in Theodore Roosevelt's America*. New York: New York University Press, 2008.

Tebbel, John. *A History of Book Publishing in the United States*. 4 vols. New York: R. R. Bowker, 1972.

——. *The Media in America*. New York: Thomas Y. Cowell, 1974.

Terrill, Mary. "About Essays, and Three." *Bookman*, April 1920, 192–95.

Thoreau, Henry David. *Walden and Resistance to Civil Government*. Ed. William Rossi. 2nd ed. 1854. Reprint, New York: W. W. Norton, 1992.

——. *The Writings of Henry David Thoreau: Journal*. Vol. 5, *March 5–November 30, 1853*, ed. Bradford Torrey. Boston: Houghton Mifflin, 1906.

——. *The Writings of Henry David Thoreau: Journal*. Vol. 6, *Familiar Letters*, ed. F. B. Sanborn. Enlarged ed. Boston: Houghton Mifflin, Riverside Press, 1906.

Trachtenberg, Alan. *The Incorporation of America: Culture and Society in the Gilded Age*. American Century Series, ed. Eric Foner. New York: Hill and Wang, 1982.

Travis, Trysh. "What We Talk about When We Talk about the *New Yorker*."

Book History 3 (2000): 253–85.

Trilling, Diana. "Humanity and Humor." Review of *One Man's Meat,* by E. B. White. *Nation,* August 8, 1942, 118.

Trilling, Lionel. "*New Yorker* Fiction." *Nation,* April 11, 1942, 425–26.

Trimbur, John. "Essayist Literacy and the Rhetoric of Deproduction." *Rhetoric Review* 9, no. 1 (1990): 72–86.

Turner, Catherine. *Marketing Modernism between the Two World Wars.* Amherst: University of Massachusetts Press, 2003.

U.S. Department of Commerce, Bureau of the Census. *Historical Statistics of the United States, Colonial Times to 1957: A Statistical Abstract Supplement.* Washington, D.C.: U.S. Department of Commerce, Bureau of the Census, 1960.

Van Doren, Carl. "Day In and Day Out: Manhattan Wits." In *Many Minds,* 181–99. New York: Alfred A. Knopf, 1924. Originally published as "Day In and Day Out—Adams, Morley, Marquis, and Broun: Manhattan Wits." *Century,* December 1923, 308–15.

——. "Short for Buncombe." Review of *Bunk,* by W. E. Woodward. *Nation,* October 10, 1923, 398.

Wallace, Henry. *The Century of the Common Man.* New York: Reynal and Hitchcock, 1943.

Wallace, Max. *The American Axis: Henry Ford, Charles Lindbergh, and the Rise of the Third Reich.* New York: St. Martin's Griffin, 2004.

Ward, A. W., et al., eds. *The Cambridge History of English and American Literature.* Vol. 17, *Later National Literature, Part II, Section XIII, Later Essayists.* New York: G. P. Putnam's Sons; Cambridge: Cambridge University Press, 1907–1921.

Ward, Douglas B. "The Reader as Consumer: Curtis Publishing Company and Its Audience, 1910–1930." *Journalism History* 22, no. 2 (1996): 46–55.

Warren, Joyce W. *Fanny Fern: An Independent Woman.* New Brunswick: Rutgers University Press, 1992.

Warshow, Robert. *The Immediate Experience: Movies, Comics, Theatre, and Other Aspects of Popular Culture.* Cambridge: Harvard University Press, 2001.

Waters, John. "A Little Old Lady Passes Away." *Forum and Century* 90, no. 1 (1933): 27–29. Reprinted in *How Writers Write: Essays by Contemporary Authors,* 23–31. New York: Crowell, 1937.

Weinberg, Sydney. "What to Tell Americans: The Writers' Quarrel in the Office of War Information." *Journal of American History* 55, no. 1 (1968): 73–89.

Wells, Benjamin A. "Contemporary American Essayists." *Forum* 23 (June 1897): 487–96.

Wertheim, Arthur Frank. *The New York Little Renaissance: Iconoclasm, Modernism, and Nationalism in American Culture, 1908–1919.* New York: New York University Press, 1976.

Westbrook, Robert. "Fighting for the American Family: Private Interests and Political Obligation in World War II." In *The Power of Culture: Critical Essays in American History*, ed. Richard Wightman Fox and T. J. Jackson Lears, 195–222. Chicago: University of Chicago Press, 1993.

Wharton, Edith, and Ogden Codman Jr. *The Decoration of Houses*. Revised and Expanded Classical America Edition. 1902. Reprint, New York: W. W. Norton, 1997.

White, E. B. *Charlotte's Web*. 1952. Reprint, New York: HarperCollins, 2001.

———. *Every Day Is Saturday*. New York: Harper and Brothers, 1934.

———. Foreword to *One Man's Meat*. New York: Harper, 1942.

———. Introduction to *One Man's Meat*, xi–xiv. New York: Harper, 1982.

———. *Letters of E. B. White*. Ed. Dorothy Lobrano Guth. New York: Harper and Row, 1976.

———. *One Man's Meat*. 1942. Reprint, New York: Harper, 1982.

———. *Quo Vadimus? or, The Case for the Bicycle*. New York: Harper and Brothers, 1939.

———. *Selected Essays of E. B. White*. New York: Harper's, 1977.

———. "A Step Forward." *New Yorker*, April 18, 1925, 21.

———. "Visitors to the Pond." *New Yorker*, May 23, 1953, 28–31. Reprinted in *Writings from the "New Yorker," 1927–1976*, ed. Rebecca M. Dale, 43–50. New York: HarperCollins, 1990.

———. "We." *New Yorker*, July 2, 1927, 12.

———. *The Wild Flag: Editorials from the "New Yorker" on Federal World Government and Other Matters*. Boston: Houghton Mifflin, 1946.

———. *Writings from the "New Yorker," 1927–1976*. Ed. Rebecca M. Dale. New York: HarperCollins, 1990.

Wiebe, Robert H. *The Search for Order, 1877–1920*. The Making of America Series, ed. David Donald. New York: Hill and Wang, 1967.

Willcox, Louise Collier. "Some Recent Essays." *North American Review* 183, no. 601 (1906): 780–91.

Williams, Raymond. *Keywords: A Vocabulary of Culture and Society*. Rev. ed. 1976. Reprint, New York: Oxford University Press, 1983.

Willis, Nathaniel Parker. "Letters from under a Bridge." In *The Prose Works of N. P. Willis: New Edition in One Volume*, 217–48. Philadelphia: Carey and Hart, 1855.

Wilson, Christopher P. *The Labor of Words: Literary Professionalism in the Progressive Era*. Athens: University of Georgia Press, 1985.

———. "The Rhetoric of Consumption: Mass-Market Magazines and the Demise of the Gentle Reader, 1880–1920." In *The Culture of Consumption: Critical Essays in American History, 1880–1980*, ed. Richard Wrightman Fox and T. J. Jackson Lears, 39–64. New York: Pantheon Books, 1983.

Winfield, Betty Houchin. *FDR and the News Media*. Urbana: University of

Illinois Press, 1990.

Winkler, Allan. *The Politics of Propaganda: The Office of War Information, 1942–1945*. New Haven: Yale University Press, 1978.

Winsor, Mary. "John Jay Chapman, Essayist." *Critic*, May 1899, 451–55.

Winter, Thomas. *Making Men, Making Class: The YMCA and Workingmen, 1877–1920*. Chicago: University of Chicago Press, 2002.

Wister, Owen. Preface to *An Apology for Old Maids, and Other Essays*, by Henry Dwight Sedgwick, x–xiv. New York: Macmillan, 1916.

Woolf, Virginia. *The Essays of Virginia Woolf*. Vol. 1, *1904–1912*. Ed. Andrew McNellie. London: Hogarth, 1986.

——. *The Essays of Virginia Woolf*. Vol. 2, *1912–1918*. Ed. Andrew McNellie. New York: Harcourt Brace Jovanovich, 1987.

——. "The Modern Essay." In *The Common Reader: First Series*, ed. Andrew McNellie, 211–22. 1925. Reprint, New York: Harcourt, 1984.

——. *Moments of Being*. Ed. Jeanne Schulkind. New York: Harcourt Brace Jovanovich, 1976.

——. "Mr. Bennett and Mrs. Brown." Hogarth Lecture, 1924. In *Approaches to the Novel: Materials for a Poetics*, ed. Robert Scholes, 211–30. San Francisco: Chandler, 1961.

Wright, Gwendolyn. *Building the Dream: A Social History of Housing in America*. Cambridge: Massachusetts Institute of Technology Press, 1983.

Yagoda, Ben. *About Town: The "New Yorker" and the World It Made*. New York: Scribner, 2000.

Yates, Norris. *The American Humorist: Conscience of the Twentieth Century*. Ames: Iowa State University Press, 1964.

——. *Robert Benchley*. New York: Twayne, 1968.

Zieger, Robert H. *The CIO: 1935–1955*. Chapel Hill: University of North Carolina Press, 1997.

Index

Woodward, William, 132
Woolf, Virginia, 9, 16, 59–61, 65, 118, 124, 158
Woollcott, Alexander, 3, 129, 131, 142
Wordsworth, William, 38
World's Work, 50, 73–74
Wright, Frank Lloyd, 62, 107
Wright, Gwendolyn, 59
Wright, Richard, 3
Wright-Cleveland, Peggy, xii

Yale, xiii, 71, 103–4, 120, 128, 156, 160, 191
Yale Record, 130
Yancey, Kathleen, xiii
Yates, Norris, 121–22

Ziegfeld, Florenz, 121
Ziff, Lazar, 108
Zukofsky, Louis, 125

About the Author

Ned Stuckey-French is Associate Professor of English at Florida State University. He is coeditor of *Essayists on the Essay: Montaigne to Our Time* and coauthor of the eighth edition of *Writing Fiction: A Guide to Narrative Craft*, the most widely adopted creative writing text in the U.S. He lives with his wife, author Elizabeth Stuckey-French, in Tallahassee, Florida.